Religion and Politics in Muslim Society

Religion and Politics in Muslim Society

Order and conflict in Pakistan

AKBAR S. AHMED

Department of Anthropology
Harvard University

CAMBRIDGE UNIVERSITY PRESS

CAMBRIDGE

LONDON   NEW YORK   NEW ROCHELLE

MELBOURNE   SYDNEY

Published by the Press Syndicate of the University of Cambridge
The Pitt Building, Trumpington Street, Cambridge CB2 1RP
32 East 57th Street, New York, NY 10022, USA
10 Stamford Road, Oakleigh, Melbourne 3166 Australia

© Cambridge University Press 1983
Reprinted 1985

Prined in the United States of America

Library of Congress Cataloging in Publication Data
Ahmed, Akbar S.
Religion and politics in Muslim society.
Bibliography: p.
Includes index
1. Waziristan (Pakistan) - Politics and government.
2. Waziristan (Pakistan) - Social life and customs.
3. Islam and politics - Pakistan - Waziristan.
I.   Title.
DS392.W3A35   1983   306'.0954912   82-14774
ISBN 0 521 24635 0

To my wife, with love

Contents

Maps and figures

Preface

This book attempts to discover, first, what is happening in the Muslim world and, second, the underlying causes. It does so by illuminating the social structure and the operative principles in contemporary Muslim society, especially Pakistan. The answers may well help us to understand the forces that are creating tension and the dialectics of social change.

I had three specific objectives in examining Waziristan: First, I wished to place the revolt of the Mullah of Waziristan within the context of similar contemporary movements elsewhere in the Muslim world and in so doing to create the Islamic district paradigm as an aid to a better understanding of that world. Second, I wanted to provide an ethnographic and contemporary account of Waziristan tribes, which have long been neglected by scholars because of Waziristan's inaccessibility and remoteness. Both the major case study of the Mullah and smaller cases involving the political agent (PA) helped me realize this objective. Third, I wished to illustrate and to emphasize the reader's need for certain information about the anthropologist conducting the study and about the circumstances surrounding it; without such information the reader cannot properly interpret the findings. Who is the anthropologist? An academic? A consultant for an international organization? An official working for the government? What are the anthropologist's biases? What was the cultural and political climate of the period? All these questions require explicit answers.

The task of anthropologists is more difficult and complex if they are natives of the society they are studying. They must guard against any possible bias toward their group that, if it were to remain unchecked, might distort analysis. They must endeavor to portray society as it is, not as it should be; they must depict actual society, not an ideal. Because they are in a position to provide special insight, it is imperative that native anthropologists document their societies. Such efforts are a necessary preliminary to the identification and solution of modern problems. By concealing or distorting our own vision of society, we ultimately deceive only ourselves.

As a native anthropologist—and also an actor in the drama—I found this book difficult to write. Personal issues are involved: ideology, loyalty, judgment. As a Muslim I respect the learned theologians of Islam—the ulema—but what is my position on the role of the mullahs in society? By discussing administration and its problems, am I in some way letting it down? By citing certain material that concerns me, am I being immodest?

I am not certain whether the problems mentioned in the preceding paragraphs have been satisfactorily solved in this volume. Grappling with the issues has been a humbling experience for me; so many difficulties remain, and so many questions are yet to be answered. I hope my attempts to discover answers and to clarify my own vision are at least somewhat illuminating and spur further discussion and debate, thereby adding to our understanding. I am tempted to agree with the answer given by M. J. M. Fischer, an anthropologist at Harvard University, to one of Iran's leading ayatullahs regarding the nature of the anthropological method. The ayatullah's rather shrewd query echoed Lévi-Strauss: Was anthropology "cooked or raw" (*pokhta ya napokhta*)? Fischer replied: "Raw, not yet a science! Perhaps it is not a science at all, but a humanist attempt at dialogue and learning, both for myself and as an aid for others" (1980, p. 244).

Part One of the book, which comprises the first three chapters, introduces and defines the models and methodology of the study and discusses the geography and history of Waziristan pertinent to an explanation of agnatic rivalry between its two tribes. The title of Part Two, "Observation," stresses my role as observer and leads to the core of my argument. Chapters 4, 5, and 6 contain an extended case study of the Mullah of Waziristan. Its preparation was facilitated by my position as political agent, South Waziristan Agency, from November 1978 to July 1980, which afforded me access to source material, including office notes and, of course, the diaries of the Mullah, which would not otherwise have been available to me. I have of course drawn for the present study only on material of a politically nonsensitive nature. Chapters 4 and 5 are based largely on written data obtained from the offices of the PA, which fact perhaps accounts for a certain discernible bias against the Mullah. Also extensively consulted, however, were Wazirs, Mahsuds, and officials of all categories.

Part Three, "Participation," comprising Chapters 7, 8, and 9, provides a counterbalance by shifting the study's focus to the role of the PA. Chapter 7 contains a series of smaller, though related, cases in which I participated and which illustrate the principles of my main arguments. Chapter 8 discusses the political agent, both past and current, as anthropologist. The last chapter addresses the methodological and conceptual problems involved in any attempt to define Islam and segmentary societies.

In a paper written on Waziristan tribes and their role in the Great Game, I indicated a few years ago the desire to pursue "one strand of the argument" (Ahmed 1979). I would like to express my profound gratitude to the Institute for Advanced Study, Princeton – especially to Clifford Geertz – for allowing me to follow during the academic year 1980–1 the strand that has become this book. For their comments on my work I warmly thank Eqbal Ahmed, Hamza Alavi, Hamid Algar, Talal Asad, Jonathan Benthall, Sir Olaf Caroe, Louis Dupree, Dale Eickelman, Isma'il al Faruqi, Ernest Gellner, Ashraf Ghani, Monica Das Gupta, David M. Hart, Adam Kuper, Ira Lapidus, Hafeez Malik, David Maybury-Lewis, Adrian C. Mayer, Muhsin Mahdi, David J. Parkin, Fazlur Rahman, Edward Said, André Singer, and Nur Yalman. I am also grateful to the following members of the Institute who commented: John Gumperz, Stephen Humphreys, Bernard Lewis, Amal Rassam, Theda Skocpol, Jean-Claude Vatin, Annette Weiner, and M. Crawford Young. Finally, I acknowledge the involvement and support, as always, of my wife.

Abbreviations

APA	Assistant political agent
APO	Assistant political officer
DIK	Dera Ismail Khan
DO	Demi-official (letter/correspondence)
IGFC	Inspector general, Frontier Corps
JUI	Jamiat-i-Ulama-i-Islam
NAP	National Awami party
NWFP	North-West Frontier Province
PA	Political agent
PPP	Pakistan People's party
SWA	South Waziristan Agency
SWS	South Waziristan Scouts
TAM	Tribal area Mohmand

PART ONE

Introduction

1

Models and method

The contemporary disorders – or movements – in Muslim society remain largely unstudied and, on the surface, inexplicable. Contrary to common thinking, the movements have followed general economic improvement, not deprivation. Revolutionary in form and content, they are inevitably accompanied by death and destruction. Their complexity, and the diverse contexts within which they appear, defy easy analysis. Perceptible beneath the ferment are the shadowy figures of religious leaders – mullah,[1] maulvi, sheikh, or ayatullah – who explicitly challenge the ideological tenets of the modern age, emphasizing the central role of God and expressing revulsion from materialism as philosophy and code of life; their target is not the king or president as symbol of the state but the modern state apparatus itself. The concept of religious war, *jihad*, is invoked, and the mosque becomes the primary base and focus of the movements; highly charged religious and political points of reference are thus provided. Tensions resulting from ethnic conflict, recent colonial and national history, and the posing of philosophic and eschatalogical questions that are difficult to answer with conviction in this age add to the complexity of the problem.

Traditionally these movements have been analyzed as revolt against legitimate authority – translated from notions of state and nationhood, order and rebellion, the major themes of modern political discussion. A corollary of this type of analysis is the placing of such endeavors simplistically within an anti-Western framework. Muslim revolts and their leaders, from Sudan to Swat, have interested the West over the last centuries and have provided the prototype of the "Mad Mullah." The implicitly hostile reaction of the West to the contemporary Muslim movements and their leaders may be partly explained as a historically conditioned response to this prototype.

The apprehensions that have revived as a result of these movements are expressed by one of the leading Western authorities on Islam:

> The Iranian revolution and the already disquieting Muslim fundamentalist movements whose hopes it nurtured, changed [the traditional West–modern Muslim equation], helped by the rising price of that petroleum with which Allah endowed his followers in such ample quantities. Once again the Muslim world became an entity jealously guarding its uniqueness, its own culture, comprising much more than just spirituality. And might not this entity again become a threat, as it had only three centuries ago when the Ottoman armies laid siege to Vienna? Might the way of life so valued by the West be in serious danger? [Rodinson 1980: vlvii]

During the colonial phase of modern Islamic history the movements were explicitly anti-West and anticolonial. Today the movements are aimed primarily at enemies *within* society.

In the last few years the movements have taken place in widely different regions of the Muslim world, from Kano, in Nigeria, to Waziristan, in Pakistan.[2] The attack in 1979 on the mosque at Mecca – the very core of the Islamic world – illustrates the seriousness and significance of the contemporary Muslim mood. Recent events in Iran provide dramatic evidence of the revolutionary aspects of Islamic movements. Other similar upheavals may have taken place, perhaps unreported because of lesser scale or drama, and more will most probably take place in the coming years.

Questions of faith, leadership, and authority are as old as Muslim society. Although every incident is unique, it is at the same time similar to others in the past. Our case from Waziristan – a religious leader challenging the established state – is a familiar story in the Muslim world today; it is equally familiar in historical accounts. What is new is the widespread concern for these issues in the contemporary world.

Recent observers of traditional societies in the process of modernizing have generally assumed that the influence of religion is on the decline. Most scholars of Islam appeared to agree with this proposition, posing as reasons economic development, migration, increased employment opportunities, and education. In fact the opposite appears to be true, and at least some of the reasons for this are, paradoxically, the same.

The Waziristan study may not tell us much about Islam, but it has a great deal to say about Muslim society. The people respond to the call of Islam regardless of their imperfect understanding of it. Islamic symbols are anchored in the society, and the realization of their affective and conative functions is of primary importance in its interpretation.

The extended case study that is the focus of this volume is based on traditional agnatic rivalry between two major tribes in a tribal agency in Pakistan, and the central actor is the Mullah of Waziristan.[3] The Mullah emerged as a political entity after building an impressive mosque – the biggest in South Waziristan, indeed in any Frontier Province agency. Operating from this base he soon gained control of the adjacent markets at Wana, the economic center of the agency. Having secured his economic base he proceeded to articulate political demands on behalf of the Wazir. In the name of Islam the Mullah mobilized the Wazirs to activate specific tribal ideology into a political movement against their cousins and rival tribe, the Mahsuds. Once his hold over the Wazirs was complete the Mullah set them on a collision course with the government administration, which he regarded as allied with the Mahsuds. The Mullah articulated Wazir animosity against the Mahsuds and damned the latter as *kafirs*, or nonbelievers. Employing religious idiom for tribal rivalry he declared jihad against the Mahsuds.

His next move was to order a general civil disobedience movement, at the climax of which he imposed a physical boycott on the Wana camp. Major clashes involving many deaths took place between the Wazirs on one side and the Mahsuds and the administration on the other. The entire South Waziristan Agency was in flames, and on the Durand line such a situation has international ramifications.[4] After obtaining clearance from the highest authority in the land, the administration acted in May 1976. In a predawn strike, the government forces destroyed the Wana markets. The Mullah's key followers were arrested and so, after a while, was he. The Mullah was tried, found guilty and jailed. The action, possibly the most severe of its kind in the recent history of the tribal areas, became and remains the center of controversy.

The Wazir Mullah defined and identified boundaries within society. His objective was explicit: the transformation of the structure and organization of society. His method was ambiguous as he alternated between a secular political paradigm and a religious–charismatic paradigm. The ambiguity allowed him large areas in which to maneuver and partly explains his social and political success among the Wazirs. Recent Waziristan history may be viewed as a function of the Mullah's emergence and politics. No Hamlet without the Prince of Denmark and no Waziristan without the Mullah. But the Mullah is only one of the main actors in the drama.

The attempt to understand the main characters in the drama within the context of their position in the social structure is fundamental to a study of Muslim society. The anthropological method may provide useful tools for the analysis of leadership operating in traditional Muslim groups confronting change and conflict. I suggest also that certain specific methodological adjustments be made in the approach to traditional Islamic studies.

The study of power, authority, and religious status, the central issues of Muslim society, by political scientists, sociologists, and historians has rested largely on traditional method and holistic analysis. These studies have tended to concern themselves with problems of rulers, dynasties, legitimacy, succession, control of armies, and finances, on the one hand, and those of orthodoxy and legality on the other. Conceptually, the canvas and the configurations are large; the ranges in area and time are also large. In this study I suggest that it may be heuristically useful to look also beneath the surface of the large configurations of Muslim society and away from their main centers of power when examining social structure and process, especially with reference to Pakistan. However, rather than the typical anthropological village, I have chosen to focus on a level of society so far neglected by scholars – the critical intermediary level, the district, or agency.[5]

Three broad but distinct categories of leadership interact at the district, or agency, level of society: traditional leaders, usually elders, government officials, and religious functionaries. The last group is the least defined and hence its locus and its role are ambiguous. Each group is symbolically defined in society by their bases, which are situated in uneasy juxtaposition at the district headquarters and, respectively, are the house or houses of the chief or elders, district headquarters (flying the government flag), and the central mosque.

Personnel from the three categories of leadership vie for power, status, and legitimacy in society. The competition is further exacerbated by the fact that the major participants are Muslims; there are no simple Muslim versus non-Muslim categories to fall back on as in the recent colonial past. Some form of alliance and collaboration between traditional leaders and district officials is characteristic of district history; it is the religious leader who must clash with the other two if he is to expand his space in society.

Once I have identified certain features in society at the district level

I shall proceed to construct what may be tentatively termed the Islamic district, or agency, paradigm of sociocultural process; from this conceptually precise and empirically based paradigm we can then predict future developments.[6] At the core of the Islamic district paradigm I shall place ethnographic analysis; it is not only most relevant but, perhaps, allows me, as a social anthropologist, to make some contribution.

I refer to the paradigm as Islamic not in a theological but in a sociological context; my study is of Muslim actors operating in Muslim society, and I emphasize that Muslim society is being examined here, not Islam. The three major categories of leadership and the society they represent are self-consciously Muslim. Questions are thereby raised, which this study proposes to examine. Which group speaks for Muslim society? How do the groups perceive society?

The district paradigm, by definition, suggests the perpetuation of one aspect of the colonial encounter. The district structure and personnel, with its official head, the district commissioner – or the political agent in the agency – were imposed by the British. Since colonial times, status and authority in the district have rested largely in district officials as representatives of an omnipotent central government. District officers were the *mai–baap* ("mother–father") of South Asian rural peasantry. The continuing importance of the district and its personnel after independence in 1947, in spite of its clear association with the colonial past, heightens tensions. Although "native," officials reflect ambivalence in their dealings with the other groups, which sometimes view them as distant and unsympathetic.[7] The power and importance of district officials are further exaggerated when normal political activities are suspended, for example, during periods of martial law. In any case the democratic process is poorly developed; elections mean that the traditional leaders, government officials, and, recently, religious figures of our paradigm masquerade as politicians.[8]

Studies in the social sciences describing models of society tend to emphasize their stability, their perpetuation through generations, and their contemporary validity. Change is analyzed as a response to external or technical stimuli. The important questions of how and why a model may be invalidated or partly fail as a result of internal stimulus are seldom asked. The present study will focus on just such questions. Let us briefly examine the Pukhtun models of society relevant to our study.

Pukhtun society may be divided into two categories: (1) acephalous, egalitarian groups, living in low-production zones and (2) those with a ranked society living on irrigated lands, usually within larger state systems. *Nang* ("honor") is the foremost symbol of the former society, as *qalang* ("taxes," "rents") is of the latter (Ahmed 1976, 1977, 1980a). Certain features of nang society correspond to those in Group B rather than Group A tribal societies familiar in the literature (Fortes and Evans-Pritchard 1970, Middleton and Tait 1970). Group B societies are acephalous and organized along the principle of the segmentary lineage system; in contrast, Group A societies contain organized, centralized states backed by force and led by powerful chiefs. Most of the nang groups live in the tribal areas. In addition, two categories of nang Pukhtun society have been identified with the Mohmand tribe (Ahmed 1980a). One may be called the tribal area Mohmand (TAM), a prototype ideal nang model, and the other may be termed the settled area Mohmand (SAM), consisting of those who settled in Peshawar District. The Waziristan tribes living in South Waziristan Agency may be identified as either TAM or nang society.

A study of Waziristan is different from a study of the Mohmands because in it we examine a nang society in crisis. The crisis itself has been generated by Muslim actors as a result of internal tensions in society. The definition of central Islamic terms therefore becomes important because the perception of such universally recognized social phenomena (*jihad* and *kafir*, for instance) differs considerably according to whether they are viewed from within society (by the actors) or from outside (by the analysts).

Because nang society is acephalous and egalitarian, the questions arise as to how and why the Wazir abandoned egalitarian organization for centralized authority, and iconoclasm for hagiolatry. The answers to the questions will enable us to examine a case where deviance from the nang model occurs *within the tribal areas* as a result of the emergence of a mullah and direct interaction with political administration. What we will witness is not the metastatic transformation of TAM to SAM but an intrinsic breakdown of TAM. The redintegration of traditional structure is made possible only by severe military action. The failure of the nang model raises a number of important theoretical questions regarding human behavior. What circumstances, what flow of incentives, material and nonmaterial, are necessary for perpetuation of ideal-type behavior? More important, why do people stop behaving according to their own notions of ideal behavior? May the failure be understood as a short- or long-term phenomenon?

The individual in Muslim society, whether official or tribesman, confronts differentiated and valid models of behavior, which allow him a wide variety of strategies and choices. He may shift social response and action to approximate one or other model. The ideal-type model does not, as indeed it cannot, monopolize the Waziristan universe. Deviation from the ideal-type, or indeed emergent alternative models especially in the articulation of political action, is evident in society. The problem is that of a multiplicity of models; their identification, where possible, will assist us in comprehending Waziristan society.

In this study we will see how social life and behavior involve a complex combination of culture, religion, politics, and indeed, the psychology of individuals as locally understood and interpreted. When questions of "morality," "honor," and "pride," and larger ones of "ideology," arise in society, man responds primarily to those symbols internal to his society, whether they originated there or were borrowed. This is especially true in short-term perspective. Such a response can clearly override rational economic and political consideration. In Waziristan, noneconomic and nonrational choices are deliberately made in spite of being seen to lead to confrontation, conflict, and disaster. In the end, the Wazirs sacrifice the material symbols of prosperity, market and trade, in an attempt to uphold group honor, unity, and loyalty.

Most studies of tribal societies ignore the presence of their administrative structure (Fortes and Evans-Pritchard 1970; Gluckman 1971; Middleton and Tait 1970). This has raised criticism in the literature and has even identified anthropology as a tool of imperialism (Asad 1973). I will illustrate how an understanding of the complex and close interaction between administration and tribal groups is fundamental to the Islamic district paradigm. Indeed, for purposes of this study the administrative organization may be conceptualized as the third "tribe" of the agency, possessing its own sets of symbols, ritualized behavior, and esoteric language – English – not generally understood by the other tribes. The political agent may be seen as the "chief" of the tribe and the South Waziristan Scouts – a paramilitary force – as its "warriors." Although a useful metaphor for purposes of analysis, the comparison must not be taken too literally. The resources that the larger state, which the third tribe represents, can muster are far greater than those available to the other two tribes.

The question of the personality of the main actors – the Mullah, the colonel, the PA – is raised as an important governing factor in the Waziristan drama. The personal makeup, the social–psychological and even physical attributes, of the actors is therefore important in understanding their relations with one another and with the tribes. Perhaps one needs to reexamine the idea of "personality" in the social sciences. Why do we oppose the question of personal factors to structural and categorical ones? If persons are the loci through which opposed forces flow then the person is also one of those forces, as I hope to illustrate in this study.

The Waziristan data will illustrate the importance of rapport between administrators and the tribes in determining policy and helping shape events. PAs often appeared to sympathize with one tribe more than another. As we will see in Parts Two and Three, obvious leaning toward the Wazirs or Mahsuds in the 1970s added to the complexity of the problem. Some PAs worsened matters for themselves by failing to establish relations with other officials, such as the commandant of the Scouts and their own direct superior, the commissioner in Dera Ismail Khan (DIK) and with nonofficials, such as the Mullah.

The Waziristan study reinforces the need to refer to the larger regional political framework when studying Pukhtun tribes, which I have emphasized elsewhere (Ahmed 1976, 1981c).[9] Life in Waziristan has been affected by larger political developments in Pakistan – indeed Afghanistan – that interacted with more local events. The Mullah clearly reflected political actions elsewhere in Pakistan. The tribes themselves were adept at recognizing and manipulating the larger framework, and the ability of the Mahsuds to identify and manipulate official networks in Pakistan partly explains their superiority over the Wazirs.

Changing politics in the province, indeed in Pakistan, and the rapid turnover of PAs suggests that the tribal agencies in the North-West Frontier Province may be in danger of, or are, pulling in different directions. On what may be viewed as the critical level of tribal administration, and the PA continues to wield immense power to influence events in his area, different policies may be followed in the tribal agencies at the same time, one PA implementing his version of the "close border policy" and another the "forward policy." A holistic plan and a long-term strategy for political administration are needed, especially in the context of the emergent politics of the region after the Soviet invasion of Afghanistan in 1979.[10] The multiplicity of models, both tribal and administrative, with specific reference to the Islamic district paradigm, must be identified and interpreted. Failure to do so may result in the mismanagement of models and lead to conflict in society, as the Waziristan cases point out.

2

Waziristan: land, lineage, and culture

Waziristan

Ahmedzai Wazirs and Mahsuds are the two major tribes of the South Waziristan Agency (Maps 1 and 2). Three other smaller tribal groups share the agency with them. The Suleman Khel and Dottani, representing larger nomadic tribes, are in the process of sedentarization and live in the Zarmelan plain and along the Gomal River.[1] The Urmar, or Burkis, is a small tribe noted for learning and lives entirely in Kaniguram.[2] Utmanzai Wazirs, cousins of the Ahmedzai, live in and dominate North Waziristan Agency and have also settled in large numbers in Bannu District. These two agencies were named after the Wazir tribe in the last years of the nineteenth century. In name and in fact, this is the land of the Wazirs. Other agencies in the tribal areas, like Malakand, Khyber, and Kurram (Map 3), are named after geographical features. The area is large and together the two agencies are almost the size of Wales.

The Pakistan census of 1972, based on what is officially acknowledged as "estimates," gives the total population of the agency as 307,514, of which approximately 247,040 are Mahsuds and 59,025 are Wazirs.[3] Census figures show evidence of high fertility trends in the agency.

Year	Agency population
1951	135,784
1961	235,442
1972	307,514

From 1951 to 1972 the total population more than doubled. Mahsud figures, in particular, indicate a population explosion, which partly explains their need for more land.[4]

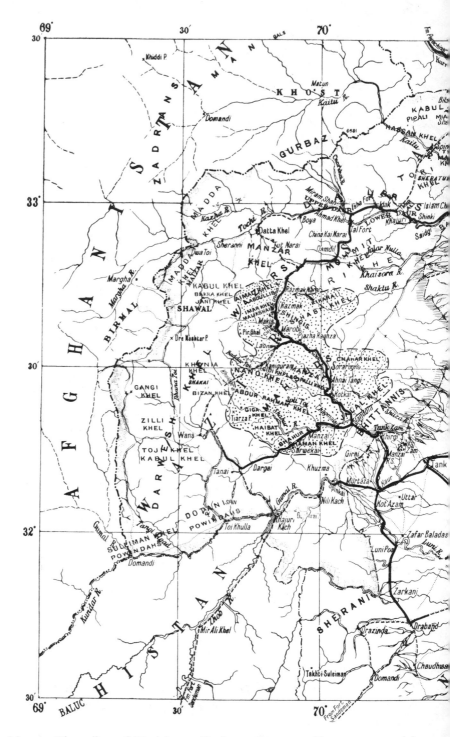

Map 1. The tribes of Waziristan. (Redrawn from an old map prepared by
the General Staff of India.)

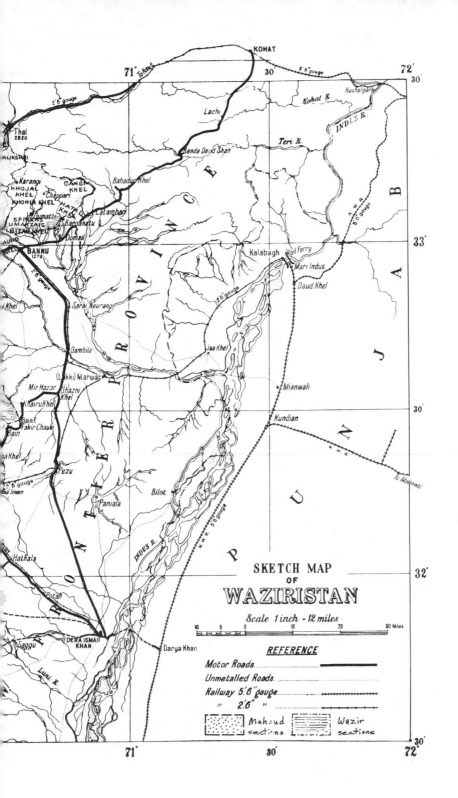

SKETCH MAP
OF
WAZIRISTAN

Scale 1 inch - 12 miles

REFERENCE
Motor Roads
Unmetalled Roads
Railway 5'6" gauge
    "   2'6"   "
Mahsud sections   Wazir sections

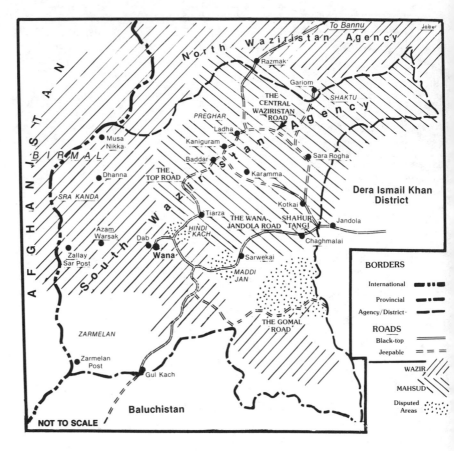

Map 2. South Waziristan Agency

Year	Mahsud population
1934	68,095 (estimated, Johnson, 1934b)
1946	88,046 (estimated, Curtis, 1946, p. 8)
1972	247,040

According to these figures Mahsud population has increased more than three and a half times in thirty-eight years and almost three times in the last twenty-six.

Although far larger in number, the Mahsuds occupy only about half the agency area. Based on their roughly equal division of the agency area, Mahsud population density is 124 per square mile, whereas that of the Wazirs is 30. The average amount of land (irrigated and unirrigated) owned by the hundred Wazir maliks ("elders") recognized as being most influential is 18 acres; that of the Mahsud maliks is 2 acres.

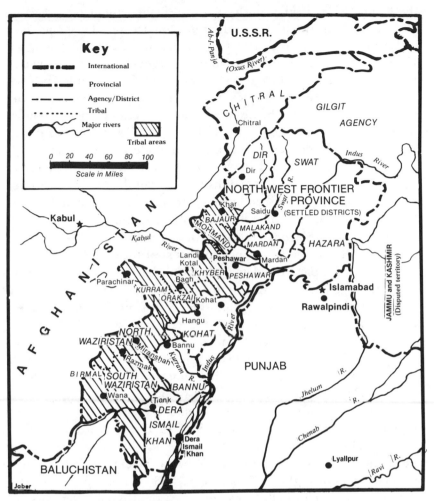

Map 3. The North-West Frontier Province

The average for nonmaliks is considerably lower. If we accept the recent population trends among the Mahsuds and project them backward into the last hundred years or so we may conclusively accept the hypothesis that a population explosion accounts for their comparatively small landholdings.

The South Waziristan Agency encompasses about 3,936 square miles (Afridi 1980, p. 7).[5] It is the largest and southernmost agency in the North-West Frontier Province's seven federally administered tribal agencies (Map 3). The agency shares borders with Afghanistan in the west and the Pakistani province of Baluchistan, separated in part by the Gomal River in the south. The two main settlements are Wana and Kaniguram. Wana, the summer headquarters of the agency, is on a rise of almost 4,500 feet in the middle of a large flat plain, and Kaniguram, 6,700 feet high, lies in the heart of the agency. Wana is 48 miles from Razmak, which is just over 7,000 feet in altitude, in North Waziristan and is on the border between the two agencies, along what is called the top road. The distance from Wana to Jandola is about 50 miles on the main agency road. It is 40 miles from Razmak to Jandola, the third side of the major triangle of Waziristan roads, known as the central Waziristan road. A recent road, about 26 miles in length, passes through the Mahsud center of the agency to connect Jandola with the top road and is referred to as the Kiss road, from the first letters of Kotkai, Imar Raghza, Shinkai, and Sam. Jandola, on the border of the agency and the Dera Ismail Khan District, is 32 miles from Tank, the winter headquarters of the agency.

For the most part, desolate valleys and barren mountains distinguish the agency. High mountains (the highest peak is Preghar at 11,556 feet) in central Waziristan, thick forests in Birmal, and desert in the Zarmelan plain illustrate the contrast in the geographical features of the agency. Fertile areas include heavily forested Birmal, the Baddar valley, which supports a fine potato crop, and recently the Wana plain, noted for its fruit. Fifteen inches of rain are estimated to fall annually in the higher regions of the agency.

The climate is one of extremes. The heat is unbearable in the lower regions in summer. The General Staff of the British Indian army noted: "The heat since the middle of May had been severe, the thermometer registering 120 degrees by day in tents, with a minimum of 90 degrees by night in Tank" (General Staff 1921, p. 44). Dozakh Tangi, "the gorge of hell," through which the Gomal River passes, is appropriately named for the heat in the summer months. In winter the cold, sharp winds are equally unbearable. Those Waziristan groups who can afford to do so tend to migrate to kin groups in search of more congenial climate for the duration of the two extreme seasons. Names like Dozakh Tangi, the Devil's Cake – a sharp, ugly mountain towering over the main agency road before it enters the Wana plain – and Giddar Khula, "the mouth of the jackal," suggest the nature of the geographical terrain as viewed by both locals and outsiders.

Waziristan lineage structure and leadership

The Wazirs and the Mahsuds are descended from an eponymous and apical ancestor, Wazir, reputed to have lived in eastern Afghanistan and descended from Karlani, a junior son of Qais bin Rashid, the putative progenitor of the Pukhtun tribes. Elders explain the name Wazir, which means "minister," as deriving from ancestors who advised the kings of Kabul. The Wazirs, until the turn of the century, were commonly referred to as Darwesh Khel (Johnston 1903), or the descendants of the Darwesh holy man Musa, who is buried in Birmal. It is safe to assume that sometime during the eighteenth or nineteenth century, Mahsuds separated from their parent Wazir tribe. However, memory of larger Wazir identity and association appears to have died out more recently. Mahsud identity with the larger and senior cousin tribe, the Wazir, is apparent in the name applied to them as recently as a few generations ago: "Muhsood Wuzeeree" (Aitchison 1933, Treaty no. 1, 1861, pp. 590–1), "Masud Waziris" (Raverty 1888, p. 536), and "Mahsud Wazirs" (Lockhart 1897).[6] Today, for all purposes the two are separate tribes and see themselves as distinct.

We witness in the Mahsuds the fissiparous tendencies in segmentary systems that at the climax lead to the birth of a distinct tribe with associated characteristics. Demographic pressures combined with political action appear to explain partly the fission in Waziristan society and the formation of a tribe. Wazir and Mahsud genealogies are shown in Figure 1 in order to relate the tribes, clans, and sections in the case studies.[7] Understanding of the genealogical charter is essential to Waziristan leadership as it explains the position of tribal sections to each other and their place in the Waziristan universe based on population, area, and history. Two population indexes, rather than actual figures, are part of Waziristan demographic mythology and are said to date back to Ahmed Shah Abdali, the founder of the Durrani dynasty in Kabul in the eighteenth century (Caroe 1965). Wazirs claim that they then numbered 60,000 individuals, including those in the two agencies, while the Mahsuds numbered 18,000. It is not clear whether the numbers refer to the entire population, the males, or the warriors, but probably they include only the male fighting population. It is also not clear to what exact dates in history the numbers refer. The Wazirs suggest that they encompass a broad period in the late eighteenth century, whereas the Mahsuds say that their figures refer to the late nineteenth century. Both tribes have a tendency to quote

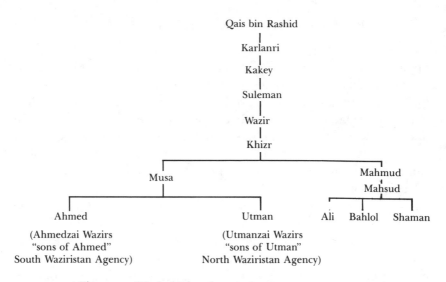

Figure 1. Wazir-Mahsud genealogy

these figures as current and contemporary. In Waziristan, these figures provide a traditional basis for the division of profits and sharing of loss, which is worked out with exact mathematical precision between and within the tribes. The system whereby profit and loss are determined in relation to the genealogical charter is called *nikkat*, from *nikka*, "grandfather" or "ancestor."

In the South Waziristan Agency, nikkat implies an inviolable law of tribal division, which is interpreted as three-fourths for the Mahsuds and one-fourth for the Wazirs. This proportion is maintained, although on the basis of current population, the Wazir share comes to one-sixth and not one-fourth, as Mahsuds frequently point out.[8] The division of the PA's year (eight months in Tank and four in Wana), the numbers of maliks (about three-fourths are Mahsud and one-fourth Wazir), and the colleges (one at Ladha for the Mahsuds and one at Wana for the Wazirs, although with a ratio of one student to one teacher in both colleges in 1980, one would have sufficed for the agency) are based on nikkat. Every aspect of administration evokes nikkat.[9] The universe is conceptualized as a division in this proportion between the two tribes. In turn, intricate mathematics divide and subdivide figures for tribal segments whether a fine is to be imposed or allowances distributed.

One of the arguments of the Mullah, speaking for the Wazirs, centered around the timber permits, an allowance distributed to the tribes (see Chapter 3). He argued that because the timber was extracted from Wazir forests in Birmal by Wazir contractors, the Wazirs ought

to receive more than the hundred permits allotted to them annually
of the total of four hundred. The Mahsuds and the administration
refuted the argument with reference to nikkat. As we shall see, in the
1970s this issue caused considerable complications for the administration and provided the Mullah with excellent material, both emotive
and economic, in espousing the cause of the Wazirs.

Figure 2 illustrates the senior position of the Zilli Khel among the
Wazirs in the charter. The Zilli Khel, the most populous and powerful
of the Ahmedzai, control the Wana and Spin plains and major
portions of Birmal, which lies partly in Pakistan and partly in Afghanistan and is the most inaccessible and thickly forested area of
Waziristan. The Zilli Khel are the dominant group and usually in the
forefront of political activity among the Wazirs. Without their active
involvement no Wazir movement can succeed, a fact the Mullah was
quick to perceive. Smaller and junior sections often find themselves
on the wrong side of the Zilli Khel, as will be seen in the case involving
the Mullah.

Although the Mahsuds view themselves as a tribe distinct from the
Wazirs, they exhibit a marked tendency to act and think in terms of
three separate clans, Dre Mahsud, literally three Mahsuds: Alizai,
Bahlolzai, and Shaman Khel (see Figure 3 for Mahsud genealogy).
Profits and losses among Mahsuds are reckoned strictly according to
nikkat, based on the semimythical original Mahsud population number
of 18,000. Of the total the Alizai claim 9,000 shares, the Bahlolzai
7,000, and the Shaman Khel 2,000. The Shaman Khel receive an
extra 1,000 shares for the non-Mahsud Urmar, or Burki, tribe, which
is associated with them. Each clan tends to speak for itself. It is
tempting to suggest that in time the three clans may well assume
separate tribal identities, repeating a process started by the Mahsuds
when they separated from the Wazirs.

Figures 4 and 5 depict the genealogies of Jalat Khan, Wazir malik,
and Abdul Maalik, Mahsud malik. Both maliks represent well-
established lineages, although Jalat Khan's is longer, and both are
prominent in the case studies.

Jalat Khan traces his ascendants to the founder of the tribe, Wazir.[10]
The generation recall suggests the importance accorded to the lineage
charter in society. Generation recall to the eponym by elders is a
characteristic feature of Pukhtun tribes. Unilineal descent in the
patrilineage defines Pukhtun identity and gives the Pukhtun traditional privileges, such as the right to carry a gun and speak in the
jirga, the council of elders (Ahmed 1980a). In contrast, ancestral
memory in village societies on the Indian subcontinent has little social

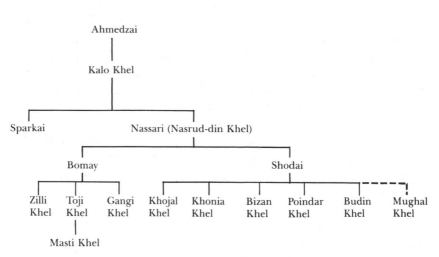

Figure 2. Wazir genealogy

or political significance, and as a consequence, generation recall rarely goes beyond four ascendants (Mayer 1970, pp. 169–70).

Nine generations separate Abdul Maalik from his ancestor Mahsud. The two genealogies shown in Figures 4 and 5 are typical of the numerous that were collected. It is noteworthy that somewhere along the line, and making allowances for genealogical amnesia and telescoping processes, Abdul Maalik appears to have "lost" more generations than his counterpart, Jalat, although both trace descent to a common ancestor, Wazir. The amnesia reflects a characteristic feature of the Mahsuds. They are less inclined to respect inherited traditions. Mahsud genealogical amnesia would be convenient when capturing Wazir lands and violating tradition.

The genealogies show, first, that elders retain genealogical memory, which emphasizes lineage affiliation as a diacritical feature in society, and second, that Wazir genealogical span is longer than the Mahsud, which suggests Wazir lineage seniority and thus access to better lands at the time of arrival in Waziristan. We know that some of the more fertile valleys and plains in Waziristan were with the Wazirs at the turn of the century. It was only two to three generations ago that the Dre Mahsuds finally wrested the fertile Baddar valley and Chalweshti from the Wazirs.[11] Indeed, the name Waziristan, the land of the Wazirs, makes the same point.

Although elders recount Wazir migration en bloc to the areas that now make up Waziristan with the armies of Mahmud of Ghazni, on his way to his Indian conquests in the early eleventh century, it is

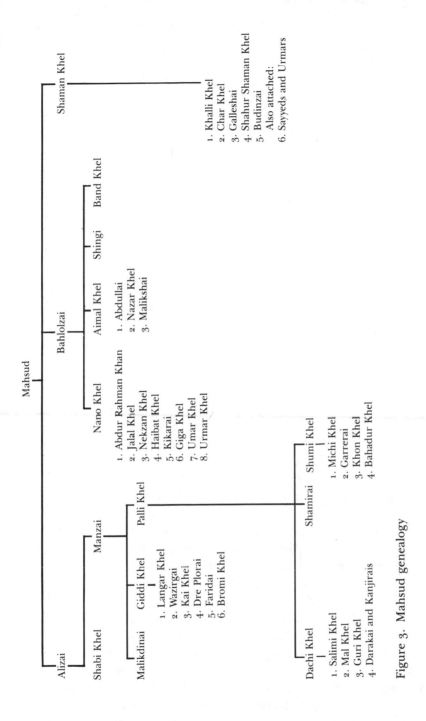

Figure 3. Mahsud genealogy

Ahmedzai
|
Kalo Khel
|
Nassari
|
Bomay Khel
|
Zilli Khel
|
Sheikh Bazid
|
Yar Gul Khel
|
Abid Khel
|
Rahkhai
|
Rahmat
|
Khon Mohammad
|
Karim Khan
|
Gulan
|
Guldin
|
Jalat Khan

Figure 4. The genealogy of Jalat Khan, Wazir Malik

doubtful that the claim can be substantiated. It is more likely that autochthonous pre-Islamic tribes converted to Islam and were absorbed by migrating waves of Pukhtun tribes well after Mahmud's incursions. I have scant evidence to support this statement except names suggesting Sanskritic or Buddhist origin from the Dre Mahsud clans, such as Shingi (Bahlolzai), Palli Khel (Manzai) and Budinzai (Shaman Khel). Place names like Hindi Kach, between Wana and Tiarza, and Gariom (from "Hariom," the Hindu invocation of God?) in North Waziristan Agency suggest Hindu origins.[12] However, a link between Mahmud of Ghazni and the Urmars of Kanigurani does appear to exist. Local myth suggests that so impressed was Mahmud on one of his Indian expeditions by their courage in defying the Hindu flame-

Figure 5. The genealogy of Abdul Maalik, Mahsud Malik

throwers at Somnath that he bestowed on them the name *oor-mar*, "flame-killers," which, in time, became Urmar.

Tribal leadership is intimately related to the issues of religion and politics in Waziristan. In the ideal, tribal structure does not admit hereditary rights of leadership and sociopolitical division according to superior and inferior status, nor does the poor ecological base allow the growth of powerful chiefs. The saying "every man is a malik unto himself" is understood literally in the tribal areas. Because every elder claims to be a malik, the title is devalued. Decisions are made through the jirga. In official dealings the tribesmen of South Waziristan are represented by about 1,000 officially appointed and recognized maliks. Among their privileges is the right to vote for National Assembly members. A Wazir malik represents about 200 and a Mahsud about 340 people of all ages and sexes. The demographic base of the malik is clearly limited.[13]

The erect posture, distinct physical appearance and confidence of the Waziristan elder in the jirga and *mulaqat* (an official meeting) convey an air of pride bordering on arrogance.[14] An impressive figure in speech and bearing, away from the administrative orbit the malik is a model of Pukhtun ideal behavior.

Two contrasting types of Pukhtun leadership within the Wazir lineage are provided by Jalat Khan and his brother Bahram Khan. Jalat is a tall, heavy, imposing man, and his black beard, black mustache curling upward, black waistcoat, and black turban lend him a rather sinister presence. The color black dominates his appearance. His brother, Bahram, represents the other, minor and not entirely successful, model in Pukhtun society. He is a dropout from the agency political system and spends his time in religious activity with the *tabligh* ("conversion"), a nonpolitical Muslim organization based in the Punjab. Bahram's beard is white as is his waistcoat and turban. He appears clean and brushed. The appearance, style, and objectives of life of the two brothers provide fine points of contrast. Jalat's conversation centers around Pukhto, *badal* ("revenge"), and *tora* ("courage"), Pukhtun themes, whereas Bahram talks of Islam and *din* ("religion") against *dunya* ("world"). A model similar to that provided by Bahram is found among the mians in the tribal areas (Ahmed 1980a, chap. 6). Tribesmen comment on both brothers with equal cynicism: "Each sees his own *gata* ("profit"), one in dunya, the other in din." It was the relevant and important model of dunya that the Mullah needed to win over in order to consolidate his hold over the Wazirs. The other model, din, was redundant to him; he himself represented din. The masters of dunya, tribal leaders like Jalat Khan, were to prove indispensable to the Mullah's politics in Waziristan.

The Pukhtun ideal type and cultural variations

Ideal Pukhtun behavior approximates the features of Pukhtunwali, the code of the Pukhtuns (Ahmed 1980a, chap. 4; Singer 1982). Pukhtunwali is perpetuated in society by historical sequences and the ecological base. Courage (*tora*), revenge (*badal*), hospitality (*melmastia*), generosity to a defeated adversary supplicating for peace (*nanawatee*) and heeding the voice of the jirga are the main traditional features of Pukhtunwali.[15] However, *tarboorwali* (cousin rivalry) and *tor* (literally, "black," upholding female honor) appear to be the two main features through which Pukhtunwali is interpreted, enacted, and judged in society (for detailed case studies see Ahmed 1980a, chap. 7; for Waziristan *tor* cases see Appendix A).[16] The Waziristan data confirm this definition of Pukhtunwali. Tarboorwali partly explains political alignment within the tribe. For instance, Abdul Maalik opposes the family of Mir Badshah and his son Alam Jan, who are his Alizai cousins.[17] Gulab Khan, allied to the family through marriage, leads the Mir Badshah party. The rivalry between Maalik and Gulab

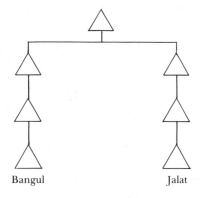

Figure 6. Bangul and Jalat, agnatic rivals

dominates the internal politics of the Mahsud. Intralineage tarboorwali has also precipitated elders, such as Jalat Khan, into the Great Game once contested between Imperial Russia and Imperial Britain. His father, a Yar Gul Khel elder of the Zilli Khel, felt slighted by the British when they favored his father's brother's son, the father of Bangul (see Figure 6). The laws of tarboorwali were activated. Jalat fled to Birmal with his family. He crossed the international border and became prominent in antigovernment activity supported by Afghanistan. Jalat returned to Pakistan in 1957, ten years after its creation, and "surrendered" to the PA. Being "forgiven" his past misdeeds by the PA, Jalat has emerged as an important figure in agency politics, as we shall see in the story of the Mullah. The rivalry between Bangul, one of the most senior Wazir maliks, and Jalat continues in contemporary Wazir politics.

Tarboorwali also provides an important key to the sociopsychological understanding of the relationship between Wazir and Mahsud. It provided ideal grounds for the organizational skills of the Mullah, who exploited it and allowed it to express itself in its most extreme forms. Thus it seems clear that the two tribes behaved as they did within the Pukhtun ideal-type model.

At this stage we may well ask how relevant is the traditional ideal type in society and does it play a significant part in daily life? The ideal type, as I shall illustrate, does exist, although it is not the only model. The Wazirs explain the emergence of the Mullah partly as an attempt to reassert Wazir "honor" in the face of the Mahsuds. The Mahsuds, too, employ the concept of "honor" to explain the deviance of Wazir behavior from Pukhtunwali in following the Mullah so blindly. The

Wazirs, they say, "dishonored" Pukhtuns by compromising their independence.

The Pukhtun ideal type, however, exists only away from the influence of the political administration. Its hold over men is diminished in the face of the power and patronage the administration represents. Politics is reduced to an art in Waziristan. Elders boast of their political acumen. To create a problem, control it, and terminate it is an acknowledged and highly regarded yardstick of political skill. A man with such skills is rewarded and recognized by society, regardless of his political standing with the administration, a fact noted by political officers.[18] Elders are conscious of the corrupting influences of political administration and the deviation it implies from ideal behavior. I heard the following sentiment in many conversations: "We have been corrupted in the offices. We spend days chasing a petty gain. It is against the dignity of the tribe and that of the elder. In the village we are different. We are real Pukhtuns." Officials, on their part, find the tribesman tedious and tiring in mulaqats.[19] The tribesman appears selfish and insatiable in his demands to officials.

This study, in part, rejects the traditionally romantic mold of Pukhtun studies that emerged from the memoirs of officers who served on the Frontier (Caroe 1965, Elliott 1968, Howell 1979, Woodruff 1965). Interaction with political administration, especially in the context of tarboorwali, forces the tribesman to be devious and deceitful, a predicament of which he is aware. The very word *potical*, from "political," has come to connote falsehood and deceit in the tribal mind. Common examples of this are comments like *der potical seray day* ("he is a very political person," that is, he is deceitful and clever) and *poticali ma kawa* ("don't be political with me," do not lie and deceive me). A new model, deviant and distinct from the ideal, has emerged. The new model is outside traditional Pukhto. It allows tribesmen to behave in a manner that the ideal type does not. Let us examine some of the social and cultural characteristics of Waziristan.

The people of Waziristan are Sunni Muslims. Prayers and fasting, two of the five pillars of Islam, are strictly observed, however educated or old the individual. Tribesmen even interrupt meetings to perform the obligatory prayers. In spite of respect for religion in Pukhtun society, the mullah remains subordinate to the lineage elder and does not usually appear on the local genealogical charter. His important functions are as organizer of the village mosque and superviser of *rites de passage*. A fuller discussion of the role of the mullah in tribal society will follow in Chapter 5.

Waziristan society is male dominated.[20] Women enjoy almost no rights and do not inherit land or property. A woman fetches from 10,000 to 40,000 rupees in bride-price, most of which is kept by her father.[21] Women lead a busy life from sunrise to sunset, cooking, collecting firewood, and looking after the house, children, and animals. Their spare, lean bodies, their bare or cheap rubber-shod feet, and their lined faces speak of a physically hard life, as one sees them walking along the roads with bundles of firewood on their heads. Men, in contrast, reserve their time and energy for politics. Some 4,000 to 5,000 males may visit the offices of the PA at Tank daily, 1,000 to 2,000 at any given time. Approximately half these numbers visit Wana each day when the PA is in residence there. Wherever the PA is, Tank or Wana, the bazaars there are crowded with men talking politics.

Individuals in the Waziristan tribes, as in other tribes in the tribal areas, are more and more becoming *dwa-kora*, or the owners of two houses, one in the agency and the other in the settled area. Mahsuds have settled in Tank in large numbers, whereas Wazirs have preferred Dera Ismail Khan.[22] Settlements in the agency are fortlike, surrounded by high, thick walls with dominating towers (Ahmed 1980a).

Although the language in Waziristan remains similar to the Yusufzai Pukhto it contains words with distinctly different meanings:[23] for example, "he lives" is *pandezhee*, not *osegee*; "runs" is *parezhee*, not *takhtee*; *kay* is pronounced as *chay*, *kena* ("sit") as *chena*; and *kh* is pronounced as *sh*, *Pukhto* as *Pushto*.[24]

When individuals from qalang society confront nang tribesmen, they show unease and uncertainty, which reflects the structural and fundamental differences in the two systems.[25] It is all the more remarkable when nang tribesmen are similarly anxious before other nang groups. In Waziristan I have witnessed nang Mohmand and Afridi tribesmen exhibit the same kind of unease. The reaction of the visitors to the desolate land of Waziristan, further isolated by poor communications,[26] and the fierce appearance of its tribes is almost one of awe: "What people: they look so dangerous always carrying knives and guns, their faces covered like bandits."[27] The travelers, however, also expressed a certain grudging admiration: "These are *really* Pukhtun." For a Pukhtun tribesman to so acknowledge another tribesman is a considerable tribute.

Qalang tribes, like the Yusufzai, have produced some of the finest literature in Pukhto. In Waziristan no art or literature has been produced. Indeed, agnatic rivalry and its often violent political forms have assumed the status of art and literature in the eyes of the Wazirs and Mahsuds. Indifference, even ill-concealed contempt, greets book learning as deviation from the Waziristan model of behavior.[28] The tribesman's question about the schoolteacher, "What worlds has he conquered?" (Ahmed 1980a, p. 325), is a general indictment of education. His is a political world; a world of action and force.

Being of the junior lineage and living in less fertile areas has induced the Mahsuds to live by their wits. Hemmed in and encircled by Wazirs in the north, south, and west, Mahsuds exhibit "back to the wall" characteristics, which partly explain their political strategy. Large numbers living in poor country also explain Mahsud movements in search of employment "down country," to Lahore and Karachi.[29] Unlike the Wazirs who cross the Durand line at will to play local variations of the Great Game, they must discover new ways of finding an outlet for their wits. Elders say, "We are surrounded by Wazirs. We have to fight for survival. We have to be more aggressive and cleverer." As a result the Mahsuds were and are more united, exhibiting internal solidarity in conflict situations.[30]

The tribes have channeled their energy inward into the politics of Waziristan for several reasons. First, unlike qalang tribes, such as the Yusufzai, the Waziristan tribes avoided service with the British. The Wazirs stayed away to a man, and the few Mahsuds who joined British service were prominent for desertion and rebellion (Howell 1979, Pettigrew 1965; also see Chapter 3). The cultural pull of Waziristan was strong. Second, few economic alternatives have been available. The Yusufzai, on the other hand, owned irrigated lands and by the turn of the century had developed complex water systems and cultivated cash crops. Third, the lure of India, for employment or adventure, was weak. Waziristan has interacted with Afghanistan (Ahmed 1979), but one rarely hears of Wazirs and Mahsuds on the Indian stage in history. Finally, by using the northern passes like the Khyber to South Asia, the major conquerors of India exposed tribes settled nearby, such as the Yusufzai and Afridi.[31] In contrast Waziristan remained largely isolated, and the tribes learned to turn their political talents inward.

3

History as an expression of agnatic rivalry

The colonial encounter in Waziristan

For all the mystification and romance of the British encounter with the Pukhtun, the tribesman saw the colonial period as an unceasing struggle against an imperial presence (Ahmed 1978, 1980a). The bitterness of the struggle was heightened by its extraethnic and extrareligious nature. Barbed wire and bombs are poor aids to communication between different cultural systems, and this was one of the most barren meetings of culture possible. To the end, it was a straightforward jihad. The retention of certain British traditions by the Pakistani administration must not be allowed to obfuscate the tribesman's rejection of British civilization.

The creation in 1901 of the North-West Frontier Province by Lord Curzon added to the mystique of the people and the area and brought them into fine focus within the context of the Great Game.[1] The nature of the Great Game provided some of the most evocative and popular writing of the British Empire, as exemplified by Kipling. Kim is a metaphor for the Great Game. The Great Game itself was an extension of the public school social philosophy and values of middle- and upper-class Victorian England. The encounters between the British and the Pukhtun in the Frontier Province also reflected the values of the Great Game. It was a "game" between worthy players, with half-times, referees, boundaries, and even rules of sorts. The entire game was cast in the almost mock-heroic mold of empire, with its concomitant concepts such as "honor" and "glory." As in a mirror the Pukhtun tribal mind reflected a similar image. "Honor," "courage," and "word" motivated individuals on both sides to action.[2] Famous names associated with the colonial encounter in Waziristan, both British (Curzon, Durand, Kitchener, and T. E. Lawrence[3]) and non-British (Mullah Powindah,[4] the fakir of Ipi, and Jawaharlal Nehru[5]), heightened its romantic mystique.[6]

Certain traditions are still preserved by the administration. The portrait of Colonel Harman, one of the earliest administrators and victims of the agency, dominates the dining room of the Wana mess, and opposite the PA's bungalow in Wana a memorial to him is maintained.[7] The western gate in the Wana camp is officially known as the Durand gate, and the main picket, situated on a conical hill rising almost 500 feet over the Wana camp bears the name Gibraltar. Bugles announce the passage of the day and play at sunset as the Pakistan flag is lowered, when, according to tradition, the entire camp comes to a halt as part of the ceremony. Officers coming into and going out from the agency are guests of honor at ritualistic ceremonies arranged in the Scouts' mess with the band, dressed in kilts and playing bagpipes, in attendance. The mess remains the focal point of social life for officers, providing camaraderie and hospitality, although as a concession to Islamic sentiment, liquor is no longer served. For fresh arrivals it provides a means of acculturation into the ways of the regiment. Other visible legacies from the past include exotic regimental silver in the mess and the impeccable Quarter-Guard, displaying battle honors won against Waziristan tribes. As in the old days, entrance to the Wana camp is restricted and almost ritualistic. The visitor must pass through a series of formalities from the lower to the upper camp. More desolate reminders of the colonial encounter are the large blocks of cement lying in disordered heaps in the bed of the Tank Zam River, along the road near Jandola. As in the Khyber Pass, these blocks were constructed during the world wars by the British to discourage any German tanks that appeared in Afghanistan from proceeding on to India (see Ahmed 1981b).

The romance of Waziristan was related to the reputation of its tribes as fighters: "The Wazirs and Mahsuds operating in their own country, can be classed among the finest fighters in the world" (General Staff 1921, p. 5). They were "physically the hardest people on earth" (Masters 1965, p. 161). Waziristan tribes were considered "the best umpires in the world as they seldom allow a tactical error to go unpunished" (General Staff 1936, p. 163).[8] The Mahsuds, in particular, were considered "tougher, spiritually and physically than even Afridis, Orakzais or Yusufzais" (O. Caroe, personal communication). Why this is so is illustrated in the following episodes:

> One of their greatest triumphs was the seizure of Kashmir Kar
> Post in 1901 which was largely due to one of their number having

spent several weeks disguised as a shepherd learning the habits of the garrison.

This success was eclipsed by the capture of Tut Narai Post in the Upper Tochi on 31st May 1917 by a gang of Abdullai Mahsuds who employed the ruse of sending two of their members disguised as women to attract the attention of the militia garrison. The gang decamped with 59 rifles and about 12,000 rounds of ammunition. [General Staff 1921, p. 6]

So turbulent was Waziristan that at one stage it was handed over to the Army High Command and administered from Delhi. In the 1930s it was estimated there were more troops in Waziristan than on the rest of the Indian subcontinent. In 1937 an entire British brigade was wiped out in the Shahur Tangi.[9] Countless British troops and officers, including five British political agents, have died here.[10] Traditionally, steel rather than glass was used for the windows of the Scouts' forts as a protection against sniping from the surrounding hills. Once in the Waziristan arena, players, civil or military, discovered rigid local rules. The game was played either according to these rules or not at all. Sudden death could result for the careless player. No place was immune; not even the Scouts' mess.[11] Most accounts introduce a personal note of "suddenly becoming a man," "growing up," or "confronting death" within a few hours of arrival in Waziristan (Masters 1965, Pettigrew 1965).

The stormy relations with the British are reflected in this account of the origin of the Mahsuds:

An apocryphal story connects them with the produce of a bevy of slave girls brought up for the delectation of the Amir of Kabul, and insufficiently guarded while encamped under Pir Ghal. True or not as the story may be, the subsequent acts of the tribe from the day we have first known them have been well worthy of the sons of those conceived in rape and born in desertion. [Johnston 1903, p. 30]

In 1849 the British occupied the trans-Indus districts, including Peshawar, after having defeated the Sikhs. Only after the famous attack on Tank by the Mahsuds in 1860, however, was a field force ordered into Waziristan. The most formidable fighting force ever assembled in the area, it was composed entirely of British Indian troops and consisted of three squadrons of cavalry, thirteen mountain guns, and nine infantry battalions. In addition there were also some

1,600 tribal levies under their own khans and maliks. This was the first time in history that an army had marched into Waziristan, but the force was not an army of occupation and it returned to Bannu after sixteen days. A pattern for the colonial phase of history, which would end only with the departure of the British in 1947, was established: raids from Waziristan and punitive expeditions into Waziristan.[12]

The special relationship between the tribes and the Afghan government was recognized by the British soon after crossing the Indus: "The sentiments and tendencies of such characters are naturally antagonistic to our rule, and they can only resort to Kabul for encouragement to persist in them" (Macaulay 1881). As one result in this century, Waziristan tribes have played "the role of the king-makers of the day" in Kabul more than once (Caroe 1965, p. 407). Kabul, it may be noted, is only about fifty miles from the border of the Kurram Agency, less than a single day's journey by truck or bus. Thus the British found it necessary to create the tribal areas.

Making a virtue of necessity, the British signed treaties recognizing the tribal areas as special areas. Although the areas were now part of British India, the treaties of the Waziristan tribes representing nang Pukhtuns stipulated that the tribes would be allowed to continue organizing their lives as they had done in the past according to custom and tradition.[13] Such treaties contrasted with those signed by Pukhtuns leading qalang feudal states.[14] The nang tribesmen would, however, in a rather ambivalent and not clearly defined manner, accept the fact that they now belonged to the larger political entity called British India. The clause stating that they formed part of what was a "special" area within that entity was clearly underlined. Pax Britannica in the tribal areas was to extend to government property, the main roads and a hundred yards on either side of them, and no more.

The creation of the tribal areas added a new dimension and complexity to the Great Game, and the British relationship with Afghanistan was often a function of their politics in the area. It also led to a series of British policies regarding Central Asia which included both Afghanistan and Russia. The policies, as their names suggest, varied from aggressiveness to neutrality in dealing with Central Asia: "masterly inactivity," "conciliatory intervention," "close border policy," and "forward policy."

The "forward policy" was followed in the creation of the tribal areas. Partly as a response to this and partly as a result of the activity of religious leaders, a series of uprisings took place in 1897 throughout the tribal areas (Ahmed 1976). These uprisings posed the most serious threat to the British in India since the Indian rebellion of 1857. The insurgency began in Waziristan. A political officer and his party were killed in the Tochi valley in North Waziristan Agency in June. The incident triggered off large-scale fighting along the Frontier led by mullahs foretelling the end of British rule. The revolt was crushed after a series of costly expeditions by the British. The failure of the insurrection indicated that the British were in Waziristan to stay.

Did the success of the British in Waziristan mean that the Wazirs and Mahsuds had patched up their differences to present a united front to the enemy? It appears not. Contemporary British records note the enmity between the two main tribes: "The relations of the Darwesh Khel (Ahmedzai Wazirs) with the Mahsuds have never been cordial, and now they might be described as distinctly strained" (Johnston 1903, p. 22). Their rivalry prevented them from joining forces against the British: "The chief weakness of the Waziristan tribes lies in their lack of unity. The Mahsuds and Wazirs have long been at feud, and a whole-hearted combination of the two is therefore unusual" (General Staff 1921, p. 4).

When it served their purposes the British intervened in the tribal rivalry. In the 1890s they prevented the Mahsuds from ejecting the Wazirs from Wana. At other times, when the stakes were small, they remained indifferent, for instance, to the fate of those Wazirs expelled from the Baddar valley by the Dre Mahsuds. On their part, the two tribes used the presence of the British to score over each other: "Each tribe has often given advice and information to the British authorities in operations against the other" (General Staff 1936, p. 165). At the Ahnai Tangi battle in the British operations of 1919–20 in Waziristan, the Wazirs supplied a large contingent to assist the Mahsuds against the British. After dispersing the Mahsuds, the British marched on the Wazirs, who sent a request to the Mahsuds for fighting men. The Mahsuds refused, arguing that but for the Wazirs they would have made peace before the Ahnai Tangi battle. The Mahsuds underlined their message to the Wazirs by escorting the British through Mahsud areas.

The Waziristan tribesmen had confronted, assessed, and rejected Western civilization as represented by the British Empire. The history of Waziristan may be read as an attempt by them to "be men like our fathers before us" (Howell 1979, preface). A senior British official's

comment on imperial endeavor in Waziristan, after he read Howell's
Mizh, is apt: "What a record of futility it all is!" (ibid., p. 95).

In order to be men like their fathers many tribesmen migrated to Afghanistan. Jaggar, so prominently mentioned by British officials (Caroe
1965, Howell 1979, and Johnston 1903), and an inveterate enemy of
the British, found it wise to migrate to Kabul with his family.[15] The
loyalty of those who remained to create a relationship with the British
was acknowledged.[16]

When the British left in 1947, Waziristan became part of Pakistan.
A new chapter opened in Waziristan history; and it opened dramatically, in keeping with the past. Upon learning that India intended to
occupy Kashmir, a Muslim state adjacent to Pakistan, Waziristan
elders declared jihad. For them it was a fight against kafirs. In the
next few months Waziristan tribes spontaneously and voluntarily
moved in large numbers to Kashmir, where they illustrated their
military talents against superior and established armies. Spearheading
other tribal groups, they scattered battalions of Dogras, the crack
Kashmir regulars, and swept aside state troops. Sikh battalions of the
regular Indian army were flown in and reached the Srinagar airport
in time to deny it to the tribesmen. Heavy armaments air lifted from
Delhi saved the situation for the Indians, but the tribesmen with their
dated .303 rifles had come close to capturing Kashmir, one of the
most important areas of the subcontinent. During the next three
decades India and Pakistan were to fight several wars over Kashmir.

A less dramatic eruption than their Kashmir adventure took the
Mahsuds into the North Waziristan Agency. Defying established
administrative and tribal tradition, Mahsuds crossed the agency borders
into North Waziristan and almost captured Razmak from the
Utmanzai Wazirs, cousins of the Ahmedzais. The British prevented
them from doing so. They have, nonetheless, over the last decades
encroached on lands in North Waziristan overlooking Razmak. By
belonging to the South Waziristan Agency but living in the North
Waziristan Agency, the Mahsuds, superb tacticians as ever, exploit
their "citizen-of-no-state" status.[17]

The government of Pakistan, after coming into being in 1947,
encouraged the settlement of Waziristan tribes in the district and
town of Dera Ismail Khan by providing land at nominal prices. The
earlier "coming down" to the settled districts and their greater emphasis
on education differentiates the Mahsuds from the Wazirs in various
ways. The Mahsuds have entered service in larger numbers, which
gives them access to official networks. They have also become rela-

tively affluent as a result of business dealings, including a lucrative truck and bus business from Tank to Karachi. There are estimated to be as many as 30,000 Mahsuds in Karachi. The Mahsuds are, therefore, better integrated into Pakistan than the Wazirs. They themselves point this out at jirgas and as an example quote the Kashmir conflict with India in which so many more Mahsuds than Wazirs embarked on jihad. These various influences, representing different values and ideas, have exposed the Mahsud mind to the larger world. They are not likely to be swayed easily by leaders claiming mystical or spiritual powers. Elders are proud of their history and will refer to past battle glories as part of their cultural tradition in conversation. The Mahsuds will state with conviction in mulaqats and jirgas, "We are the greatest Pukhtun tribe; the greatest Muslim tribe; there are none like us."

The recent British period of history has been interesting – full of action and flair – but what has it to tell us about the emergence of the Mullah in Waziristan? First, the Mullah was not responsible for creating Wazir-Mahsud rivalry in Waziristan but merely reformulating it afresh. Given their fierce resistance to the British to maintain independence, the surrender of Waziristan tribesmen to the Mullah's authority appears all the more remarkable. Second, by appointing maliks and distributing allowances to them the British succeeded in creating rifts in an egalitarian society. In time, the maliks were seen as corrupt and servile by tribesmen, and their impotence created a vacuum for leadership, which men like the Mullah could hope to fill. Third, although the British departed in 1947, they left behind the administrative structure through which they had ruled. Both the political administrative structure and the hierarchy of personnel with all associated functions and values, remained intact. To many, in an increasingly different postindependence world, the inherited structure appeared alien and out of tune with the times.

Political administration

After the formation of Pakistan in 1947 the Wazirs and Mahsuds in South Waziristan Agency tended to stay out of each other's way except for occasional and minor clashes, usually on borderland such as Maddi Jan. No protracted or complicated clashes are noted in the 1950s and 1960s. The PA dealt with each tribe and its problems dyadically. He had his share of problems – "Pukhtunistanis," disgruntled maliks, kidnappings – but for him they were of a routine nature.[18]

The distance from the provincial capital, Peshawar, and the poor communications allowed the PA a greater degree of authority and autonomy than his counterparts had elsewhere in the frontier. The PA, especially at Wana, was often cut off even by telephone for days from his superiors in Peshawar, and had to decide on his own critical matters that demanded immediate action. He was, as the tribes pointed out in jirgas, the *badshah*, "king," of the agency.[19] The emergence of the Mullah was to change all that in the 1970s.

The laws of Pakistan, criminal, civil, or revenue, do not apply in the tribal areas.[20] No licenses or permits are required to carry a gun, symbol of Pukhtunness. The tribal areas are off limits to all except duly authorized personnel. Check-posts, including the Scouts' fort at Jandola, supervise ingress to and egress from the agency. Political parties are officially prohibited from functioning in the tribal areas. A special paramilitary unit, the Frontier Corps, and not the regular army, mans the tribal areas for military purposes.

The political administration of an agency revolves around the person of and in the office of the PA (Figure 7).The PA has been described as "half-ambassador and half-governor" (Spain 1962, p. 24) and in the days of British India usually belonged to the Indian Political Service, an elite cadre (see Appendix E for names of PAs since the creation of the agency).[21] The PA's main duties are to keep general peace, to maintain the roads, and to protect government property. The PA is assisted by an extensive field and office staff.[22] One assistant political officer and two assistant political agents are in charge of the agency's three subdivisions: Sarwekai and Ladha for the Mahsuds, and Wana for the Wazirs. The political nature of the PA's duties is reflected in his designation, political agent, and contrasts with that of his counterpart in charge of a settled district, the deputy commissioner, also called district magistrate for purposes of court work and revenue collector for revenue functions.

On his posting to an agency, information about the PA is carefully researched by tribesmen.[23] The character and wisdom of a PA are important in the political handling of the tribes. In the South Waziristan Agency this is especially true because it contains two major politically opposed tribes and the PA must remain neutral. The tribes use various devices, fair and foul, to win him over. Pressure groups demanding his attention include tribal elders (*mashar*), tribal emerging groups (*kashar*), students (as in Tank), and religious men (*ulema* and mullahs). Dissatisfaction with the PA, or his junior field officers, is expressed by sniping, explosions on government property, and even

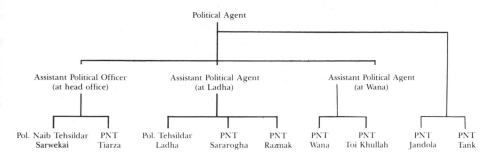

Figure 7. Administrative organization, South Waziristan Agency

kidnapping.[24] Government organizations, too, demand the PA's constant attention. These include the Scouts (tensions between the colonel and the PA are notorious), the development departments and the PA's own staff. The PA, in the midst of these currents and their pulls, must remain and be seen to remain neutral. His ability to command and make difficult decisions under adverse circumstances involving considerable danger is severely tested at all hours. The pressure on him is unrelenting.[25] One political agent, who "could not take any more," was driven to despair and committed suicide.[26] The agency has been the graveyard of political reputations and, for those successful, a jumping-off place to higher posts. The agency is therefore considered one of the more difficult and important agencies in the tribal areas.

The PA can affect honor and authority, the central issues of Waziristan society, for his powers to coerce and patronize are vast. He may use either the stick or the carrot in implementing policy. Mahsuds quote a proverb when talking of the naked use of the PA's power: *Politikal de tira barshawi, achawee de na,* "the political agent should brandish his sword but should not use it" (Afridi 1980, p. 49). Nevertheless, use of the stick has been sanctioned by custom and the Frontier Crimes Regulation; he may arrest and jail offenders or their male kin wherever he can lay hands on them and seize their property, usually at Tank (buses are the most visible and effective contemporary pressure), and in more serious cases blockade and even destroy settlements. Tank property "serves in some sort as a hostage in Government's hands for the good behavior of the tribe" (General Staff 1937, p. 15). To assist him in wielding the stick are two bodies of troops, the paramilitary South Waziristan Scouts, a corps of some 4,000 tribal soldiers, under an army colonel with headquarters at Wana, and the *khassadars* (tribal levies). Traditionally considered "the biggest and most warlike corps of all" (Masters 1965, p. 153), the South Waziristan Scouts still hold pride of place in the Frontier Corps. Their motto in Pukhto reflects their traditions: "brave men die in the battlefield" (*narina pa medan key mari*).[27] In the early years of the agency the PA was the commandant of both bodies of troops. He still commands the *khassadars* directly, who number about 3,000 in the agency.

The PA's patronage covers vast and varied areas, from heading the newly established Tank Zam public school to sanctioning social and economic projects (schools, hospitals, roads, etc.) and allotting contracts to the builders.[28] (The tribesmen thereby profit from the project itself and from the contract to build it.) As director of the Rural Works Program (which involves annual sums of 400,000 to 500,000 rupees), the PA has approval over rural development plans. He disburses, at his discretion, various allowances and secret funds to tribesmen for political work. He also approves scholarships, food rations, and domicile certificates (Appendix D).[29] The last confers rights and obligations in the agency and is an essential document of identification in Pakistan for admissions to educational institutions, employment, and so on. Finally, under his signature are issued the charcoal and timber permits.[30] In a favorable market the latter fetches up to 5,000 rupees. When discussing the powers of the PA of the South Waziristan Agency, tribesmen are quick to point out that not even the signature of the president of Pakistan can convert a scrap of paper into legal tender worth thousands of rupees.

The PA lives and travels in a style reflecting the colonial origins of his office. He moves officially, with his entire office, twice a year – from Tank to Wana in May, when it becomes hot in the plains and from Wana to Tank in September, when the chill becomes distinct. The year is divided according to nikkat, eight months for the Mahsuds and four for the Wazirs, and the tribes voice their objection if a PA overstays the stipulated period. Traditionally the move takes place on the fifteenth day of the month, accompanied by ritual and watched by the tribesmen with interest.

The house at Tank, built at the turn of the century, is characteristically colonial with its high roofs, deep verandahs, spreading lawns (which require ten gardeners), and tennis courts.[31] Equally luxurious is the Wana house. Both houses remain fully functional for the visit at short notice of important officials, such as the president or prime minister of Pakistan, both of whom traditionally stay with the PA when at Wana. Perhaps inspired by Kubla Khan's pleasure garden in

Xanadu, a former PA decreed as the "PA's garden" the magnificent rambling, walled garden outside the western Durand gate at Wana.

On tours, the PA is accompanied by a personal escort (*badragga*) of thirty Waziristan tribesmen, who are on duty during alternate months. A personal bodyguard, consisting of five Mahsuds and one Zilli Khel Wazir, protect him around the clock wherever he is. Duty with the PA is considered highly prestigious, partly because it affords access to him. For that reason the eldest personal bodyguard, a Shaman Khel Mahsud, has been in service since the mid-1940s, and refuses to step down for a younger man.

Although it would be logical to assume a growing political pressure to cut down the privileges of the PA, traditional leadership takes the opposite viewpoint. Maliks would preserve the apparent grandeur surrounding the PA. The maliks view it as reflecting the status of their agency and therefore themselves. Wazir and Mahsud elders who accompanied me on a visit to Zhob Agency in Baluchistan were constantly overheard comparing favorably the facilities of *mizh potical saib*, "our political agent sahib," to those of the political agent at Zhob Agency. The maliks are quick to question attempts at economizing: "Where will the unemployed go?" "How will it affect nikkat?" "Why challenge tradition?" They believe in upholding established tradition, for they themselves are part of the tradition.

Between 1895, when the first PA was posted, and 1980, fifty-two PAs have held office in the agency. As many as sixteen of the British PAs were once army officers. After the creation of Pakistan only two PAs have been from the Defence Services. The last British PA, who stayed on to serve in Pakistan, was assassinated by a Mahsud in May 1948.[32] Before 1947 the British PAs faced considerable personal danger. In contrast, no Pakistani PA has been killed so far. Nevertheless, the life of a Pakistani PA is not entirely free of danger. Early in 1980 machine-gun fire shattered the windscreen of the jeepster in which the PA of the North Waziristan Agency was traveling and shots were fired at the PA's bungalow at Ghalanay, Mohmand Agency. The average tenure of a PA in South Waziristan is a little more than one and a half years, but this average has been considerably altered during the last ten years, which have seen nine PAs come and go (and six commandants, although a commandant holds office for a fixed tenure of three years). The Mullah's emergence in Waziristan is directly related to this rapid turnover of officials.

Shahur Tangi, circa 1920.

Waziristan settlement.

Kaniguram.

Timber transport on camel in agency.

Wazir.

Mehr Dil attacks Nehru, on left. Political agent steps in between.
Razmak, 1946.

Emblems of British regiments engraved in Shahur Tangi.

Ladha fort.

Wana Mess.

PA's Mahsud bodyguard outside PA's bungalow, Wana.

PA's bungalow at Tank.

Constabulary post overlooking tennis courts in PA's bungalow, Tank.

Durand gate, western gate of Wana camp and Scout soldier, 1980.

PART TWO

Observation

4

Strategy and conflict
in Waziristan

The emergence of the Mullah

The story of the Mullah begins in 1920 with the migration, from the Bannu District to the Baddar valley in the South Waziristan Agency, of Maulvi Khan, a Bizan Khel Wazir.[1] The mosque at Baddar required a mullah, and the maulvi had responded to the invitation of the elders. After a few years, Maulvi Khan moved to Wana, which was then primarily a military camp with a few scattered tribal settlements around it. Of the latter the PA of the time recorded: "There are only about 120 houses altogether of these tribes living in Wana, where they will be found chiefly at Moghul Khel village just outside the camp" (Johnson 1934a, p. 8). An appointment as mullah in their small *kacha* (mud) mosque was offered to the maulvi by the Mughal Khel, a cousin lineage to the Bizan Khel (see Figure 2). The maulvi soon established his reputation in Wana as a man of piety and devotion. He distributed *taweez* ("religious talismen") and acted as a *desi hakeem*, a native medicine man.

A son, his first, was born to him in 1931 in his Bizan Khel village in Bannu District and was named Noor Muhammad ("light of the Prophet Muhammad"). Shortly after this event, the maulvi moved his entire family to Wana. It was during this time that the father of Pasti Khan, an elder of the Mughal Khel, obtained permission from the political authorities to construct another and bigger mosque for the settlement. The mosque, also kacha, was built and came to be known as the mosque of the Mughal Khel.

Maulvi Khan sent his son to the Dar-ul-uloom in Multan in the Punjab for religious schooling as a *talib* ("religious scholar," from the Arabic). The school was organized and supervised by Maulana Mufti Mahmood.[2] After completing his education, Noor Muhammad returned in the early 1950s to assist his father in the mosque. His knowledge of Islamic learning and his fluency in Urdu, gained from his education at Multan, were to be of considerable assistance to him in his career. When Maulvi Khan died in 1963, Noor Muhammad succeeded him as the mullah of the Mughal Khel mosque and as desi hakeem. Shortly before his father's death, he had organized a delegation of Wazirs, including Jalat Khan and Haji Pasti, to call on the commissioner, DIK. They requested that the grant of lease for the mosque be extended to one hundred years and additional land be provided for expansion. After considerable correspondence and meetings between the concerned officials, the requests were granted. An executive committee headed by the Mullah, and including Haji Pasti, was formed to deal with matters pertaining to the mosque. When it became necessary to name someone as sole spokesman for the mosque and executant of the land deed, the Mullah was suggested. Having secured an administrative footing the Mullah launched a vigorous drive to collect donations for a new, *pakka* ("cement") mosque on the same site. His powers of oratory and persuasion were established in his appeals for donations. The Wazirs agreed to impose a tax to be collected for the mosque of half a rupee on every camel entering the Wana market; two rupees were contributed monthly by each Wazir khassadar. Elders like Jalat Khan who rallied to the Mullah also made handsome personal contributions.

Two important economic developments in the agency coincided with the construction of the new mosque. First, a market – *adda* – sprang up between the mosque and the main road (see Figure 8). It had started in the late 1950s and early 1960s as a cluster of tiny mud shops. The Scouts had protested on the grounds that these encroachments violated their rules, which prohibit civil construction near Scouts' posts, forts, and camps. Numerous letters passed between the commandant, the PA, and the commissioner, and many meetings were held. The market, in spite of several setbacks, continued to grow. Because it was on Mughal Khel property it came to be known as Adda Mughal Khel, or adda. Eventually, some 400 shops, not more than a small room or two each, were constructed. About 250 shops were of cement and brick, and the others were kacha. The adda became a thriving center for commerce and trade in the agency. Cloth, crockery, household appliances, and edibles filled the shops to bursting. Every day, heavily loaded camel caravans arrived with wood from Birmal and tires and electrical goods from Afghanistan and departed with wheat flour, vegetable oil, and other foodstuffs. The adda lay in the Wazir area and, although some shops were sublet to Mahsuds, the Wazirs dominated the market. Its growing success

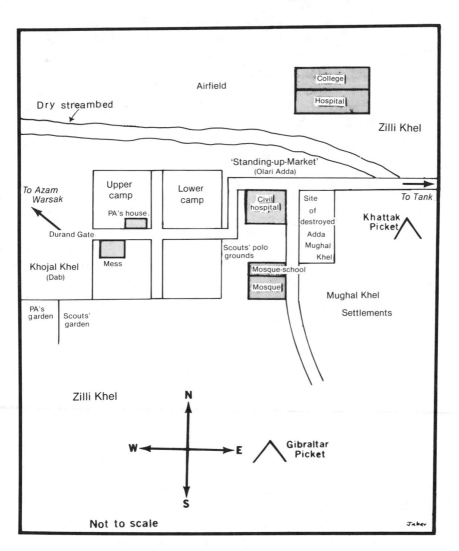

Figure 8. Mosque, market, and camp at Wana

reflected growing Wazir prosperity and provided a powerful symbol of Wazir identity. The mosque was now popularly called Adda Mughal Khel mosque, that is, mosque of the Mughal Khel market.

The importance of the adda to the Mullah and his organization was emphasized later in the official analysis of the entire drama. "It was through the Adda that Funds were generated and the *Chalweshti* [fighting men] was being maintained. Through these Funds, the supply line was being maintained, the requirements of Arms and

Ammunition being met, and on the top of it bribes were given by the Maulvi to the people whenever the situation demanded" (Political Agent's Office, 1977, p. 16). The mosque and the market were linked by their guiding genius, the Mullah.

The second economic development came in the form of a major dam, the Gomal Zam Project, started by the government of Pakistan in Wazir territory. Wazirs provided labor and were given building contracts. The project was later abandoned, but it succeeded in generating local money for a few years.

The new mosque, a magnificent structure costing between 700,000 and 800,000 rupees, was soon completed.[3] The minarets and domes were resplendent with tiles and glass of many hues. The interior reflected depth and space. A stream passed through the mosque and the variety of colored fish that were farmed in it fascinated visitors. No monument as splendid had been seen in that or any other agency until then. Elders from other agencies came to marvel at the mosque and to compliment its builder. The Mullah basked in his accomplishment and concentrated his energies in further expanding an organization around the mosque. He built a *madrassah* ("religious school") adjacent to the mosque, with dormitories for talibs, most of whom were sons of Wazir elders. A set of rooms was built for the Mullah on the second floor of the mosque, overlooking its courtyard. As a mark of deference, people now referred to him as maulvi sahib and not by his name.

It was felt that walking about on foot, especially to the Wana camp, was not in keeping with his growing status. It meant being jostled and accosted by maliks, petty officials and the common Wazir. The Wazirs, therefore, organized a collection, and a car was purchased for the Mullah in 1966. In those days even leading maliks of the agency, like Gulab Khan, walked on foot, and the Mullah's car added to his prestige and status. In time the purchase of a new car, usually a Toyota, for the Mullah assumed the significance of a rite, performed at least twice a year.

Having secured the religious base in the mosque, the Mullah proceeded to expand his sphere of activity. He secured shops in the adda for those talibs who graduated from the madrassah or accommodated them in neighboring mosques in the Wazir area. In the latter half of the 1960s the Mullah began to test overtly the political waters of the agency. His name began to appear in official correspondence. In May 1966 the political agent wrote to his assistant political officer: "It has been observed that a few days back Mufti Mahmood of

Paniala, District D.I. Khan, went to Wana on the invitation of the Maulvi Noor Mohammad where they delivered speeches in the Adda Mughal Khel Mosque criticising the Government for un-Islamic laws in the country" (PA to APO, May 28, 1966).[4]

A copy of the note was sent to the APA at Wana with instructions to "please send for Maulvi Noor Mohammad and warn him in suitable terms that we will not allow the Government criticised by anybody anywhere in the Agency and any such action in future will be interpreted as hostile towards the Government." The PA "hoped the Maulvi will not only desist from such like acts in future but will keep away from politics as well, if he wants to maintain his present position in the Agency" (ibid.).

In an incident some months later, the Mullah exhibited his capacity to turn a situation adroitly to his advantage. The opportunity presented itself to him in the sighting of the moon, which announces the festival of Eid at the end of Ramadan, the month of fasting. Throughout the Islamic world minor discrepancies arise as to the hour, or even day of the sighting. The following official note relates the episode well and I shall, therefore, quote it in full:

> Maulvi, being on very good terms with Subedar Sarwar Shah (Signal Corps) and Subedar Major South Waziristan Scouts, asked them to pass on information received from any of the Scouts Post/Picket in the Agency regarding the sighting of the moon. Sarwar Shah passed on the information to Maulvi on the 11th evening that no reports about sighting of the moon had been received from any Scouts Post/Picket in the Agency. The same evening the Subedar Major also called on the Maulvi. Maulvi Noor Mohammad told the Subedar Major that since the moon has not been sighted, he, in consultation with other Maulvis, decided to celebrate Eid on the 13th January, 1967, although he himself had heard the decision of Roheeth Hillal Committee on radio on the 11th evening. He further requested the Subedar Major not to fire any gun that evening so that the people in the vicinity of camp may not get an inkling that the Eid will be celebrated on the 12th January, 1967.
>
> The Subedar Major complied with his request and did not fire a single shot though the decision of the Government that the Eid would be celebrated on 12.1.1967, was known to him. Since it is customary that fires and shots on such occasions by the Scouts, the people generally thought that Eid would not be celebrated on 12.1.1967. The Commandant S.W.S. told me that he had a word in this respect with my predecessor but as he was under transfer

> he did not take any notice of it. And hence under the instruction
> of Maulvi Noor Mohammad, Khatib Jamia Masjid, Mughal Khel,
> the people of Wana celebrated Eid on the 13th January, 1967
> while the rest of the Agency celebrated Eid on 12.1.1967." [APA,
> Wana, to PA, February 10, 1967]

The Mullah had used his contacts with official networks to obtain special information and thus establish his authority among the Wazirs. The incident is widely quoted in Waziristan as an example of the powers of the Mullah in manipulating official contacts and asserting his will over the Wazirs. It illustrates his shrewd understanding of both administrative working and tribal psychology. He was to use this gift with skill in the coming years.

It is about this time that the Mullah first interfered, though with caution, in the political affairs of the agency. In the following case he once again exhibited his political shrewdness and skills. An old land dispute between the Gangi Khel and Masti Khel Wazirs in Dhanna, a few miles from Wana, had flared up. Masti Khel elders formed a jirga and called on the Mullah in Wana. They were prepared to accept nanawatee, which implies admission of defeat. A primary feature of Pukhtunwali, nanawatee is ideally then also agreed to by the rival party. The Mullah, making a flimsy excuse that he was preoccupied, refused to negotiate on their behalf and turned back the jirga. In the meantime the dispute took a serious turn and in the gunfire that followed, four males, two from each group, were killed. Death turns a temporary conflict into a vendetta, which could involve badal lasting for generations. The situation further deteriorated as allied groups of the contestants began to converge on Dhanna. The Masti and Gangi Khel elders were desperate and looked around for mediation. The Mullah saw his opportunity. His talibs were sent out to announce his spiritual powers, through which he could impose peace. He demanded unconditional agreement to his decision in advance. The elders of the two parties gladly accepted his terms. Having established general credibility the Mullah arrived at the right psychological moment and announced peace terms that were unanimously accepted. The Mullah was now being recognized as a man both of piety and political skill; a man of leadership and a man to turn to in times of crisis.

The Mullah, continuing to distribute taweez as cures for the ill and providing council for the grieved, was soon reputed to possess healing powers, of which taweez were the symbols. Payments were made to him in gratitude for such favors; dyadic links were cemented with prestations. Economic favors were exchanged for spiritual patronage.

The Wazirs had found a spiritual leader they could trust, and he was becoming the symbol of their revived pride and identity. An emotionally contagious atmosphere surrounded him.

Apart from the religious functions he had assumed, the Mullah imposed a general Wazir peace in the area, fining and punishing those who quarreled among themselves. His peace patched old tarboorwali enmities like the one between Jalat and Bangul (see Chapter 2). He also began to arbitrate actively between groups in conflict. Clearly he was appropriating the roles both of the traditional elders in a jirga and of the political administration.

Larger developments in Pakistan helped provide a suitable background for the Mullah's emergence. In December 1971, Bangla Desh was created after the secession of East Pakistan from Pakistan. The successful ethnic struggle led by a charismatic leader against the central government provided ideas to others in Pakistan. An air of uncertainty lay over the land after the trauma of the December war and the loss of East Pakistan. The uncertainty contrasted with the relative surface calm and stability of the Ayub Khan era (1958-69). Matters were made worse by the large number of prisoners, more than 100,000, taken by India after the war. Many Pakistani Muslims considered this fact, along with the ignominy of defeat, unique in the annals of Islamic history. From the South Waziristan Agency some 18,000 tribesmen, mostly Mahsuds who were soldiers in the army or in the Scouts serving in East Pakistan, languished as prisoners-of-war in Indian camps. Families of the prisoners asked questions and demanded answers from the Pakistan authorities. The mood of the country was one of deep crisis; people were bewildered and in despair.

In this atmosphere Mr. Z. A. Bhutto emerged as the political leader of Pakistan, rallying a dispirited nation. Initially he seemed to offer a viable model of politics. The Mullah watched and learned. Indeed, there were certain similarities between the two men. Both were relatively young leaders with considerable political skill and organizational ability who relied on their charisma and oratory to gain followers. Both were men of vision: One wished to transform Pakistan society; the other, Wazir society. Both spoke in the language of hyperbole and poetic populism. To their critics their demeanor bordered on arrogance, because they brooked no opposition. Their critics also accused them of crass opportunism. For better or worse, the politics of Pakistan in the 1970s was to be cast in the mould of Mr. Bhutto.[5]

The Mullah in the first years of the 1970s launched a vigorous campaign to establish his dominance over Wazir minds and in Wazir society. For instance, he forbade the use of the radio in the adda, calling it un-Islamic. He then listened to its programs punctiliously, and from the information he heard he would "predict" national events at the Friday congregation in the mosque. His announcement of the National Pay Commission is one such example. The Mullah informed his following that he was praying for an increase in the pay of the poorly paid (about 200 to 250 rupees a month) Wazir khassadars and Scouts' soldiers. Increase in official salaries was being debated nationally during 1972–73, and an announcement on the matter was imminent. Forbidden to hear the radio and generally being illiterate the Wazir tribe remained largely unaware of the national debate. When the government announced an increase in salaries the Wazirs took it as an example of the Mullah's powers to predict and influence events. The khassadars were particularly impressed and increased their monthly individual contribution for the mosque fund from two to four rupees.

The Mullah now imposed various taxes on almost every aspect of commercial activity at the adda, ostensibly to support the mosque. Every shop paid a monthly contribution of ten rupees. Smaller charges were imposed on items sold, for instance, two rupees for a camel-load (usually of wood), one-fourth of a rupee per crate of apples, and half a rupee per animal. The khassadars, to display their loyalty, further increased their monthly contribution to five rupees. Fines brought in more money. A shop owner violating the radio ban could be fined 500 rupees by the chalweshti and also beaten up by them. Mir Askar, a Khojal Khel elder who remained defiant throughout, was regularly fined and manhandled by the chalweshti. Wazir maliks who received a timber permit were expected to donate half of its market price to the Mullah. Estimates of the income from these sources vary from 20,000 to 30,000 rupees daily. The Mullah kept half the sum, and the other half was divided among the chalweshti, who organized its collection, and the Mullah's followers. No audit of these sums was conducted nor were the figures made public.

Unlimited money now allowed the Mullah to live a life of ease, and the swelling number of followers demanded he do so. His dressing and personal habits were becoming fastidious. It was said he changed his clothes twice or three times daily and, according to those with discerning noses, his scent a similar number of times. His hands and beard, scented and impeccably clean, and his somewhat plump appearance signified a man of wealth and leisure.

About this time the Mullah began to imitate and develop some of the more formal aspects of bureaucracy associated with the PA. Mulaqats were arranged with him after formal, often written, requests through the chalweshti hierarchy. He issued chits to his followers ordering official schools or dispensaries to provide admission, and he wrote notes asking officials to give interviews "to the bearer of the note"; his requests were honored and his whims humored. Armed guards escorted him wherever he went. These were the visible symbols of his growing importance in and to society. By appropriating some of the form and content of the PA's functions, he was setting himself on a collision course with that office.

A celebrated example of the Mullah's spiritual power was provided by the selection of Pirzada to the junior administrative post of xaib tehsildar.[6] The son of Muhammad Yar, an elder of the Zilli Khel, Pirzada and his father had visited the Mullah in the mosque in public to request prayers on Pirzada's behalf. The Mullah promised special prayers, as a result of which, he declared, Pirzada would be selected as naib tehsildar. He knew, through his contacts with the lower rungs of the administration, that Pirzada was the only candidate for the post. When the news of Pirzada's selection was announced, the Wazirs were once again given "proof" of the Mullah's powers. Pirzada's brother, Shahzada, and his father swore undying loyalty to the Mullah, which they were to honor to the end. The Wazirs bestowed the title of *de janat mata*, "pillar of heaven," on him.

Other stage-managed incidents were interpreted by talibs and chalweshti as signs of the Mullah's special power and authority over men. One such man was the new commandant, Colonel Ali Gohar (1972–3). Finding the colonel sympathetic, the Mullah cultivated him assiduously and requested his assistance in building an unmetalled kacha road, about ten miles long, from Wana to Tatti Kach. The colonel obliged by offering a construction crew of a hundred Scouts' soldiers. The Wazirs provided additional free manual labor as well as funds, and the road became an excellent example of self-help in rural development. The Mullah extolled the virtues of the colonel as a "true Pukhtun" in his sermons. During his one-year tenure, the colonel would be a considerable asset to the Mullah.

On an official visit to Wana, Arbab Sikander Khan, governor of the NWFP (1972–3) and head of the National Awami party (NAP), abandoned protocol and called on the Mullah in his rooms in the mosque late at night. The visit confirmed the Mullah's national stature in the eyes of the Wazirs. Such episodes emphasized to the

Wazirs the need for unity and submission to the command of the Mullah. To them he was becoming the quintessential figure of their finer ideals and aspirations.

After Arbab Sikander's visit the Mullah introduced the theme of Pukhtun nationalism into his speeches and sermons.[7] This indicated an alignment with the NAP, which favored Pukhtun nationalism, and opposition to Mr. Bhutto's party, the PPP, which held power in the center in Islamabad. It was also rumored that the North-West Frontier government, under NAP pressure, contemplated the transfer of control of Wana Subdivision to Baluchistan. The implication of acquiring a separate administrative status and thus escaping Mahsud domination was clear to the Wazirs.

The visit of the deputy speaker of the Baluchistan government, a NAP supporter from the Zhob Agency, was interpreted as a harbinger of the rumored administrative arrangement. It also illustrated the progressing deterioration of the relationship between the Mullah and the PA. In a speech made in the Wana mosque the visitor from Baluchistan warned: "If anyone uses a pen against Maulvi Noor Muhammad we will break that pen and if anyone raises a hand against him we will break that hand." These lines were to be often cited by the Wazirs in the coming years.

The Mullah stepped up his praise of Colonel Ali Gohar in his sermons "as a true and brave Pukhtun," which drove the wedge deeper between the PA and the commandant. The PA, in contrast, was dismissed as a "fool" and "politically incompetent" (Noor Muhammad n.d., p. 89).

Playing the Pukhtun nationalist tune, the Mullah resorted to explicit ethnic themes. While praising Colonel Ali Gohar, he condemned the PA and APA as "cowardly," dismissing them as *kharai* – from Peshawar – and "tools of Punjabi domination."[8] In the context of frontier politics and ethnic tensions, *Khar*, or Peshawar, where the PA lived, and Swabi, the home of the colonel, represent two mutually opposed and distinct prototypes. Khar traditionally supports the center in Islamabad, and is strongly opposed to the politics of the NAP. Swabi is just as strongly the hotbed of Pukhtun nationalist politics. Their respective languages act as defining barriers. *Kharis* speak Hindko, akin to Punjabi, and Swabi is the home of orthodox Yusufzai Pukhto, where it is spoken with self-conscious pride.

The Mullah's new crusade for Pukhtun nationalism was short-lived. Only a few months after Bhutto dismissed the NAP government from the NWFP, the Mullah appeared to be moving to the PPP:

> It has reliably been learnt, and as already reported, the Maulvi
> has been making overtures to Hayat Muhammad Khan Sherpao
> [leader of the PPP in the NWFP] and Mr. Khurshid Hassan Mir,
> Minister, for permission to set up a Branch of the Pakistan
> People's Party at Wana under his patronage. The rumours which
> are afloat today are his emissaries have finally succeeded in
> receiving Hayat Muhammad Khan Sherpao's blessings and that
> the latter has sent word to Malik Bashir Advocate and Muhammad
> Farooq, General Secretary, PPP, D. I. Khan to come to Wana and
> formally hoist the PPP flag here. [PA at Wana to commissioner,
> DIK, June 16, 1973]

If the PPP leadership did not, at least the PA saw clearly through the
Mullah's game:

> The other day his open crabbing against Maulvi Mufti Mahmud,
> instead of startling me in fact intrigued me because he intended
> thereby to make us less wary about his game. A very young man
> as he is, his game, however, is too transparent to escape the notice
> of those who have had the opportunity to meet hundreds like
> him." [Ibid.]

The view that the Mullah was not serious about the PPP was to prevail
in official circles for the coming years:

> After the fall of NAP Government in the Province, Maulvi Noor
> Mohammad has given out to have joined PPP but this fact does
> not seem to be true. I believe that Maulvi Noor Mohammad who
> has become an important and wealthy man over the past 8/10
> years is a party by himself. A clever, power loving man, conscious
> of the lukewarm policies of the Political Administration, well
> established in the midst of orthodox ignorant Wazirs can very
> well play the role of religious leader. [APA, Wana, to PA, March
> 30, 1975]

The Mullah, indeed, appeared to be "a party by himself" and advised
his followers "to join different political parties in order to gather
information" (Noor Muhammad n.d., p. 138).

The Mullah had been biding his time before challenging the
traditional leaders of Wazir society, the maliks and the *pirs* (religious
leaders). When he felt strong enough he came into the open and
poured forth scorn and venom on them. As a result, traditional and
somewhat ineffective leaders like Malik Pasti, the Mughal Khel elder,
and such established religious figures as the pir of Wana came under

considerable pressure from the tribe. They held their peace "to save their self-respect." An occasional bomb blast (at Malik Pasti's home) or ambush (of Khojal Khel elders) made sure the point of the Mullah's authority was not lost on recalcitrant elders.[9] Officials in the political administration read the Mullah's attack on their traditional allies, the maliks, as a prelude to challenging established authority:

> His first target was the institution of Maliki. He started condemning the Maliks openly and at times when he abused them on the pulpit. The idea was to weaken the institutional arrangements so that he could bulldoze his way by shattering all the norms and forms of administration. The Maliks started feeling uneasy but owing to his deepening influence on the tribe they found themselves absolutely helpless. They had no other option but to join his umbrella where they felt they could shelter themselves against the wrath of the *teeman* [populace, common people] who would go into a state of frenzy at the slightest provocation by Maulvi. [Political Agent's Office 1977, p. 4]

Dismissing traditional leaders as "government toadies" who only worked for their own selfish interests. the Mullah built up an alternative leadership. Around himself he gathered together the *dolas kassi* ("twelve men"), mainly from the Zilli Khel, which assumed the status of his cabinet and conducted affairs on his behalf. The cabinet included eloquent men like Ba Khan, Zilli Khel, a kashar and therefore not a traditional malik. The chalweshti was streamlined to ensure immediate implementation of his decisions. Those who opposed his wishes were incarcerated for short periods in a jail organized for this purpose. Many traditional Zilli Khel elders, like Jalat, supported him wholeheartedly because they saw in him a viable focus of opposition to their traditional rivals, the Mahsuds. The Mullah in bypassing traditional leadership, and exposing it as impotent and corrupt, had created a powerful base in the teeman. The teeman, which included women and children, reflected their confidence in him through expressions of personal loyalty. Traditional leaders had been outflanked by the Mullah's approach to the hearts of the Wazirs. The Mullah had become the very embodiment of Wazir aspirations.

From being a traditional mullah serving the tribe, he had now emerged as a leader representing and speaking for the tribe. The transformation from subordinate to superordinate position in society was as visible as portentous; however, the passage was smooth and not marked by any dramatic event. The Mullah was impressed and somewhat awed by his own growing popularity: "There was such a multitude of people which reminded people who had performed *haj* of Arafa [where the Holy Prophet preached]" (Noor Muhammad n.d., pp. 21–22). He perceived a sense of destiny pervading his actions. Addressing himself, he noted: "God Almighty has given you status and influence matched by few men in history" (ibid.). In his diaries he did not refer to himself in the first person, a traditional practice of Muslim royalty. Indeed, the theme of royalty was not far from his mind: "When they insisted you address the gathering they introduced you as *the uncrowned king [badshah] of Wana*" (ibid.). The title was underlined thrice by the Mullah. There was another claimant to the title in the agency, however, and it is a notorious principle of history that no realm can support two kings.

The Wazirs rampant

The timber problem, which manifested itself through the timber permit, remained a chronic sore in the agency administration and provided the Mullah an opportunity finally to consolidate his leadership. He organized a general agitation against the system of the timber permit. To begin with, the Wazirs agreed to object to receiving the timber permit at Tank, which they perceived as a Mahsud town: "The Ahmedzai Jirga came to me in this connection today and told me that they were not prepared to receive their Timber Permits at Tank, and that their feelings may be conveyed to the Political Agent." In addition, any Wazir breaking the agreement would be fined: "They have also decided that anyone who pays a visit to Tank in connection with his Timber Permit share will be subject to a *kanra* [fine; lit., 'stone'] of Rs. 20,000 (Rupees Twenty thousand)." (APA, Wana, to PA, March 6, 1972). The APA suggested that the PA concede to the Wazir demand and come to Wana to distribute the permits: "In case they are adamant then it would be advisable that the Political Agent pay monthly visits to Wana for distribution of Permits to Ahmedzai Wazirs" (ibid.). The Mahsuds, in retaliation, insisted on the PA's presence in Tank according to tradition and nikkat. The dolas kassi responded by issuing the following orders included in a note from the APA to the PA:

> (1) The Wazir Members of the Permit Committee should be stopped altogether from purchasing the permits for the time being.
> (2) All the *wesha* [timber] lorries including those of Mahsuds

going out of Wana should be stopped and no wesha traffic should
be allowed.

(3) The road contractor on Tanai-Gul Kach Road should be
stopped from carrying out the work.

(4) Drummers should be brought to Adda Mughal Khel and
drum beating should be started as a protest against our orders.
[APA, Wana, to PA, March 8, 1972]

In the same letter the APA, fully conceding Wazir demands, suggested that the permits be delivered to "Maulvi Noor Muhammad
Sahib of the Adda" for distribution among the Wazirs. The Mullah
was now addressed as "sahib," a formal term of respect for those in
authority, and was designated as "of the Adda." His leadership as the
spokesman of the Wazirs in times of crisis was officially acknowledged.

For the present the PA thought it wise to follow his APA's suggestion, but the problem of the timber permits remained unresolved. As
a way out of the impasse the PA formed a Timber Committee
consisting of four leading maliks of the agency, two from each tribe.
The committee, the PA calculated, would democratize the process
and disengage him from distributing the timber permits. Noor
Muhammad was appointed chairman of the committee. The committee would henceforth handle all timber problems. Upon coming
into being the committee fixed a price of 1,200 rupees for a permit.
The holders of permits were compelled to sell them to the committee
which, in view of its monopoly position and political authority, resold
them at considerably higher sums to middlemen. As the timber trade
and market were situated in the Wazir area, the Mahsuds were
ignored in the back-door dealings that followed. The Mullah had
discovered a rich source of income. The Timber Committee assumed
the function of a parallel administration, and through it the writ of
the Mullah ran unchallenged in Wazir territory. Certain smaller clans,
like the Khojal Khel, continued to oppose the Mullah, but various
measures, including assassination attempts and fines, subdued their
opposition.

The Mahsuds reacted strongly to the developments and charged
the Mullah with dishonest handling of the timber money, which had
allowed him to acquire property in Dera Ismail Khan under assumed
names. The administration, too, was aware of these developments:
"The income from Committee and other sources of taxation by
Maulvi was meant for the chosen few and for the Maulvi's personal
benefit. He had his business partnership with many people, bought

land squares at D.I. Khan and made investments under cover names" (Political Agent's Office 1977, p. 6). The position of the administration and of the Mahsuds on the Mullah was beginning to coincide; both were reaching the limits of their tolerance. Mahsud hawks began to beat drums in the agency and called for a mobilization. The conflict between the Wazirs and the Mahsuds was in the open. Each tribe declared its area out of bounds to the other tribe.

The Mullah countered by adopting several lines of action. Most effective were his sermons in the mosque. In these he declared jihad against the Mahsuds. Having raised Wazir emotions to a high pitch he condemned the Mahsuds as kafir. The Mahsuds had dominated and exploited Wazirs against the spirit of Islam, he argued. They were no better than Hindus. The time had arrived to rid themselves of the Mahsuds. The imminent jihad would be between good and evil, between Muslim and Hindu. God was on the side of the Wazirs. If, he declared in his fiery sermons, a Wazir killed a Mahsud it would be the equivalent of killing a Hindu kafir. If, on the other hand, a Wazir was killed by a Mahsud he would become *shaheed*, one who dies for Islam, and win paradise because he had been killed by a kafir. The rhetoric inflamed the Wazirs. By deploying religious arguments in a fundamentally tribal conflict the Mullah was bringing about an internal fusion in society between the spiritual and the social.

Simultaneously, the Mullah brought up the issue of an alternative route, hitherto closed, along the Gomal River to the settled districts. The Gomal road, which would bypass the Mahsud area, would be the first major step in obtaining a separate agency for the Wazirs. A separate agency would deprive the Mahsuds of the entire timber funds and would also reduce the importance and size of the present agency. Above all, for the Mahsuds, it would allow their agnatic rivals to escape from the agency arena and establish their own identity.

The Mahsuds, not being able to dismiss the Mullah as an "unbeliever," stepped up their attack on his character (debauched, homosexual, practicer of black magic, etc.), which indirectly reflected on Wazir morality. The Mahsuds impugned the Mullah's "Pukhtunness" and accused the Wazirs of being without shame, of deviating from Pukhtunwali. Mystification of Pukhtunness was a strategy employed by the Mahsuds to counter the accusation of being kafir by the Mullah. An ethnic counterattack was made to a religious attack. Feelings on both sides ran high. The battle hysteria divided Wazirs and Mahsuds sharply, and the two camps began to prepare for armed confrontation.

The PA, faced with the multidimensional aspects of the growing Wazir-Mahsud problem, decided in early 1973 to take firm action. First, he abolished the Timber Committee. The timber permits were now sold from his office. In the context of the hysteria being built up in the agency the action did not please or suit any party. Although the Wazirs continued to buy the permits and resell them at inflated prices, they resented the dissolution of the committee. The Mahsuds insisted that the permits should be sold in the open market and not at fixed prices.

Second, the arrest of the dolas kassi and chalweshti was secretly ordered. The PA also ordered the adda to be blown up on the following day if they refused to surrender. Blowing up the adda would cost the Wazirs millions of rupees. The shops did a thriving business and were full of goods. Besides, most owners kept a safe on the premises for their money. As the PA's relations with the commandant were severely strained, a fact advertised and exploited by the Mullah, the action was ordered when the commandant was away from the agency. Unfortunately for the PA, the commandant arrived in Wana late at night and, it was widely rumored, upon learning of the plans passed on the information to the Mullah (Noor Muhammad n.d., p. 102). The Mullah immediately called an emergency meeting of his key men. He observed that in the past "whenever the Scouts came to arrest our people they ran and hid in fields and mountains." Tomorrow, he commanded, "no one will offer themselves for arrest and if necessary they will fight" (ibid.).

At the crack of dawn, heavy guns were placed around the adda, which was surrounded by the Scouts. The APA, Wana, leading the official party, demanded that the dolas kassi and chalweshti come forth and hand themselves over to him. The Mullah's men were prepared. The chalweshti commander, designated *jernail* (from "general") by the Mullah, returned the message that "he was not General Niazi [the commander of the Pakistan Army in East Pakistan, who surrendered to the Indians in December 1971] and would not surrender alive" (ibid., p. 103). The APA issued written orders on the spot for the adda to be blown up. These orders were countermanded by the commandant. Confusion and a sense of anticlimax prevailed. A stalemate had developed, and by the end of the long, cold day it was apparent that the Mullah had won a major moral and political victory for the Wazirs: "The 22nd of February, 1973," he observed in his notebook, "has added a new chapter to the history of the Ahmedzai

Wazirs" (ibid., p. 102). He exulted that "two to three Wazirs faced each Scout's sepoy and all night the sepoys shivered in the rain and cold" (ibid., p. 103). The Mullah had publicly defied and humiliated the political authorities and got away with it.

Shortly after, the PA made another attempt to curb the Mullah's influence by arresting some of his Wazir supporters. The Mullah convened an emergency jirga at Wana. He ordered "all Wazir Maliks and leaders present themselves at Adda Mughal Khel in three days and anybody absent will be severely dealt with." The administration was warned to release his men before the jirga or face dire consequences (ibid., p. 106). On the third day, the atmosphere in Wana was highly charged as some 2,000 armed Wazirs gathered to await the Mullah's orders. Into this rally drove the commandant, bringing with him the Mullah's men, who had been unconditionally released by the PA. "I expect he will not go awry again and repent his wrong actions," commented the Mullah of the PA (ibid.).

Acts symbolizing humiliation of the administration now became commonplace in Wana. For example, a dog, representing the PA, was placed on a cot, carried in a large procession, and then given a sound thrashing. This symbolic representation of relations between the administration and the Wazirs was to be repeated in the following months.

The PA was further isolated by the Mullah's careful cultivation of the commissioner at Dera Ismail Khan, whom he termed an "honourable and intelligent officer" (ibid., pp. 88–90). The Mullah helped to create misunderstanding between the two officials by adopting a series of successful strategies. An example of one such maneuver involved the PA's ban on timber export from the agency for a certain period. The Mullah visited the commissioner in Dera Ismail Khan and obtained a permit from him. After his return to the agency the permit was used, and a truck, laden with timber, proceeded to Jandola. On the PA's standing orders the truck was detained, and the Wazirs informed the commissioner on the telephone that his permit had not been honored by the PA. The result, the Mullah noted with satisfaction, was increased pressure on and further isolation of the PA (ibid.). Politics at various administrative levels had become personal and bitter, and the two tribes were playing officials off against each other.

Provoked beyond endurance the PA broke the official chain of communication, bypassing the commissioner, DIK, and corresponded directly with the home secretary at Peshawar in April 1973 to express his despair about agency affairs. He referred to the visit of the chief secretary, NWFP, and his attempts to solve the main agency problems.

> The upshot of the tiresome meetings which the Chief Secretary had undergone was that the Commissioner D. I. Khan would give the Political Agent an unqualified assurance that Mahsuds business at Wana would not be interfered with by the Ahmedzai Wazirs of that place and thereafter the Political Agent would be responsible to ensure the lifting of the blockade by the Mahsuds of Ahmedzai Wazirs of Wana in South Waziristan Agency. [PA to Home Secretary, April 3, 1973]

The PA also mentioned the attempts of the commandant and commissioner, DIK, to frustrate him:

> My numerous complaints about, leave alone, non-cooperation but total opposition of my legitimate directions and authority by the Commandant, S. W. Scouts, never went beyond the office of the Divisional Commissioner. Despite my receiving a handsome apology from a noble and superior officer like Brigadier Nasirullah Khan Babar, Inspector General Frontier Corps, for the conduct of the Commandant S. W. Scouts, the Commandant persists in non-cooperation and behaving contrary to my directions in which apparently the Commandant has the support of the Divisional Commissioner. [Ibid.]

In an exceptional gesture of despair the PA concluded his note with a request to the government to transfer him from the agency [ibid.]. A new PA would be posted the following month. The demoralization of the administration had reached its nadir.

The Mullah's campaign to discomfit the PA and thereby ensure his early transfer continued unabated. A course of action charted out by the Mullah was repeated at Wazir jirgas:

> No one should see the PA, SW; however, the Ahmedzai Wazirs may keep their relations good with APA Wana. If the Government is not going to transfer the present PA, SW, then the Ahmedzai have no objection to it but no Ahmedzai will see him. Defaulters will be liable to pay penalty of Rs.20,000. Maulvi urged for allowing vehicle traffic on Gomal Road. He added that PA,SW is trying to make friction among the Ahmedzais but they should remain alert and may not disturb their unity. [Political Agent's Office (1966–80), Situation Intelligence Report of Wana tehsil, May 20, 1973]

Those who still saw the PA were punished: "After the speech of Mullah Noor Muhammad, Khudaimir Matak Khel, (member of dolas kassi) announced that Malik Hakim is fined for seeing PA,SW, some days back. The amount of fine is not known and will be told to them after three days" (ibid.). On leaving the agency the PA analyzed the situation for the government and predicted dire consequences if firm action were not taken:

> As I have repeatedly pointed out the only mischief in South Waziristan Agency is at Wana; at Wana all the commotion is created in Adda Mughal Khel a protected area; and the source of mischief is Maulvi Noor Muhammad . . . . I would respectfully urge the Divisional Commissioner with all the emphasis at my command that the only course of action which presents itself to me to overcome a great up-heaval which may result in confrontation of Mahsud and Wazir tribes of this Agency and may lead to fatal encounters amongst them, Maulvi Noor Muhammad (JUI) and his brother Niaz Muhammad who are permanent residents of the Agency living in the protected area should be externed under section 36 of Frontier Crimes Regulation for a period of three years. [PA to commissioner, May 24, 1973]

Although the PA's transfer was seen as a victory for the Mullah, it did not mollify him. It only appeared to whet his appetite for more active interference in administrative matters. Shortly after, the Mullah lost an ally when Colonel Ali Gohar was transferred before the completion of his tenure. Certain high officials in Peshawar and Islamabad may have suggested this action to balance the transfer of the PA and indicate support for his office. On his transfer the colonel was given a memorable farewell: "On 20.6.1973; the Ahmedzai Wazirs of Wana gave a warm send off to Lieutenant-Colonel Ali Gohar. Those who organized the send off were the Ithihad-e-Qabail, *dolas kassi* and Maulvi Noor Muhammad. A ceremonial gate had been erected near Malik Jalat's pump by the members of Ithihad-e-Qabail" (APA Wana to PA, July 1, 1973). Both the colonel and the PA were seen as victims of the Mullah's politics. Among the Wazirs in and around Wana, the Mullah's supremacy was unchallenged.

Along with the cry for jihad against the Mahsuds, other action was taken by the Mullah to pour fuel on the Waziristan fire. For example, a Mahsud was paid by the Mullah's men to stop and loot a Wazir bus on the main agency road in the Mahsud area. The Mullah's direct complicity was suspected in these incidents: "It is no more a secret that the Maulvi paid some money to a Nano Khel Mahsud who looted the Ahmedzai Wazir bus and then the storm broke. Maulvi blared the incident and its pathetic detail on loud speaker and his crowd started swelling day by day" (Political Agent's Office, 1977, p. 7). The Wazirs retaliated by performing similar acts in their area against Mahsuds. Traffic between Wana and Jandola, on the main road of the agency, was virtually suspended. Such incidents over the next years further strengthened the Mullah's argument for a separate road, indeed, agency, for the Wazirs.

In the summer of 1975, Wazir and Mahsud war parties, *lashkars*, clashed with each other in several places. At Maddi Jan, a traditional border of the two tribes, a major encounter took place in which several men on both sides were killed and several others wounded. The agency had become a battleground for the two tribes.[10]

Surveying the scene in mid-1975, the PA noted: "For the past five years the political administration in South Waziristan has been confronted with the intractable problem of 'Adda Mughal Khel,' where a third force more powerful than the Wazirs and Mahsuds has emerged in the personality of Maulvi Noor Muhammad" (PA to commissioner, May 28, 1975). He contemplated the immediate past: "Within a week of my taking over, the Governor NWFP visited Wana in the 2nd week of August, 1974. The Ahmedzai Wazirs demanded (i) separated Agency and (ii) opening of the Gomal route. These two demands were repeated more vehemently before the Federal Interior Minister, Khan Abdul Qayum Khan, during his visit of Waziristan in March, 1975" (ibid.). The PA suggested firm action against the Mullah and tallied up his official victims: "In the meantime I suggest very strongly that we should strike at the root cause of this trouble which has created enormous bad blood between the tribes and has so far tolled one Commissioner, two Political Agents and one Scouts Commandant" (ibid.).

Late in the summer of 1975 the Mullah ordered a total boycott of the administration until his demand for the opening of the Gomal route was met. The Mullah commanded that Wazir khassadars quit their posts, schools close, and government servants boycott their offices. Further, shops were to hoist black flags, the chalweshti were to wear black arm bands, and the timber trade was to cease (Noor Muhammad n.d., pp. 108–16). No shop in the adda, or in Wazir territory, would be allowed to sell any commodity to government personnel. A Wazir disobeying the Mullah's orders would be fined up to 50,000 rupees by the chalweshti. In an expression of overenthusiasm, Wazir khassadars not only stopped performing their duties but smashed their official quarters, the pickets and posts placed along roads and by government buildings. Furthermore, the Mullah declared, the authority of the APA, Wana, would not be recognized by the Wazir tribe (ibid.). In a "warning" to the Scouts the Mullah stated that "until now the Ahmedzai Wazirs were firing in the air as a protest and not as they were bad marksmen" (ibid., pp. 59–60). He further added, "in future if their dictatorial attitudes do not change he will teach them a lesson and the Wazirs will rain bullets from the hills and cripple their artillery" (ibid.). In retaliation the administration fined Wazirs, suspended those in service, and cancelled their privileges, such as mulaqats. These sanctions did not break Wazir ranks. The Wazirs had effectively paralyzed life in Wana subdivision.

The Mullah's boycott had several aims. It was meant to threaten the administration into submission, show the power of the Wazirs to the Mahsuds, and consolidate the Mullah's authority. The Wazirs were ordered to prepare lashkars to capture the Gomal road. A separate agency, of which he would be de facto ruler, was now the Mullah's main demand and declared ambition.

An abortive attempt was made by the PA to stem the drift to chaos by striking at what he called "the root cause." He ordered the arrest of the Mullah. The Mullah was found in the mosque, and under cover of darkness a strong Scouts' escort accompanied him to DIK. The news of his arrest spread like wildfire among the Wazirs. The atmosphere in Wana was electric. Armed groups assembled for consultation and action: "Even the ladies (mothers, wives, sisters) of the houses brought out fire arms for their men and said after the arrest of Maulvi Sahib we do not want to see you alive" (ibid., p. 15). Wazirs blocked the roads leading to the Wana camp and surrounded the airfield in order to prevent reinforcements from arriving by air. Talibs, including girls, attempted an assault on the camp. "The Wazir nation," noted the Mullah with satisfaction, "were prepared for shahadat [death in the cause of Islam]" (ibid.). Such was the intensity of Wazir feelings that the administration felt it politic to release the Mullah within twenty-four hours of his arrest. The Mullah's return to Wana was triumphal. Elders, accompanied by women and children, had prepared a hero's welcome for him. The authority and prestige of the administration lay in the dust.[11] The Mullah was incensed with the PA: "He is a fool and cannot remain here any longer." He had dared to arrest the man the Wazirs "will jump into the fire for" (ibid., p. 124). The Mullah planned to avenge his humiliation.

At this juncture the PA was posted out of the agency, and a new PA was appointed. Before the PA left, however, the Mullah hatched an elaborate assassination plot. "Arrangements for murder of PA were made on the Gomal road," but "the PA left secretly early in the morning on 24th June via the Tiarza road under Scouts escort and thus made good his escape" (ibid., pp. 36–37). The PA had taken the top road, which passes only through Mahsud territory.

The new PA, a Daur tribesman from North Waziristan Agency, took up his post on June 25. As a Daur, his sympathy for the Wazirs was presupposed. On his first day in office he declared allegiance to the Wazirs and in a dramatic reversal of policy promised to open the Gomal road. He was to last four months. A letter to the commissioner from the new PA reflected the radical departure in agency politics and clearly expressed his position. He complained of Mahsud obduracy, pointing out certain leaders:

> Malik Gulab Khan Shingi especially his cousin ex-Captain Sher Badshah and his few supporters create hurdles. . . . they are still creating mischief and have sent messengers to "New Shahzada" [grandson of Mullah Powindah] at Latakka with the request that all the Maliks and Elders of Mahsuds have given Gomal to Ahmedzai Wazirs and he should come out with commoners [i.e., teeman] to oppose this decision. [PA to commissioner, September 6, 1975]

Among the Wazirs the Mullah's authority was total and mesmeric in both the temporal and religious realms. He would not lead the Wazirs to the promised land but bring the promised land to the Wazirs. The Mullah now virtually controlled affairs in Wana subdivision. Truly, he was the "uncrowned king of Wana."

The Wazirs vanquished

The new PA promised to open the Gomal road for at least forty days and gave written assurance to this effect to the Wazir tribe. Armed with this agreement, large, well-organized lashkars moved to Gomal and occupied strategic positions with the stated view of securing the road permanently. The Mahsuds were furious. Wazir occupation of the Gomal route violated the fundamental principle of nikkat. "The Mahsuds," it was noted, "made their position very clear that they would wait until the expiry of the forty days period and if the Government failed to honour its commitment, they would go into a bigger action against the Establishment" (Political Agent's Office 1977, p. 11).

The Mahsuds had not been idle. They had launched a vigorous campaign against the PA, accusing him of being bribed by the Wazirs to favor them. Official contacts and networks in the country were mobilized in an attempt to discredit him and thereby ensure his premature transfer from the agency. In order to apply pressure on the administration to act against the Wazirs, the Mahsuds resorted to traditional methods. They attacked government buildings such as Scouts' forts and removed telephone poles, seriously impairing communications in the agency. At Tiarza, in Mahsud territory, some 2,000 Mahsuds surrounded and attacked the Scouts' post. The fifty Scouts' soldiers inside found their situation desperate. Water supplies had been cut off to the post. It was only heavy artillery fire that dispelled the attackers. Law and order had ceased to function in the agency.

The acute political suspense generated a mood of imminent disaster in the agency, at the height of which the political agent was transferred. The new PA surveyed the scene and has left us a record of his reactions: "One feels like covering one's face with shame while reading the letters written by the then Political Agent who remained in a state of constant agony throughout his tenure" (ibid. p. 5). On November 23, 1975, the forty days expired and the tribes waited for the next move of the administration. The PA appeared to take charge of events with resolution. To start with, he orderd the immediate closure of the Gomal road. The scouts moved into the Gomal area, prepared for action. The Frontier constabulary also strengthened certain posts on the agency border. The following weeks saw scattered and persistent exchanges of fire between the Wazir and government forces. The constabulary, in the face of Wazir attacks, had to abandon certain posts. Exposed to wind, cold, and hunger the Wazirs conducted guerilla action in the Gomal area, but as winter set in, Wazir resolve weakened. In the barren mountains and in the severe cold of December they faced the problem of logistics. It was estimated that the operation was costing them about 100,000 rupees daily.

The Mullah opened a new front to divert attention and keep the Wazir war spirit from flagging. He ordered the main agency road to be blocked. In late December 1975, a Wazir lashkar gathered at Dargai in the Maddi Jan area for this purpose. Traffic was entirely suspended and the agency was cut off from the outside world. The Wazirs occupied strategic positions and dug in to defend them. Senior representatives of the provincial and central government flew in to Jandola for discussions with the PA. The prime minister of

Pakistan ordered the opening of the road. He sanctioned air action if required, the destruction of the adda, the arrest of the Mullah, and the closure of the Fort Sandeman road, in Baluchistan, to the Wazirs if they refused to lift the blockade. Army tanks were moved into the agency from the settled districts.

On December 22, the PA moved with a strong force of Scouts from Jandola towards Wana to enforce the opening of the agency road. Simultaneously, another force moved with the APA, Wana, toward Jandola from Wana. A general order was passed by the commandant to shoot on sight any armed Wazir. All movement by Wazirs, on foot or in vehicles, was banned. A fierce and bloody encounter took place at Maddi Jan, in which five soldiers were killed and more wounded. It was estimated that 30 Wazirs were killed or wounded. Other clashes also took place on that day causing loss of life.

The Wazirs remained defiant and a few days later once again blocked the agency road. The sequence of events would be repeated, it appeared. Orders were issued from Islamabad to open the road "at all costs." The PA warned that the adda would be blown up as a first move against the Wazirs. The Scouts moved in considerable strength from Jandola, but they faced no opposition. The Wazirs had melted into the night and the roads were deserted.

The Mullah had left for the North Waziristan Agency to request support from the Wazirs of the agency. His trip also afforded him a convenient alibi should he be held guilty for the clash at Maddi Jan. The involvement of Wazirs from North Waziristan would extend the theater of conflict beyond the agency borders and create serious complications for the government. Kabul was watching developments in Waziristan with interest. Ideal material was at hand for their Pukhtunistan propaganda, which claimed that Pukhtuns in the Frontier Province wished to secede from Pakistan. The affair was cast as a Pukhtun struggle for autonomy against the central government. Fortunately for the administration the Utmanzai Wazirs of North Waziristan, though sympathetic to their cousins in the south, were prevented from joining the conflict. The Mahsuds had successfully applied pressure through the governor and PAs of both the South and North Waziristan agencies to isolate Utmanzais from their Ahmedzai cousins.

Among the Mahsuds the following of Abdul Maalik made vigorous but unsuccessful attempts to bring some semblance of order into the agency. As the single member of the National Assembly from South

Waziristan, Maalik represented both tribes. Advocating accommodation with the Wazirs, he argued that matters could be resolved through a jirga. For him, this served the double purpose of ensuring Wazir support and weaning Mahsud loyalties from his rivals in the Gulabi bloc, which was so deeply involved in the Wazir dispute. Maalik went to the extent of laying the entire blame on his own tribe: "The Mahsuds are unbeatable at *shaitani* ['devilry']," he argued. "They can bite [*chak lagai*] at the right time and finish an opponent." He contrasted the Wazir as "simple and less cunning." Indirectly he was pointing a finger at his rivals who led the dominant Mahsud bloc. To canvass among the political leaders of Pakistan, Maalik spent a considerable time in Islamabad at the National Assembly. His absence from the agency also allowed him to avoid making decisions that would condemn him in Mahsud eyes as a traitor to their cause. So high were the feelings in the administration and among Mahsuds against the Wazirs, however, that his efforts were in vain. Abdul Maalik was seen by the administration as a mischief maker who encouraged the Wazirs to embarrass the Gulabi bloc. For his troubles a warrant of arrest was issued against him. Abdul Maalik spent many uncomfortable months underground in the towns of Punjab eluding the Mahsud khassadars of the PA sent to arrest him. The warrant and his opposition to the agency administration effectively removed him from the agency scene until 1979, when he emerged once again as an active leader of the agency.

In contrast, the followers of Gulab Khan, his rival, were riding a crest in the agency. The leadership of Gulab's bloc devolved on Sher Badshah; he was the iron fist under Gulab's velvet glove and was to prove a shrewd and implacable foe of the Mullah. He led the Mahsuds with a formidable combination of tribal strategy and knowledge acquired in the British Indian army. In order to neutralize Abdul Maalik and his efforts on behalf of the Wazirs, Sher Badshah sent a telegram in March 1976 to the prime minister of Pakistan, Z. A. Bhutto, with copies to the key officials involved in the drama: the interior minister, Pakistan; the governor, NWFP; the chief minister, NWFP; the chief secretary, NWFP; the commissioner; and the PA. The telegram read:

> We refer you to our previous resolution passed at Spinkai Raghzai [South Waziristan] by Dre Mahsuds and sent to you all in the form of a telegram. Abdul Maalik is rejected by Mahsuds as our representative in the assembly. If he could he would butcher the

whole tribe for personal petty gain. In the present dispute he was heavily bribed by the Wazirs. He is great dakoo [dacoit] and big robber. He is a traitor and anti-state.

Maalik's followers countered in a similar vein. The Waziristan pot was boiling and threatened to spill over.

Wazirs and Mahsuds, in or out of government, sided with their tribes. Pakistan politicians, too, took sides. To Pukhtun nationalists the Mullah posed as a champion of Pukhtun rights against the central government, and to the ruling leftist Pakistan People's party he appeared as the champion of the poor. As Wazirs also live in Afghanistan across the Durand line, there was considerable international interest in the situation. Kabul adopted a generally pro-Wazir stance, casting the affair as a revolt of the Pukhtuns against the authority of Pakistan. The issue was now operating on three levels: tribal, national, and international.

After the Maddi Jan incident in December, a notice was publicly issued warning the Wazirs that if they continued their intransigence, air strikes would be used against them and the adda blown up. The Maddi Jan action had shaken the Wazirs, and they retired to lick their wounds. The Mullah went into a period of contemplation. In April 1976 he appealed in a letter written in Urdu to the Pukhtun chief minister of the province:

> Although the Wazirs own irrigated lands and thick forests the Mahsuds have better educated people and more in government service. From the time of the British they have exploited and humiliated Wazirs. Now that the Awami [Peoples] Government is in power and the light of democracy shines in the land the hearts of the poor Wazirs feel that the star of hope has risen and the sun of exploitation is sinking. [Noor Muhammad 1976]

The Mullah went on to request the opening of the Gomal road and ended the letter by declaring his unshaken belief in the ideology of Pakistan. "The administration of the agency to humor the Mahsuds," he complained, "has warmed the *bazaars* of tyranny [carried injustice to an extreme]" (ibid.). The letter drew no response from Peshawar.

To avoid the possibility of a breach of peace the PA ordered a security deposit, to be produced in one month, of 300,000 rupees from both tribes. The Mahsuds deposited the security, but the Wazirs refused to do so. Tension built up over the next weeks and was defused only when elders from outside the agency attempted to bring the two tribes together for negotiations. The tribes agreed to meet in

May at Tiarza, in Mahsud territory. The Mahsuds, as hosts, prepared a traditional tribal lunch on May 17, and it was hoped a solution would be produced.

The Wazirs immediately on arrival invoked the laws of nanawatee. They requested a Mahsud commitment in writing regarding the opening of the Gomal road. The Mahsuds saw the Mullah's hand in this move and rejected the proposal. The Wazirs refused to eat and returned to Wana in a huff. Their request for nanawatee, they claimed, was rejected in violation of Pukhtunwali. Both tribes felt grieved and offended. The attempt to outwit each other through tribal idiom, in this case nanawatee, is described by the PA:

> The Wazirs took animals of nanawatee, concealed in a truck with an intention to embarrass the other side and let the cat out of the bag melodramatically without giving any reaction time to the other side. The Mahsuds received the Wazirs with some degree of spontaneity and the negotiations started soon after the address by the Political Agent. I told them that they should avail of this opportunity which had come to them after a long period of agony and disorder. The Mahsuds hurriedly arranged a "counter nanawatee" and begged the Ahmedzais not to open up the question of Gomal again. They pleaded that they could live peacefully like their ancestors and gave maximum assurances of their good conduct in future, The Mahsuds also offered the nanawatee on the Holy Quran but the Wazirs were not prepared to listen to anything. They refused to take their meals which were arranged by the Mahsuds at Tiarza. Thus Maulvi's strategy of disorder flouted all our efforts for a peaceful settlement. The Wazirs came back in anger and propagated that despite their being "wronged"even their nanawatee was not accepted by the Mahsuds. [Political Agent's Office, 1977, pp. 14-15]

Seizing this opportunity the Mullah once again whipped up fervor among the Wazirs by declaring that their appeal for nanawatee had been rejected by the Mahsuds against the laws of Pukhtunwali. War was the only honorable way out. Large lashkars attacked the Mahsuds living west of Tiarza, in Shakki. The Mullah ordered fresh lashkars to surround the Wana camp. In his diaries he described the Wazirs as prepared for shahadat. Traffic and commerce came to a standstill. Once again, law and order had collapsed in the agency.

The PA obtained clearance from the governor who, in turn, cleared the matter with the prime minister, and Plan Alpha was set in motion. Plan Alpha was the destruction of the adda and the arrest of the

Mullah and his key men. Notices were issued of government intentions, warning Wazirs to stay clear of the adda. On May 26, shortly
after midnight, the Scouts surrounded the deserted adda and their
heavy guns opened fire.[12] Simultaneously, raids were conducted on
the houses of the Mullah and his men. The Mullah had been tipped
off and escaped into the night. The shops in the market were blown
up and then set on fire. The conflagration was awesome, and flames,
forty to fifty feet high, burned all the next day. The Ahmedzai tribe
promptly paid up the 300,000 rupees demanded by the PA as security
and declared their intention in writing of remaining peaceful in the
future.

The fire did not die out completely for another four or five days.
Bulldozers were then imported into the agency and worked for weeks
leveling the ground; today the entire market area appears like a
freshly plowed field.[13]

The administration captured a considerable number of items from
the adda, including guns and ammunition which were used as proof
of the Mullah's subversive activities. Among the Mullah's possessions
found in his rooms were what the administration termed "morally
subversive literature," such as books on black magic, his diary (hand-
written in four notebooks), and a wide variety of contraceptives.[14] All
these items were used as evidence against him. The Wazirs dismiss
the evidence as "planted" and further proof of the attempt at character assassination of the Mullah.

The Wazirs claim that cash and valuables worth millions of rupees
were stolen from the adda. Paradoxically, the Mullah's chalweshti
were at least partially responsible for the loss. When tension was high
and talk of blowing up the adda was in the air, the chalweshti, to
underline the unchallenged authority and position of their leader,
refused to allow the more nervous shopkeepers to move their valuables.

The Mullah, after a few days of hiding in the hills near Wana, finally
appeared in Dhanna, adjacent to Birmal, where he sought shelter for
the next few weeks: "Maulvi Noor Muhammad ran away and took
shelter at various places and that is how the history of Adda Mughal
Khel came to an end. He assumed the role of a 'Hassan Bin Sabah'
and his Mephistophelean empire became an obvious threat to the
authority of the Government. The demolition of Adda was nothing
but a crying call of the time" (PA Order, September 24, 1976, p. 7).[15]

The PA was determined to capture the Mullah, and increasing
pressure was applied to his supporters. Movable and immovable

properties were seized, and settlements were systematically blown up, including that of Ba Khan. Secret political negotiations were also conducted. About three months later a dishevelled and somewhat shaken Mullah surrendered with his key followers, including the jernails and the cabinet. His brother, Niaz Muhammad, remained at large with the Birmal Wazirs.

The Mullah "was confined in a Bungalow in the Upper Camp and was properly looked after" (Political Agent's Office, 1977, p. 17). He was treated as a political prisoner, and securities from the Wazirs were demanded for his release. They were not forthcoming. According to the official story, when the PA asked the leading Wazir maliks for surety for the Mullah's future good behavior they declined, replying, "who can guarantee the surety of a *badshah*?" Apparently the less important maliks were equally evasive and gave the same answer, and therefore the PA had no recourse but to order a trial through jirga.

The PA, with a jirga of elders, including Pasti and Mir Askar from the smaller Wazir clans, tried the Mullah and his men under the Frontier Crimes Regulation. On October 9 the PA announced judgment. The accused were found guilty on numerous charges. The Mullah was sentenced to ten years "rigorous imprisonment," his property confiscated, and his entire family expelled from the agency. He was sent to Haripur jail in Hazara District, across the Indus. Nine of his supporters received sentences ranging from one to five years. The presiding officer at the trial, the PA, recorded: "The trial was conducted in an absolutely just and fair manner. It was a representative jirga of all the Ahmedzais and they fully satisfied themselves about the charges levelled against the accused" (Political Agent's Office, 1977, p. 18).

The Mullah's mosque had been confiscated in the previous month: "In order to maintain public peace on the one hand and encourage pristine religious education, I therefore order that the mosque is hereby taken over by the Government along with the madrassah and the properties therein under Section 21 (C) of the Frontier Crimes Regulation. There can be no better application of this Section than this case" (PA Order, September 24, 1976, p. 7).

The arrest and subsequent trial of the Mullah by the PA generated controversy. Wazirs claimed that honor was violated because the Mullah had surrendered on *itbar* ("trust") after the PA had promised him "leniency" and waived the question of trial. The PA denied any such agreement with the Mullah or his men. A personal animosity between the mullah and the PA was suggested by the supporters of the Wazirs. As a consequence, the lives of the PA and his family were threatened by the Wazirs. It was rumored that a purse of half a million rupees had been collected to assassinate him. On his transfer, the government felt it wise to post him outside the country.

The action in Wana and events leading up to it had been followed with interest in Kabul. Propaganda had shaped the conflict as a simple Pukhtun struggle for autonomy against a Punjabi-dominated central government. Indeed, not since the merger of the NWFP states of Swat, Chitral, Dir, and Amb in 1969 had such a live issue presented itself to Kabul. The situation was tense with possibilities. Kabul propaganda emphasized the ethnic nature of the Mullah's struggle and argued that such key men in the drama as the central interior minister, the chief secretary of the province, and the political agent were non-Pukhtun and thus could not be sympathetic to Pukhtuns. Although the NAP argued along similar lines, its voice had become ineffective since 1975 as its leadership languished in the jails of Sind in connection with the assassination of Mr. Sherpao, the PPP senior minister of the province. However, the inaccessibility of Waziristan, combined with the rather isolated position of Wazirs in Pakistan, prevented news of the Wana action from spreading far.

After the destruction of the adda in May, the Wazirs stood in disarray while the Mahsuds became jubilant and the administration acted smugly self-righteous. The Wazirs, especially those in the Wana plain, the Zilli Khel, had been carried away by the persuasive rhetoric and organizational skills of the Mullah, and the adventure had cast them in the role of villains in the eyes of non-Wazirs. They were "second class" and "disloyal citizens," claimed their critics. Crude allusions and taunting remarks—to contraceptives, for instance— added to Wazir resentment. "Are you a Muslim first or Wazir?" was a common jibe the implied question being, "Do you follow the laws of Islam or those of the Mullah?"[16] Without their leader, the Wazirs were cowed but defiant.

Meanwhile the Mahsuds had become the dominant tribe of the agency. They and their friends interpreted the action in Wana as the culmination of brilliant tribal strategy. Caroe's description of them as a wolf pack was apt. They had proved themselves united, purposeful, and masters of strategy. Posing as "loyalists" in the episode, they basked in the favor of the administration, receiving various rewards. Those in the forefront of the drama and loyal to the PA received official recognition from him in such forms as increased allowances and even the creation of new malikis. Wazirs complained that the PA was now "in the pocket" of the Mahsuds. Indeed, Mahsud elders would agree with this assessment and say, "We always use the PA for our own objectives but allow him to think he is using us."

Not all Mahsuds supported the action in Wana. Some, like Alam Jan, while not countenancing the Mullah's tactics, disapproved of the severity of the action. The wound would never heal, they argued. Others like Abdul Maalik remained sympathetic to the Wazir position. Although these were only a few voices, they raised questions that created moral debate in Mahsud society. The administration, whose main charter is to keep the general law and order, maintained that peace was restored in the agency, a potential revolt against the government crushed, and a larger conflagration averted.

5

Order, ideology, and morality in Waziristan

Order and administration in Waziristan

In terms of traditional political analysis two interconnected facts of Waziristan life are evident after May 26, 1976, if the prima facie evidence is to be relied upon: the termination of the Mullah's role and that of the Wazir movement in the agency. The adda was removed from the face of the earth, the mosque and madrassah "captured," and the Mullah put behind prison bars. The key symbols of the affair were thus rendered ineffective. Can we then deduce that the Wazir cause had been abandoned? The administration and the Mahsuds answered in the affirmative: aberration, partly acknowledged by the Wazirs, had been corrected. Harmony and unity had been restored: "This brought complete normalcy to the Agency and the Wazirs and Mahsuds started working together" (Political Agent's Office 1977, p. 19). The prima facie evidence, however, can be read differently.

Wazir strategy centers on four specific objectives, which determine contemporary Wazir politics and belie the argument claiming "normalcy" in the agency. The first objective is to secure the release of the Mullah, which however, is linked with larger political developments in Pakistan. After the fall of Z. A. Bhutto in 1977, the army, which had come to power in Pakistan, assumed an increasingly rightist political stance. The Wazirs felt that the time was ripe for the release of the Mullah. They had the support of Maulana Mufti, then courted by the generals for his role in Mr. Bhutto's downfall. The case was frequently "recommended" by Islamabad to the government of NWFP and just as frequently turned down. The Mahsuds have a powerful lobby in Peshawar and, as we will see in Chapter 7 (case IV), they are capable of mobilizing civil and military networks effectively.

The Wazirs were hopeful when a member of Maulana Mufti's party, the Jamiat-i-Ulama-i-Islam (JUI), became central minister for

Tribal Affairs. The minister expressed his position publicly regarding the Mullah by visiting him in jail at Haripur. In early 1979 the minister promised the Wazirs (indeed he made the same pronouncement to me): "The Mullah will be out in a few weeks. I have been assured by the highest authorities." A few weeks later the national press announced that the minister was out of office; the Mullah remained in prison. The Mahsuds were proving more skillful than the Wazirs.

The second objective of the Wazirs, which the Mahsuds similarly frustrate, is a new adda. The majority of Wazirs are prepared to accept an adda outside Wana, although the hawks in the Mullah's cabinet, like Ba Khan, insist on the old site. Mahsud hawks would like Azam Warsak, about nine miles west of Wana, to be the site of the new adda.[1] During my tenure as PA I saw the building of an adda as fundamental to a new relationship between the major tribes, apart from its own intrinsic importance. The adda has been officially disallowed, however, for a variety of reasons: It may create a fresh "law and order" situation in the agency or it may invite complications "in view of the situation prevailing in Afghanistan." Implicit threat of Mahsud pressure keeps the issue from being officially considered. The Wazirs, while awaiting an adda, congregate by the main road outside the Wana camp for purposes of trade and commerce. Felt tents have sprung up in the temporary market, which is known as *olari adda*, or the standing-up market.

The Wazir's third objective centers around the mosque and the *madrassah* and presents a more complicated picture. Because the three parties in the agency (the Mahsuds, Wazirs, and administration), adhere to the Sunni sect of Islam, they all hold the Wana mosque in reverence. Nevertheless, subtle nuances can be distinguished in the Wazir position. To them the mosque has been "captured" and thus desecrated. Until it is "returned" to them it is to be boycotted. The religious function is here subordinated to the political one. The point of Wazir ethnicity is explicitly made. Except for loyalist maliks, such as Pasti or Mir Askar, the Wazirs all boycott the mosque. The once active madrassah is a dying institution for want of pupils. Mullahs from outside the agency are discouraged form serving in the Adda Mughal Khel mosque by threats and acts of violence. The nose of one was knifed. His successor barely escaped with his life when unknown assailants fired on him in the dark, riddling his clothing with bullets. The culprits remain untraced. The attackers by night are the friends and visitors by day. "They may come to meet you with broad smiles and make tall promises of loyalty," the PA had warned his successor (Political Agent's Office, 1977, p. 20).

The opening of the Gomal road is the Wazirs fourth objective. Seen as a Pandora's box of troubles by the administration, it is kept closed to all nonofficial private traffic and the agency is thus deprived of one of its major routes.

The attainment of these objectives may be remote, but their active pursuance by the Wazirs keeps tensions high. Visiting officials are usually welcomed by noisy sniping at the Wana camp, especially at night. In November 1976, Bhutto's entourage was kept highly nervous most of the night by machine-gun and rifle fire from surrounding hills. Occasional kidnappings of officials makes them somewhat reluctant to work outside the Wana camp. The most serious incident involved a senior officer in the Public Works Department who was kidnapped with his entire badragga some months after the adda was blown up. Officials also refuse to live in government accommodations unless they are provided in the camp. The bungalows of the newly completed hospital and college buildings outside the camp remain empty. Even the mullah employed to supervise the Wana mosque returns to the camp at night.

Such tension in the agency while effectively conveying the Wazirs message also acts as a barrier between the tribes. Mahsuds visiting Wana or Wazirs visiting Tank make sure that they leave by sunset to avoid any unpleasant occurrence. The problem is reflected in the administration. In 1980 the nephew of the Mahsud elder Gulab Khan was posted to the position of tehsildar in Wana to assist in the problem of the Afghan refugees. Because he was a Mahsud, his usefulness as an administrator was curbed in the Wazir area.

The Mullah follows events in Waziristan closely. Some even accuse him of still meddling in agency affairs. He is able to communicate with his flock from Haripur jail through the recently discovered marvel of the cassette recorder. His instruction, counsel, and warnings are heard and circulated among the Wazir, as is his message of hope and better days to come. His brother, Niaz Muhammad, still at large in Birmal, remains his main representative in the agency, supervising the collection of donations and conducting negotiations on his behalf. Memory of the Wazir cause and movement is not allowed to die out.

The memory is kept alive in various ways. In November 1978, Asaldin, a Sirki Khel Wazir, appealed for justice to the president and chief martial law administrator of Pakistan, General Muhammad Zia-ul-Haq, in a petition entitled "Attempt to Murder on December

22, 1975" against the then political agent, SWA, and commandant,
SWS. Copies were sent to, among others, the chief justices of the
Supreme Court of Pakistan and of the Peshawar High Court. In the
petition, written in English, Asaldin described how, on December 22,
1975, "the South Waziristan Scouts opened Gun fires on Spin Village
which is at a distance of four miles from Tanai Scouts post towards
south on Wana-Gul Kach Road and Machine Gun fires on our bus."
Two men were killed and three, including the petitioner, wounded in
the bus. Asaldin listed the killed and the wounded in his petition as
follows:

> 1. Bahram S/o Payo Nir caste Jai Khel Wazir of Manra (Killed)
> 2. Khan Badshah S/o Baji caste Toji Khel Wazir of Birmal
> (Killed)
> 3. Malik Qalandar Khan, Karmaz Khel Wazir living close to
> Shin Warsak (wounded)
> 4. Zangi Khan, Salimi Khel Mahsud, living as Hamsaya of Zilli
> Khel Wazirs at Shin Warsak, Mali of APA's Garden. His leg was
> fractured
> 5. Asaldin, Sirki Khel Wazir (petitioner) of Kazha Punga, leg
> fractured.

Of what happened subsequently he said: "I was taken to District
Headquarter hospital Dera Ismail Khan for treatment. Then to Lady
Reading Hospital, Peshawar, and finally to Makki Hospital, People's
Colony, Lyallpur, where I got recovered after six (6) months treat-
ment. In all I spent a sum of Rs. 20,000/- on my treatment, for which
I can produce the relevant bills for perusal."

The petitioner accused the main officers involved in the action of
attempt to murder. He reminded the head of state,

> We Wazirs took active part in Kashmir *Jihad* of 1947–49 and
> Indo-Pakistan War of 1965 and also in 1971 and thus proved our
> loyalty to the state. But in spite of our loyalty, our shops have been
> blown up with Gun fires . . . because the Pakistan Peoples Party
> did every thing in their power to undo the tribesmen and this was
> why our business at Adda Mughal Khel was put on fire through
> Gun fires and we were put to a loss of millions of Rupees.

The conclusion carried a reference to the larger political events of
Pakistan:

> If Mr. Zulfiqar Ali Bhutto, former Prime Minister of Pakistan is
> being tried for the murder of Nawab Muhammad Ahmed Khan
> Qasuri by the Government whose case is pending trial in the

Supreme Court of Pakistan, I feel the above officers must realise the strong clutches of the Law of the country–because they are not above the Law of the country and in my view they should be tried–because they have deprived so many families of their legitimate income and by killing them with Gun fires etc.

A more eschatological argument, characteristic of such applications, was also given:

We all would appear before the Almighty God on the "Dooms-day" irrespective of one's status one has in this world and if no justice is done to me, I would seek justice in the Court of Almighty God–because here the Rules framed by the former British Government is still being followed in spite of the slogans that "Nizam-e-Mustafa" [rule of Islam] would be introduced shortly.

The petition did not produce any results, but it provided concrete evidence that the Wazirs had not forgotten.

The administration, particularly, felt the need to explain the Wazir unrest and movement. Numerous theses purport to give reasons for recent Waziristan history, but most rest on simple assumptions. The first explanation is based on a cynical calculation. When faced with a choice between 250,000 Mahsuds and 50,000 Wazirs, the administration sided with the stronger party and thus opted for the easier solution. Material motivations are behind other official explanations: "It is necessary to trace out the history of the 'saga' right from the beginning, the saga of confrontation between the Wazirs and Mahsuds. As you know that the whole affair is linked up with the question of Timber Permits" (Political Agent's Office 1977, p. 1). The motives of the Mullah were also explained as material: "income from the Committee and other sources of taxation by Maulvi was meant . . . for the Maulvi's personal benefit. He had . . . bought land . . . and investments under cover names" (ibid., p. 6).

Simplistic theories of political administration are not, however, a monopoly of provincial minds. In the centers of power in Pakistan, also, "agitator–conspirator" theories tend to be accepted as explanations of expressed political discontent. Law and order will be restored and dissatisfaction disappear if the agitator is removed from the scene, it is believed. Such analysis is based on the form rather than the content of the problem and time and again, the arrest of the agitator has increased the volume of discontent. In jail his popularity artificially accelerates and he becomes the symbol of hope against the tyranny of the ruling group. Nonetheless, the agitator theory has prevailed, and every major figure has subscribed to it: President Ayub when he jailed Mr. Bhutto, President Yahya when he tried Sheikh Mujib-ur-Rehman and, in turn, Prime Minister Bhutto when he jailed Wali Khan, and so on. The agitator–conspirator theory was now applied to the Mullah. Once he was arrested the Wazirs would forget him. The theory was to be refuted once again.

An explanation of the Waziristan crisis that combines psychological and administrative factors holds personal tension between senior officials, such as the PA and the commandant, responsible. One of the indirect causes during the 1970s for the strained relations between the PA and the commandant was Mr. Bhutto's "lateral entry" system into the civil service of Pakistan. Some military officers were inducted laterally as political officers, and this encouraged others to exhibit their skills in the political field. The officers of the South Waziristan Scouts were no exception. Commandants tended to interfere in matters outside their jurisdiction. They envied what they saw as the glamor, stature, and privilege of the PA's post. A good personal relationship between the main actors is crucial to their ability to understand and to shape events. In this instance, a poor relationship between the commandant and the PA exacerbated the problem.

Actors often appear to be in complete command of the stage, but while they are manipulating their audience, they are also being manipulated by others. An example is the relationship of the Mullah and the colonel in 1972–3. The Mullah assumed he was manipulating the colonel for his own ends. The colonel, in conversation with me drew the opposite picture. It was he who stage-managed the emergence of the Mullah, playing on the Mullah's ego by suggesting that the time was ripe for him to declare his leadership to the world. He supported this claim by quoting incidents referred to in the last chapter. It was he who tipped the Mullah off when action was contemplated against him and the adda; and it was his refusal to take seriously the PA's order to arrest the Mullah's men that ensured that the action ended in fiasco. Although he assisted him to emerge in Waziristan, the colonel had a poor opinion of the Mullah and thought him "corrupt and cowardly." Perhaps part of the explanation for the actions of the colonel may be viewed in the light of the larger politics of the province. The colonel sympathized with the NAP, and embarrassing the political administration would have embarrassed the opponents of the NAP, the PPP.

The Islamic district paradigm may provide another explanation for the Waziristan crisis. As we know, there appears to be a structural conflict between the three categories of leadership in Muslim society. In our case the "appointed" chief the (PA) and the "anointed" chief (the Mullah) could not function in one frame. Expansion of the latter's role into Waziristan politics meant a clear encroachment on the former's space. It was a "zero-sum" relationship. Every unit acquired by the Mullah detracted from the total of the PA. Every political concession won by the Mullah and every malik swearing personal loyalty to him reduced the PA by that sum of prestige and authority. Though both functioned in the same arena and were locked in a zero-sum equation, the two represented disparate bases of power. The criteria, ascribed or achieved, on which their social ranking was based were diametrically opposed and illustrate the differences in their leadership roles. The PA was an official, nominated by the government. Authority was *ascribed* to him by the stroke of a pen and could be as abruptly removed by another stroke. In contrast, the Mullah had *achieved* his status and authority through his personality and organizational skills. For him, each unit of political power that he won and each member of his constituency was a personal achievement.

The Mullah of Waziristan

Was the Mullah's primary motivation religious? It would appear not. Although he employed a specifically religious idiom, his objectives remained explicitly political. His actions were patterned on military themes rather than religious ones. The Mullah was adept at converting mundane information into what appeared to be spiritual powers, as we saw in Chapter 4. The Mullah, it seems, wished to control Islam rather than be controlled by it. Moreover, he wished to harness Islam in the cause of the Wazirs. Part of his genius as a strategist was to impose a religious frame on secular agnatic rivalry; part of it was to identify the need to couch the problem in semiotic terms for tribesmen.

The building and organization of the mosque provided an ideal platform for the Mullah to be seen and heard by the Wazirs. Its central position at Wana made it the most important religious institution in the agency. From involvement in religious affairs based around the mosque it was a logical step first to organize a madrassah for disciple-students and then to extend his influence into the adjacent market. The combination of religious and economic functions established a powerful political base. At this juncture the Mullah was a hero in search of a role. He found the role as champion of the Wazir cause against the Mahsuds. Perhaps in a different age and in a different land he may have succeeded in his objectives; the Wazirs may have obtained a separate area to live in, and the Mullah may have been acknowledged as its "uncrowned king."

The Mullah appeared to possess no consistent theory of politics, however, no grand conception of the social order: his thought contained no cosmological explanations for phenomena, no mystical content.[2] A generalized ambition appears to have driven him – the ambition of a saint who would be king. Visions and prophets, kings and crowns, these were the ideas inside the Mullah's mind. His personal notebooks emphasize the themes of sainthood and royalty. Gatherings paid homage to him as the "uncrowned king of Wana," he often confided to his diary. In the Islamic ideal saints and kings do not sit comfortably in one chair; they exist as opposing and contrary models. The Prophet's saying reflects the opposition between the spiritual and the material: "The nearer a man is to government, the further he is from God; the more followers he has, the more devils; the greater his wealth, the more exacting his reckoning" (Al-Muttaqi 1974, p. 151). Waziristan society, too, saw din ("religion") and dunya ("world") as opposed categories. The Mullah wished to cross from the world of din into that of dunya.

Was political ambition, then, the Mullah's main objective? No clear or consistent answer is available. With his growing power the complexity of his political objectives increased. The desire for a separate agency, couched in different demands, reflected an explicitly political ambition. Had such an agency been granted, the Mullah would have been elected as its National Assembly member. His political skills would have almost certainly won him a seat in the central cabinet usually reserved for one of the seven tribal area members. His objectives, however, remain clouded and, indeed, seem to shift with the situation. The answer to the pursuit of power may partly lie in the irrational. Power as an end in itself is a sufficient objective to many leaders. The greater the power, the more dangerous the abuse, said Edmund Burke in 1771. Burke's warning applies as does Lord Acton's phrase about the corrupting effect of power.

Once the Mullah had established his base at Wana, he played the politics of Pakistan, inasmuch as it could benefit him in Waziristan. In the early 1970s he assumed a political stance in accordance with that of the NAP but appeared to change sides when the NAP government was dismissed. When courting the PPP, the Mullah used its idiom in his speeches, "exploitation of the masses," "people's rights," and "Islamic socialism" and dropped that of "Pukhtun rights." His free-wheeling style allowed him to shape his position according to the prevalent ideology on the larger stage. It is difficult to escape the con-clusion that the Mullah based his politics on opportunism; indeed as we know, he had exhorted his followers "to join different political parties in order to gather information" (Noor Muhammad n.d., p. 138). There is a clear answer as to why the national parties encour-aged the Mullah in spite of knowing his background. Through him it allowed them a foothold, however tenuous, in Waziristan; it was either the Mullah or nothing. By law, political parties are not permitted in the tribal areas.

Can we view the Mullah's movement as an act of ethnic assertion against the state, such as the periphery–center struggles common in the literature? Or did it contain the seeds of secession, an explicit attempt to break away through armed rebellion? These questions must remain unanswered as must an interesting question that follows from them. Was the Mullah aware of the larger implication of a successful movement for an agency? The Bangla Desh case was fresh in Pakistani minds. The Mullah's triumph would have been the first of its kind in the trans-Indus provinces of the North-West Frontier and Baluchistan and almost certainly would have encouraged other nascent movements. Did the Mullah wish to go this far? His critics affirm so; the Wazirs disagree, arguing that he wished to represent their legiti-mate demands within the context of Pakistan.

An acute paradox was inherent in the situation for the Mullah. A religious leader could not overtly espouse an ethnic secessionist move-ment supported by Kabul in the context of Pakistan politics, with its marked emphasis on religious ideology. In Pakistan, the more suc-cessful the Mullah was in advocating parochial ethnic philosophy, the farther he would move from a position of religious leader repre-senting a universalistic tradition. The dilemma is reflected in the Mullah's action immediately following the destruction of the adda in May 1976.

The escape of the Mullah from the mosque on that night raises an important question and provides us with an important clue to his thinking. Why did he not cross the border into Afghanistan, where he would have received a hero's welcome? Ajmal Khattak, of the NAP, had escaped from Bhutto earlier and was well lodged in Kabul. The Mullah's crossing into Afghanistan would have identified him irrevocably as pro-Pukhtunistan and therefore, according to the logic of regional politics, anti-Pakistan. His political and cultural moorings would have been altered. His surrender was thus a matter of choosing between the two alternatives.

The Wazirs, the Mahsuds, and the administration each saw the Mullah in a highly different light. His very title became symbolic of the different viewpoints.[3] The Wazirs referred to him as maulvi sahib, not using his name in deference. The administration was more prosaic, and official correspondence generally refers to him as Maulvi or Mullah Noor Muhammad. The Mahsuds contemptuously just use the term *mullah*, equating him to the prototype religious functionary subordinate to the tribal elders, the *mashar*. Thus the Wazirs elevated him to the position of a respected religious leader transcending local loyalties, officialdom remained cautiously neutral, and the Mahsuds emphasized their Pukhtunness, thereby suggesting the inferior placement of the mullah in the Pukhtun lineage universe.

The personal character of so puissant a prophet has to be beyond reproach. To his detractors the Mullah appeared to conjure up the dark spirits that lurk within man; to them he was a Hasan-i Sabbah (PA Order, September 24, 1976, p. 7) and "diabolical" (Political Agent's Office, 1977, p. 4). They execrate him as the reincarnation of shaitan, the devil. The word is freely applied to him in official reports emanating from the PA's office. The Mahsuds, too, refer to him as shaitan. To them, proof of his intrinsic evil is displayed in the titles of the Urdu books he possessed, *Bengal ka jado* ("the magic of Bengal") and *Talismani Chakar* ("the magic of the talisman"), and his moral turpitude in the numerous batches of condoms found in his rooms. *De jado starga*, the magic eye installed in the door of his rooms is another proof of his powers of evil. He personified *kala ilm* ("black knowledge"). When entering the Kaaba in Mecca, as a triumphant victor, the Prophet announced, "Truth hath come and falsehood vanished." To his critics the Mullah stood for the same maxim in reverse: Falsehood hath come and truth vanished.

Mahsuds are contemptuous of the Mullah. To them his personal habits hint of darker psychological elements: "He used scent and eye make-up. Can he be a man?" Mahsud elders, like Gulab Khan, were appalled at Wazir "worship" of the Mullah: "What sort of maliks were they? The Mullah fined them, hand-cuffed them and jailed them in his own private jail. Yet they worshipped him. They were *beghairat* ["without shame"]." To Mahsuds this casts the Wazirs as invidious, cowardly, and even heretical. The Mullah, to the Mahsud, was an unmitigated scoundrel, a shaitan. Does the role of the Mullah as shaitan tell us more about him or his followers? In the context of the long-standing tribal rivalry the slurs may have been part of a deliberate Mahsud strategy to reflect on Wazir character.

To the Wazirs the Mullah appeared as an honorable and sympathetic religious leader determined to establish their honor and rights: "Maulvi Sahib made us united. He gave us pride and hope." Other, more material advantages are also enumerated: financial aid, shops, employment, and even education. To the Wazirs he had promised a visionary future, and they believed in him. Even after leading them to a disastrous defeat they had faith in him. To the teeman he remained *de janat mata* ("pillar of heaven"). He symbolized the spiritual renaissance of the tribe. Through him they were both ethnically and spiritually sublimated, expressed, and defined. Religion is not merely metaphysics. It bears within it a sense of intrinsic social obligation; it not only induces intellectual conformity, it enforces emotional commitment. The Mullah not only induced intellectual conformity, he enforced emotional commitment, still explicitly expressed in society.

The Mullah relied largely on his charisma, composed of his powerful rhetoric, forceful personality, and organizational skills, to win the hearts of his followers. His hold over the Wazirs is all the more remarkable as he was palpably not a *qazi* ("judge"), learned in *shariat* ("holy law"), and he was not a saint or sufi, with a reputation derived from life-long abstinence, meditation, or scholarship. None of this mattered to the Wazirs.

The Wazirs needed a savior figure who could deliver them from the Mahsuds. The ground was ripe for the emergence of a leader who could organize both cultural and religious forces on behalf of his followers. A Pukhto proverb sums up the relationship of the believing follower to his *pir* ("saint"): "Though the pir himself does not fly his disciples would have him fly" (Ahmed 1973, p. 19). The Wazirs saw their pir in miraculous flight.

Identifying the Mullah's main supporters and opponents in Wazir society may tell us something about him. His supporters are reflected in his "inner cabinet," the members of the dolas kassi and chalweshti, and fall into three general categories: first, established maliks, such as Jalat Khan; second, emerging leaders who were not officially recognized maliks but were effective organizers and speakers, like Ba Khan; and third, young firebrands like Pirzada's brother, Shahzada, still fresh from the madrassah and representing a new generation and a high, even passionate, degree of commitment. One cause of the Mullah's success among the Wazirs was his ability to bring such disparate elements under his flag. Personal loyalty to the Mullah remained the common bond among them. The loyalty was reinforced by other links forged from the mosque, where younger members served their apprenticeship in his madrassah as his talibs, or from the adda, as in the partnership with Ba Khan.

The loyalty of the inner group has stood the test of the apparent failure of the Mullah and its political consequences. In spite of Jalat's falling out of official favor, Ba Khan's houses being destroyed, and Shahzada being sentenced to jail, their loyalty to the Mullah remains undiminished. Some members of the inner cabinet continue to express their loyalty in highly visible action. Ba Khan regularly visits the Mullah in Haripur jail to provide information and to obtain advice. Other Wazirs prefer to present a unified position on the Mullah to the world, whatever they may feel about him in their hearts.

Two main elements within Wazir society opposed the Mullah, and both remained his targets. The first, the Mughal Khel of Wana and the Khojal Khel of the Dab settlements near Wana, resisted the Mullah to the end because of economic and social reasons. They were economically better off than their Zilli Khel cousins, which created jealousy in society. The Khojal Khel had converted their lands to cash crops, such as fruit, before other Wazirs, and they enjoyed irrigation facilities in their villages, some of which were provided by the administration. Both the Khojal Khel and the Mughal Khel had interacted politically with the administration at Wana and as a result were more responsive to education. Their members were in government schools and service in spite of local pressure long before other Wazirs. They remained cynically unmoved by the Mullah, and their better economic standing and education encouraged their isolation among the Wazirs.

The second source of opposition was the traditional leadership, whether maliks or pirs. A populist strand is evident in the Mullah's arguments. He spoke for the teeman, the common people. In the main the maliks and pirs of Wana capitulated to him. They were either intimidated into leaving the political arena or they were incorporated into his organization. He thus exploited and used traditional leadership structure while, at the same time, transcending it. In private, elders resented the skillful way in which the Mullah had bypassed them into their own homes through links with women and children. These links allowed Mahsuds to hint at improper and immoral behavior on his part. A group loyal to the Mullah *within* the household ensured pressure on the elder.

Although resenting the Mullah elders found it politic to hold their peace in public. For example, in the governor's jirga at Tank in early 1980 the Wazir maliks en bloc requested the Mullah's release. Wazir demands were again equated to the person of the Mullah. The request expressed clearly the strength of the jailed Mullah after four years of absence from the agency: it also demonstrated the attempt by traditionally anti-Mullah maliks like Pasti, who had been publicly humiliated by the Mullah, to appear to be loyal.[4] Wazir ethnicity dominated political alignments in public. For the Wazirs, the Mullah's charisma remains undiminished.

Max Weber's definition of charisma underlined continued success and the ability to distribute patronage (Bendix 1960; Gerth and Mills 1961). The response of followers to charismatic leaders is partly motivated by material expectations, he argued. Patronage, which may take different forms, reinforces the personal mystique of the leader. Repeated failure to provide for his followers is translated as a sign of failing charisma. The story of the Mullah of Waziristan would suggest a partial rejection of Weber's thesis. The Mullah's charisma has continued to dominate Wazir minds and actions since 1976, in spite of his being in no position to grant favors.

Wazirs have come to look on the Mullah as symbolic of their group honor and identity. His movement to challenge and transform structure, its disastrous end notwithstanding, remains a memory of heroic endeavor and exhilarating tribal unity for the Wazirs. His charisma rests on properties that are nonmaterial. The Mullah on trial, like Christ on his cross, may well have asked heaven if he had been deserted. If we are allowed to take the neo-Durkheimian liberty of equating heaven with society, the answer would be in the negative. Charisma may be viewed as much a function of the contemporary needs of society as an expression of the innate qualities and compulsions of an individual.

Mullahs in Muslim society

Islamic groups that provide religious leadership may be broadly divided into three overlapping categories. The first two are defined by their function in society and the third by genealogical links with holy ancestors. The first, the *ulema*,[5] distinguished by religious and legal learning, include *mufti, qazi, maulana,* and *maulvi*: the second category includes esoteric, sometimes unorthodox groups like the sufis; and the third distinguished by religious genealogy and descent and thus claiming superior social status, includes *sharif* or *sayyid* (descended from the Prophet) and mian (descended from holy men).

The ulema represent the orthodox, bureaucratic, formal, and legalistic tradition in Islam. They interact with the state at the highest level and advise the kings and captains of Islam. In contrast, the mystical orders largely restrict themselves to rural areas, shunning worldly pursuits, and avoid formal interaction with administration. Such orders command the hearts as well as the minds of their followers. The holy lineages and their members, sayyid, sharif, or mian, are accepted in society as associated with holy ancestors. They command a vague and generalized respect, especially if they live up to idealized behavior, which is pacific, dignified and neutral between warring groups and clans.

The difficulty in placing the mullah in any one category is not taxonomic but is related to the ambiguity and elasticity surrounding his social role. Not quite the learned mufti, sure of his orthodox Islamic knowledge, nor the sufi, sure of his inner Islamic faith, the mullah is forced to define and create his own role. He may, indeed, borrow from all three categories, elevating himself to maulvi in one place (as in this study) and to mian in another (Ahmed 1980a, p. 167).

Early in Chapter 1, I accepted the *Oxford English Dictionary's* definition of a mullah as one "learned in theology and sacred law" to serve our general purposes. Let us examine the origin of the word. The word derives from *mawla*, a tutor, helper, guide, used for *God* ("He is the *mawla* of the faithful") in the Holy Quran.[6] Other derivatives are *mawla* and *moulay*, "my lord," implying king and saint in North Africa, and *mawlana*, "our master" (the title given par excellence to Jalal al-din Rumi). In South Asia the word *mullah* does not signify superior status, saint, or king but a religious functionary in the village.

In general, the mullah occupies a junior position in the religious hierarchy and is defined as "a lesser member of the religious classes" (Algar 1969, p. 264). The mullah restricts himself largely to the village level of social and political life except in extrordinary circumstances. He appears to thrive in crises.

Noor Muhammad was a Wazir, that is, a Pukhtun from Bannu. He was not a sayyid or mian. The distinction is important in the Pukhtun universe. Sayyids and mians are traditionally accepted as embodying superior lineage because of their links to the Holy Prophet and holy men. Their claims to superiority are backed by marriage rules and idealized behavior patterns. Pukhtuns, notoriously endogamous and reluctant to give their women to non-Pukhtuns, are prepared to waive the prejudice for sayyids (Ahmed 1980a; Barth 1972). The mullah is more often than not a poor Pukhtun of a junior or depressed lineage.

Translation of role from religious to political spokesman *within* the boundaries of society was thus inevitable once the Mullah's following grew. No lineage structure constrained him; as the son of a migrant member of a junior lineage he remained outside the local lineage charter yet a part of the larger Wazir tribe. From a mullah supervising religious functions he became a leader promising specific political goals.

Among Pukhtuns the mullah remains subordinate to the lineage elders and usually does not feature on the genealogical charter (Ahmed 1980a). The observation is confirmed by archival material based on contemporary records for Waziristan (Bruce 1929, 1938; Curtis 1946, General Staff 1921, 1932, and 1936; Howell 1925; Intelligence Section 1930; Johnson 1934a 1934b; Johnston 1903; and Watteville 1925). Pukhtun elders see political activity as their preserve and restrict the role of the mian or mullah to specified religious functions (Ahmed 1980a, p. 162). Of these the main functions of the mullah are to organize and supervise the local mosque and the *rites de passage* based on Islamic tradition. The mullah in a Muslim society has no proselytizing function. He must, perforce, explore other areas if he is to enhance his role and authority in society.

The mullah may rise to power in extraordinary times, rallying Muslims against invading non-Muslims (Ahmed 1976). In the tribal areas, mullahs have led widespread revolts with singular courage and conviction against the British as in 1897 (ibid.). Their bold stand provided a contrast to those quiescent elements in society who preferred to sit on the fence in the struggle against the British (traditional leaders and native bureaucrats, in terms of the district paradigm). Men such as Adda Mullah, Manki Mullah, Palam Mullah, and Mastan Mullah, and in Waziristan, Mullah Powindah and the Fakir of Ipi, seemed to appear from nowhere to mobilize society and lead the struggle. Some, like Mastan Mullah of Buner in Swat, known as *sartor baba*, claimed or were believed to possess magical powers in their fight for Islam.[7] The struggle, to the mullahs, was interpreted as jihad, a holy war for Islam to be conducted irrespective of success. Their uncompromising devotion to the Islamic cause, as they interpreted it, and consequently its militant expression provided the British with a prototype of what became popular as the fanatical "mad mullah" or the "mad fakir" (Churchill 1972, p. 29).

The role of the mullah is negligible in cases where the invading army is Muslim. In such a situation an ambiguity is inherent in the conflict. Jihad cannot be invoked against Muslims. When the Pukhtun tribes fought Mughal armies representing a Muslim dynasty, they were led by traditional tribal leaders rather than by mullahs (Mackenzie 1965).

In spite of their leadership in times of crises and their service during normal times, a certain explicit antipathy to the mullah is expressed by traditional Muslim writers and intellectuals, whether Pukhtun or non-Pukhtun.[8] They find him a poor advertisement for Islam. Contemporary Mahsud scholars appear to conform to this view.[9] Traditional leaders are, of course, clear about his role. Mahsud elders have firmly kept the mullahs "in their place," and they quote examples of the leading Mahsud mullahs. A popular example is of Mir Badshah squelching Fazil Din, the son of Mullah Powindah, in public when the two were in Kashmir with the Mahsuds in 1947–8 for jihad: "Don't give us advice on how to conduct battles and matters that don't concern you. You just lead prayers and wash the bodies of our dead comrades according to Islam. We have other men to lead us in battle." Mahsuds repeat stories of their elders' publicly putting even the Mullah Powindah in his place by the statement: "You are a mullah. Stick to your traditional business only." Gulab Khan recounted how his father and Mehr Dil rejected the Mullah Powindah's proposal in jirga that Mahsuds not deal with the British government: "This is no concern of yours and we will have good relations with them."

Mahsuds, in commenting on the Mullah of Waziristan, would assert *mizh charta mullah predo*, which roughly translates as "we would never allow a mullah to emerge." Part of Mahsud strategy, as we saw, was to mystify Pukhtunness as a method to cut the Mullah down to size. By emphasizing the humdrum and subordinate role of the mullah in ideal Pukhtun society they were, at a stroke, denying the spiritual or special properties claimed by the Wazir Mullah.

In turn, religious leaders like Shahzada Tajudin, the grandson of the Mullah Powindah, accuse Mahsud maliks of being *asli shaitan*, "true devils." They were "toadies of the British" and "sold out" their tribe and their religion for allowances and favors, he argues, a view shared by the Mullah of Waziristan.

A discussion of mullahs raises the related issue of the definition of

saints and holy men in Muslim society. I have argued elsewhere that it
is misleading to use the gloss "saint" for mullahs (Ahmed 1976) as
some anthropologists have done (Bailey 1972; Barth 1972, 1981). The
problem of placing mullahs in the saint category is made explicit in
this study. Mullahs such as the Wazir one and the Nalkot Pacha of
Swat who aspire to spiritual status through shortcuts, usually employ
transparent tricks and clever devices in order to convince people of
their special powers. The sayyid and mian, assured of their position,
do not need to resort to such tricks and devices to further their claim
to leadership. The Wazir Mullah, as we know, had installed in his door
a wide-angle door viewer sent by a follower from the Arab Gulf States.
He could thus "foresee" and predict who his visitor was, what he
looked like, and what he wore. The Mullah's capacity for seeing
through opaque doors was further evidence of his powers. Wazirs
believed that he possessed "the magic eye," *de jado starga*. Even some
educated agency people believed that the door viewer was a magic
device.[10]

The Nalkot, in his village in 1976, explained to me the devices he
employed as part of his stratagem to impress followers. His favorite
was to stitch a thin piece of wire under the skin on his stomach and
then, in front of a selected gathering, "eat" another bit of wire. As the
audience watched in amazement he would slowly pull out the first
wire. Similar stories are related about the Mullah Powindah in
Waziristan. The mullah's grandnephew, Ahmedo Jan, one of the
leading elders of the agency, related various devices his ancestor
employed to illustrate his powers. A favorite was to predict that the
niswar ("snuff") his followers were addicted to would turn to feces if
they did not give up the habit. At night he would arrange for dog feces
to be placed in the niswar containers. On rising in the morning, his
followers would marvel at the powers of Mullah Powindah.

"Am I to blame," the Nalkot asked me, "if people are so simple and
believe everything they see?" People not only believed in his powers
but some elevated him to the role of "saint." In anthropological
literature, the Swat village quack, blatantly manipulating people around
him with mumbo-jumbo and chicanery, has become the model of a
prototype Islamic Saint—with a capital S (Bailey 1972; Barth 1972,
1981). To categorize the Nalkot, or the Mullah of Waziristan, as
"Saint" is conceptually inaccurate and empirically misleading.[11]

A relevant question with theoretical ramifications for my nang
TAM model of society may be thus posed: Could a mullah have risen
to similar power among the Mahsuds? The answer is complex but

may be given in the negative. Mullah Powindah had assumed power in the early years of this century among the Mahsuds. He was a man who possessed exceptional leadership qualities, but his role was restricted by the Mahsuds to that of a religious leader conducting jihad against the British. His attempts to influence the Mahsuds politically or economically were unsuccessful. The reasons lie in a combination of factors, including demographic and educational ones, which differentiate the two tribes.

The emergence of mullahs, pirs and fakirs dabbling in politics is a constant phenomenon in the tribal areas. Unchecked, such men may create considerable problems for the administration, especially in times of general regional tension.[12]

The nature of the Islamic jihad

For the orthodox Muslim the crime of the Great Mughal emperor Akbar, the most famous case of imperial heresy in South Asian Islam, lay in his attempt to redefine Islam;[13] for the majority of Muslims of Waziristan the crime of the Mullah lay in his redefinition of jihad. From the time of the Prophet, scholars of Islam have held different opinions on the exact nature of jihad. Still, its importance for the believer is not in doubt. The Holy Quran is explicit regarding the central role of jihad in Muslim activity. Sura II, "*Al-baqarah*," one of the most important sections of the Holy Quran, commands Muslims to "fight in the way of Allah against those who fight against you, but begin not hostilities. Lo! Allah loveth not aggressors" (Pickthall 1969, verse 190). Verse 191 of the same sura actually employs the term *kafir* with reference to the preceding verse. Jihad is an all-encompassing struggle, a total commitment. "Go forth," Muslims are exhorted, "and strive with your wealth and your lives in the way of Allah!" (ibid., Sura IX, verse 41).

Following the Holy Quran, the Prophet affirmed the importance of jihad: "In Islam there are three dwellings [stages], the lower, the upper, and the uppermost. The lower is the Islam of the generality of Muslims. If you ask any one of them he will answer, 'I am a Muslim.' In the upper their merits differ, some of the Muslims being better than others. The uppermost is the jihad in the cause of God, which only the best of them attain" (Al-Muttaqi 1974, p. 211). However, he clearly pointed out a nonmilitary form of jihad. Sufis, tracing their spiritual links to the Prophet, quote him as identifying two forms of jihad: the lesser jihad as holy war and the greater jihad as the struggle against one's own passions. The importance of the moral life, the struggle to control one's *inner* passions, is thus emphaized (Hodgson 1974, vol. 2 p. 228). Modern Sufi scholars, too, emphasize "personal striving" in defining jihad (Algar 1969, p. 263). Contemporary Muslim scholars with differing perspectives on Islam (Khomeini 1981, Maududi 1948, Rahman 1979) agree that "the means of jihad can vary—in fact, armed jihad is only one form" (Rahman 1980, p. 63).

Ibn Khaldun, however, emphasizes the difference in waging jihad aginst people of the Book (Jewish and Christian) and against "pagan" groups.[14] Defensive warfare is legitimate against the former as is offensive war against the latter. Jihad is also defined a "war to defend the frontiers of the Dar al-Islam against infidels" (Hodgson 1974, vol. 2, p. 120). Examples are cited in history of rejection by the ulema of a call to war by Muslim rulers in the face of a Muslim enemy. The fall of the Samanid dynasty of Bukhara was due to the ulema's persuading people not to resist the advancing Kara-khani forces on the ground that fighting among Muslims was worse than the fall of a government (ibid.). The *Oxford English Dictionary*, reflecting the traditional Western view, defines jihad as a "religious war of Mohammedans against unbelievers." (1975, p. 653).[15] Traditional Oriental scholars suggest a similar definition: "the Holy War against infidels" (Holt, Lambton, and Lewis 1970, p. 908). Recent Western scholarship discusses jihad mainly as an instrument against the European colonial venture (Dale 1981, Peters 1979).

For our purposes, jihad may be defined as "a holy struggle in the way of Allah." There are thus no theological sources to support jihad against fellow Muslims.[16] However, jihad becomes operative when *takfir*, declaring someone an unbeliever or non-Muslim, is involved. The point leads to the more complex argument of who is a Muslim. The Holy Quran and Prophet define *Muslim* as a person who pronounces the *shahada* or *kalima* (there is no God but Allah, and Muhammad is His Prophet). The Mahsuds fitted neither the nonbeliever nor the heretic category. To condemn them as kafir was in itself an act of considerable audacity. The Mullah's jihad clearly rested on a weak theological but strong sociological base.

Of interest here is the Mullah's successful employment of the concept of jihad, which has a range of interpretation in a specified situation involving Muslim combatants.[17] In fiery sermons delivered in the mosque the Mullah condemned the Mahsud as kafir. Those who would die fighting them or their allies in the administration would attain shahadat. Struggle, death, and paradise, the eternal

Muslim paradigm, were lucidly predicated for the Wazir mind. The Wazirs had little alternative but to obey the call to jihad because their options were limited in society, but acceptance of the jihad did not mean that they did not question its morality. Was the jihad Islamic or was it a Wazir jihad? Was the Mahsud a kafir? Was it proper to oppose the legal government of the land? For the Wazirs, such questions were disturbing, made even more so by the failure of their resolution. It may be concluded that the Mullah's jihad was neither "holy" nor for "Allah."

6

Economic development and reinforcement of ideology in Waziristan

The Waziristan case is not one of tribal culture tamely adapting to new economic conditions; rather, that culture plays a major part in shaping the political consequences of the new economic conditions. Traditionally, income was derived from political activity such as raiding settled districts, allowances from the administration for good behavior, or limited agriculture. Such income was small and irregular. It reinforced ideal-type behavior and social organization. Two important sources of wealth, however, opened during the last years of the 1960s and the early 1970s: the expanding Arab oil economies, and a vigorous policy of economic development in the tribal areas by the government of Pakistan (Ahmed 1977). Fundamental changes in society thus ensued: men migrated overseas to work in the Arab States, and attitudes toward ideal-type behavior changed in regard to trade and commerce.

There is evidence that junior, or depressed, lineages saw employment abroad and the economic opportunities at home as an avenue of escape from their positions in society (Ahmed 1980a, 1981a). Working in the Arab States allowed them to send remittances home, thus enhancing their economy. Their involvement in trade and contracting within the agency allowed them to challenge the maliks. In most lineages tarboorwali was being translated from political into economic forms. In the late 1970s the maliks entered the race, and junior sons were sent abroad or began accepting contracts in the agency. Such contracts were more often than not then subcontracted.

Few statistics exist of migration from the agency. The total number is said to be anywhere between 20,000 and 30,000 men from a total agency population of about 300,000. In random samples I discovered that almost every malik—whether senior or junior, formally recognized or self-appointed—had a male relative from the extended family working abroad. As obtaining a visa is expensive and difficult, the malik's connections with the government prove helpful. In the Arab States the tribesmen are employed in hard manual labor performed under extremely harsh conditions, making roads and buildings or driving trucks. Most send regular sums of money back to their families. On return they construct houses and invest in businesses.

The impact of the new money and ideas on traditional hierarchy, authority and, indeed, morality (as the Waziristan *tor* cases in Appendix A illustrate) may be extensive (Ahmed 1981a).[1] The implications for change in the ideal-type model are many. In our case we know that Wazir remittances from abroad assisted the Mullah's cause in Waziristan. No estimates exist of the sums provided to the Mullah before 1976, but Wazirs suggest they were enormous. Even after the Mullah was jailed, monthly donations from remittances collected by Niaz Muhammad (estimated between 80,000 and 100,000 rupees) continued and still help to carry on the struggle. Closer at hand, however, were the new local sources of income.

Development projects and schemes were provided with unrestrained generosity in the tribal areas during the Bhutto era (Ahmed 1977). Such economic development was not politically innocent but a rather shrewd move on Bhutto's part to outflank his Pukhtun rivals in the NAP, based in Charsadda and Mardan, by wooing the hitherto neglected tribal areas. If, as rumor had it before the general elections in 1977, he had announced adult franchise for the tribal areas, allowing each adult a vote, the widespread development projects would have stood him in good stead with the *teeman*, the tribe. He would have been able to successfully bypass the maliks and their exclusive privilege to vote for Assembly members. Adult franchise was not granted in 1977, however, and the maliks retained the right to vote. The vote meant continued benefits for the maliks, including development projects.

Double benefits accrued to the maliks who accepted such projects: the project itself, whether a water tank or primary school, for their settlement and, by established tradition, the right to be nominated by the administration as contractor. Because the government is eager to open up new areas, it is prepared to placate the malik whose authority would allow a development scheme to be implemented. Unfortunately, work on the projects is often shoddy, but profits are large. The resulting problems in diplomacy for the political administration are many.[2]

The growth in the number of development projects also tells a story. Before the creation of Pakistan the tribes had rejected development schemes as symbols of British imperialism and a method of penetration. The lack of the most basic facilities, such as primary schools is understandable only in this context; "a record of futility," a British officer had called it (Howell 1979,p. 95). The mullahs, especially, condemned education, because it was organized by and identified with the British.[3] The student risked being labeled a kafir. Maliks blame the attitude of the mullahs for illiteracy in Waziristan. Abdul Maalik would say: "The mullahs argued that if we were educated we would become kafirs. But by remaining illiterate we have become kafirs in this country." In the face of severe opposition some Mahsud elders, like Mir Badshah, persisted. Today, as a consequence, his sons hold high office in Pakistan: Alam Jan is a general in the Pakistan army, the first Mahsud to reach that rank, and his younger brother Saeed Khan was returned as member of the National Assembly for the agency in 1977. Another son, Inayatullah, holds a law degree and in spite of his young years has shown promise in agency affairs. Unfortunately for the Wazirs, there were no Mir Badshahs among them, and they have lagged far behind the Mahsuds in education.

It is, therefore, not surprising that when Pakistan came into being in 1947 there were only 8 schools (primary, middle, and high) in the agency. Within ten years 34 more had been opened, and 1967 saw 50 schools in operation. By 1980 the total was 213. The proliferation of schools suggest their general acceptance in Waziristan society. The principle of nikkat has been observed in the distribution of schools, and about a quarter are in Wazir territory. Most of the Wazir schools, however, are either in or near Wana, notably Dab, and are attended by children of nonlocal government employees.

The location of the two colleges of the agency, one at Ladha and one at Wana, sanctioned in the mid-1970s, also reflects nikkat. Because most students prefer to study in the settled areas (usually Tank or Dera Ismail Khan), the colleges are not thriving. For the eleven Wazir students in the Wana college there are eleven teachers; the ratio is about the same for the Mahsud college at Ladha. The lack of enthusiasm of the college students is matched by that of the teachers who face serious problems living in the agencies (see Chapter 7, case III). It is interesting to note that the Mahsuds, who have more and older schools in their areas, are less susceptible to mullahs than are the Wazirs.

Education was not the only area that saw rapid expansion after

1947. Seventeen animal hospitals have been established since 1947, when none existed. The nine civil hospitals and dispensaries in 1947 were confined to Scouts' posts and were only for officials. Today there are forty-five civil hospitals and dispensaries in the agency for tribesmen.

In 1979–80, 43 million rupees were earmarked for government development projects in the agency. The projects included the building and expansion of communications networks, roads, bridges, irrigation wells, public health facilities, and schools, and all generated local employment and income. Tribesmen are also employed by the administration as *badraggas* (escort) and as mollifiers of the leading maliks of the area. The latter accept their monthly pay as sinecure and are often absent, some working in the Arab Gulf States.

During the 1960s and early 1970s, a variety of seeds were introduced in the Wana plain, and wells were driven for irrigation. The plain was found ideal for certain kinds of fruit, and apples, pears, apricots, and plums were successfully cultivated in village gardens. Apples soon became a major cash crop and were exported from Wana to other parts of Pakistan. This provided a source of income for the Mullah, who levied a tax of one-quarter of a rupee on every crate of apples meant for export. A crate fetched from 80 to 100 rupees in the market, and the Wazirs could pass the tax onto the consumer.

In addition to development and agricultural sources, wealth was generated from other nontraditional and noneconomic sources. One was the timber permit, and another was the election to the Assembly. During the 1977 elections, agency candidates admitted to spending hundreds of thousands of rupees in "buying" the votes of the maliks. The tribesmen themselves do not employ euphemism. Votes are negotiated and paid for. The successful candidate, Saeed Khan, is said to have spent about 1.7 million rupees to ensure the outcome. Unfortunately, he lost his investment when martial law was declared in the country soon after the election: all political activity was suspended and the elections declared null and void.

Development projects sometimes face unexpected and unusual opposition. The "electrification of Waziristan" project is one such example. Shahzada, grandson of Mullah Powindah, opposed the introduction of electricity to Waziristan in the 1970s. It would, he reasoned, end the isolation and therefore the independence of Waziristan. Shahzada drew effective Freudian comparisons with the electric poles being erected along the main roads. The pole was the penis and the insulators attached to it on top were the testicles of the devil, and therefore they deserved to be destroyed. His followers set out to castrate the devil. A vigorous nocturnal campaign was launched in early 1979 to dislocate and damage electric poles wherever they were found unprotected. Fortunately, the tribes and especially the maliks disagreed with Shahzada on this issue. Because I was new to the agency the matter caused me considerable perplexity and took some time and effort to resolve.[4] By summer, however, the electrification program was once again resumed.

All the new sources of income implied some form of patronage and were therefore responsive to political pressure. These sources were effectively tapped by the Mullah and diverted to his political organization. The more wealth the Mullah accumulated, the more followers he was able to organize: more followers meant more influence with political administration, and more influence resulted in greater patronage of the Mullah. The new wealth identified his movement as it supported it. His automobile, for instance, new every few months, was a symbol of Wazir wealth and prestige and was a calculated gesture of defiance and assertion aimed at those who opposed him.

It seems, however, that in spite of wealth and the indexes of modernization – schools, roads, tube-wells – that appeared in society, the Wazirs were not prepared to change their traditional ideas and social life. On the contrary, instead of accepting new ideas and values, the Wazirs seem to have been gripped by a powerful social compulsion to reformulate and regroup along traditional lines. The lesson is clear. Contrary to conventional wisdom, society does not always proceed on a lineal path forward when it is modernizing.

PART THREE

Participation

7

The anthropologist
as political agent

Reconciliation and reconstruction

After the Mullah was removed from Waziristan, the Wazirs claimed that they were misrepresented by their opponents. They wanted a chance to prove their Pukhto and, their "honor." When I took charge of the agency in November 1978, I was determined to give them that chance. I set out to demonstrate that the behavior of a contemporary tribal society immersed in its particularistic code will approximate the society's notions of the ideal type if the circumstances are provided. The path was fraught with danger for me. Romantic models applied in the field do not necessarily correspond to empirical behavior. The policy could backfire and, in a critical time, create complications with the Mullah or across the Durand line.

The Wazir response to my overtures sprang partly from the nature of the Pukhtun model; to establish, or reestablish, themselves as men of "honor". Partly it was a strategic move to end their isolation without having to compromise their main objectives. The Mullah from his cell in Haripur jail appeared to have declared an unwritten armistice.

Social life was slowly returning to normal in the Wazir areas and a delicate equilibrium was being established when the Russians entered Afghanistan in December 1979. Refugees flocked to the agency in increasing numbers and anti-Pakistan elements living in the agency were contacted by foreign agents to create trouble.[1] The moment appeared opportune for supporters of the Mullah to begin disturbances and to put pressure on the government for his release, but the Wazir equilibrium held. The Wazirs responded to critical events in the agency in terms described as "loyalist" by the government; henceforth they could not be called "second-class" or "disloyal citizens".

Shortly after I took charge, Niaz Muhammad sent me a letter from his sanctuary in Birmal through a mutual friend. In it he argued the cause of the Wazirs. He requested that I observe and hear for myself and reach my own conclusions: "All the Wazir tribe want from you," he wrote, "is application of balm [*marham pati*, literally "balm and bandages"] to their wounds," and toward the end of the letter he affirmed, "The question of opposing administration or Government does not arise" (N. Muhammad, personal communication). In my reply I promised to do my best.

The "balm" was applied through word, gesture, and deed. Whereever I could I made it a point to express confidence in the Wazirs as a tribe. Rejecting recent practice, I accepted invitations to meals organized by Wazirs in their settlements. In the summer of 1979, Jalat Khan arranged a lunch for me in the guest rooms (*hujra*) of his village to which some 300 elders and officials were invited. Ba Khan and the father of Shahzada also invited me to lunches. Not to be seen as leaning toward the Zilli Khel, I also accepted invitations from the Khojal Khel, in Dab, near Wana. On such occasions the Wazirs expressed their loyalty and I promised neutrality in agency matters. Informal after-lunch talk, sitting on the floor on rugs, provided valuable information and helped establish rapport.

It was also ensured that Wazirs received material benefits. Their annual timber permits were increased in 1979 as was their food grain quota. Nikkat was maintained by requesting the government for extra shares to satisfy the Mahsuds. The prestigious Waziristan Public School project was to be located in Wana. The Zilli Khel responded enthusiastically by accompanying me to a site that I had selected north of the Wana camp and offering fifty acres of land free to the government for the school grounds.

As a gesture of confidence in the Wazirs I took to taking walks at sunset outside the Wana camp alone or with a single companion. Hill and gully around the camp provided cover for anyone contemplating a shot or knife stab. I was aware of violating established agency precedence. Many hints were dropped that I ought not to expose myself and trust Wazirs to this extent because they were "intrinsically unreliable." The threats of the Wazirs to kidnap officials as hostages for the release of the Mullah were put to a test. The PA would be an ideal bargaining point. No attempt was made or contemplated, to the best of my knowledge. The balm being applied to the Wazirs was apparently soothing them. The time was ripe for a major psychological breakthrough to the Wazirs. I chose to perform an act of cultural significance to them. I decided to visit the shrine of the Wazir ancestor Musa Nikka, in Birmal, the most inaccessible part of the

Wana mosque.

The Mullah defends himself in the jirga, 1976.

Site of destroyed Adda in foreground, mosque in center, and Wana camp on right. Gibraltar picket is visible on the peak behind the mosque.

On the Durand line in Birmal. The PA is standing in the center. Jalat standing second from left and Ba Khar fourth from left in the front row.

PA receiving the surrender of Birmal Wazirs against the backdrop of the Durand line, 1980.

The surrender of arms and ammunition by Mahsuds to the PA at Wana. Abdul Maalik fully visible in front row. 1979.

Maees Khan, Mahsud Robin Hood.

Jirga with Sappar Khan seated. Abdul Maalik third from left.
Gulabi and Nemat Kharoti on PA's left. At PA's bungalow, 1980.

The grave of Musa Nikka.

New Scouts post at Zarmelan looking toward Afghanistan and Gomal river on Durand line.

tribal areas. The journey proved to be a turning point in my relations with the Wazirs.

In visiting Birmal I was taking a calculated risk. Estimated to be nearly fifty miles to the northwest of Wana, it had no government or modern facilities, no roads, schools, or hospitals. Because of its inaccessibility, authoritative writers have made errors regarding Birmal and its shrine. Raverty records that Musa Nikka is on the "Tonchi river" in the North Waziristan Agency (1888, p. 536). Historically it is a notorious shelter for "hostiles," "proclaimed offenders," Afghan agents (Johnson 1934a, p. 5), and "Pukhtunistanis." Even one shot fired in the air from a distant peak during the trip would be reported and exaggerated by national and international intelligence agencies. Nonetheless, I felt the risk was worth taking. The Wazirs would be delighted to have the shrine of their ancestor visited and honored.

Apart from the popular cultural purpose of the trip, it would also be an important political move. For the first time a political officer would visit Birmal. Such a visit has wide implications in the tribal areas. If the PA can manage his first journey successfully, the area is declared "open" to other departments. Actual administrative control of the agency would shift right up to the border and, I felt, in the coming years stand Pakistan in good stead.[2]

It was arranged that I would visit Birmal as the guest of the Wazirs. The relationship of host and guest was made explicit. Honor and trust were involved. My dishonor would reflect on the Wazirs.

Departure time and destination of journeys in the agency are disclosed by the PA at the last moment for reasons of security. Even if the timing is announced to the escort, the destination is kept a secret. Information about the Birmal trip was thus closely guarded, and not even my seniors were informed. The obvious problem of when to inform the many Wazirs who had to accompany us as hosts was solved by the APA Wana. We invited them for tea on the afternoon before the trip. When the Scouts' Quarter-Guard sounded the bugles at sunset, the camp gates were closed as usual and the Wazirs were perforce guests for the night. Although they speculated that some such trip was being planned, the information was contained within the camp. We provided a red herring by dropping hints to the staff about a tour to the Gomal River in the south. So effective was the ploy that the agency surgeon, himself a Manzai Mahsud, accepted the rumor as gospel truth and positioned himself with his escort by the Jandola gate, east of the Wana camp, at the appointed hour, whereas we, of course, left from the Durand gate, west of the camp.

We left Wana well before sunrise. No roads or paths existed west of Wana when the standard maps had been made more than half a century ago (Surveyor-General 1922–3, p. 38–H) and none did now. After heading due west, we turned north. Our journey through ravines and streambeds was slow and bumpy. On either side, running north to south, were mountain ranges between 8,000 to 10,000 feet high, mostly covered by forests. After climbing up to the Srakanda Pass we descended into the Birmal area.

Once we entered the Birmal valley, Jalat and Ba Khan took charge of me and shouldered the Mahsud bodyguard aside. Through their protective gesture they were pointing out that we were in the most exclusive Wazir area. They rightly calculated that if an enemy wished to embarrass them personally by firing on me or our convoy this area provided the ideal opportunity. They were acutely aware that the honor of the Wazirs, as hosts, was at stake. At one stage my jeep was separated from the rest of the party for a short while. Had Jalat and Ba Khan decided to take me hostage during this time in order to bargain for the release of the Mullah, they could have done so. Indeed, when I joked about this, Ba Khan took offense saying, "the Wazirs now have two chiefs." He was restoring the PA to the role of chief of the agency, alongside the Mullah, a considerable concession for a key member of the Mullah's cabinet.

Upon arriving at the shrine of Musa Nikka we offered our prayers. The grave itself was made of mud and plaster. On behalf of the government I announced that a dome would be built over the grave. Two primary schools and a dispensary were also sanctioned, to be started as soon as sites could be found. At lunch I chided the Wazirs for being so involved in agency politics as to neglect their revered ancestor. The Wazirs took the point. After a brief excursion to Suwwey Warra ("small rabbit"), a knoll on the Durand line that overlooked the irrigated and large plains leading to Urgun, an Afghan district headquarters, we began the return trip and arrived in Wana by sunset. Within hours of our departure from Suwwey Warra, Afghan fighter jets flew along the Durand line, our trip perhaps having been mistaken for a military maneuver.

The news of the trip to Birmal was reported in the *Khyber Mail* on June 3, 1979. Its effect on the Wazirs was considerable. Those fighting alongside their kin in Afghanistan took time off to write and congratulate me for "removing the *parda* ['veil'] of Birmal." Even Niaz Muhammad congratulated me in a letter, reminding me of his goodwill in not spoiling the journey, through a hostile act such as gunshots. Wazir mulaqats and jirgas for months afterward would begin with a recitation of the Birmal trip as evidence of their loyalty and hospitality. The Wazir sense of self-respect was being restored. The Mahsuds turned the trip into an argument for the nikkat principle and requested me to visit a holy ancestor of theirs, Borak Nikka, near Tiarza. I promised to visit Borak Nikka once we moved to Tank for the winter.

Apart from the cultural goodwill generated among Wazirs, important political consequences followed the Birmal trip. In a gesture of friendship, the Zilli Khel donated land for a new Scouts' post at Zallay Sar, west of Wana and just short of the Durand line. The post controls three routes, including the Birmal route, which converge at Zallay Sar on the path to Wana. Usually such exchanges of land are effected with considerable effort, cost, and often fighting. The Scouts' posts of Zallay Sar and Zarmelan, also established during this period, were the earliest government footholds in the area. For the first time the Pakistani flag flew on the Durand line in the agency; the governor of the NWFP recorded his "appreciation."[3]

The trip to Birmal also helped to flush out Pukhtunistanis from that area. In a jirga near the new Zallay Sar Scouts' post, the first one ever conducted in this remote area with the PA, a large group of well-known Birmal Pukhtunistani Wazirs surrendered to me. They were made to feel welcome at the jirga and thereby honored. An appropriately dramatic backdrop to the ceremony was provided by the mountain range along the watershed of which runs the Durand line. The surrender helped to encourage other groups of Waziristan Pukhtunistanis to do the same.[4]

Thus the government has made slow but steady attempts to reconcile the Wazirs within the agency framework, and Wazirs have made a slow but steady response. Even so, the relationship remains fragile and is marked by tension and sometimes violent demonstration of support for the Mullah.

Waziristan cases

The extra attention to the Wazirs could have been interpreted as a drift away from the Mahsuds had not equally strenuous efforts been made to keep the Mahsuds in good humor.[5] The exercise to placate both tribes is a complicated one involving shifting alliances between and within the major Mahsud political blocs, emerging leaders, and breakaway groups. It is also an exhausting and testing one. Visible and constant neutrality in intertribal affairs, between Wazir and Mahsud, had to be matched by the same in intratribal matters. The smaller tribes like the Suleman Khel and Burkis could not be ignored either.[6]

The cases that follow provide insights into certain principles of tribal administration, social structure, and organization and allow us to test the thesis regarding ideal behavior. Case IV is different from the other cases in nature because it took place in the settled area, but it also supports my thesis: When ideal behavior is not invoked, the tribesman is free to employ a different range of strategy, fair or foul, to achieve his objectives. In doing so he may violate established law and administrative precedence. Although some of the cases involve the Wazirs, they differ from those discussed previously in that Pukhto and honor are at issue rather than Wazir ethnicity. The influence of the Mullah and the effects of his movement are thus of secondary concern.

Case I: The Mahsud arms surrender. The Shabi Khel are notorious for their truculence even among the Mahsuds. Their history during the British period is one of murder and mayhem. They are responsible for one of the earliest murders in the agency, that of Lt. Col. R. Harman in 1905, commandant of the Scouts, and for one of the last deaths, that of Maj. J. O. S. Donald in 1946, a PA. Not unnaturally, many Shabi Khel have felt it wise to cross the border and settle in Afghanistan. Some Shabi Khel have done well there; one was reported recently to be an executive engineer in the Public Works Department. Such families exhibit divided loyalties between their ancestral homes in the agency and their adopted land.

During 1979, as developments in Afghanistan made their impact on the agency, some groups crossed the border to return with arms and ammunition for the purpose of creating mischief. In June 1979, I learned of a heavy cache of arms brought from across the border into the Bromi Khel section, deep in Shabi Khel territory. Included were said to be 10,000 rounds of cartridges contributed by the ruler of Afghanistan, Tarakki himself. Mischief on a grand scale was being planned. Investigation confirmed the report, and the administration immediately moved into action. Privileges, such as khassadars and food-grain rations, were suspended for the entire Bromi Khel. A Shabi Khel official serving in Wana was placed under arrest—a harsh revival of the established administrative tradition of treating tribal officials as "hostages." The APA, Ladha subdivision, held jirgas and sent for the three Bromi Khel elders suspected of organizing and bringing the weapons. They refused to see him and instead took to the hills. A stalemate was reached. Mashud internal politics now intervened. As Abdul Maalik was related to the accused, his opponents played on the incident to embarrass him. They argued that Maalik was unfaithful to Pakistan at this critical juncture of its history. The propaganda, which cast him as both un-Islamic and anti-Pakistan, built up public opinion against Maalik and put pressure on the administration to deal severely with him.

Abdul Maalik was sent for and told that he could assist the administration while also clearing his name by bringing the concerned elders to Wana "on the PA's surety." Maalik went to the Bromi Khel and returned with a negative answer. The Bromi Khel wanted an *itbar nama*, a written guarantee of surety, that the PA would not arrest them. They claimed that the PA had betrayed his word in the case of the Mullah. I replied that the word of the PA should be surety enough. Maalik returned to them with this message. We met a few days later and he announced a date when he would arrive with the elders. He had persuaded them to accept the word of the PA. On the appointed day the elders arrived at the Wana camp. In my office they appeared nervous until assured they would not be arrested. I had given them my word. They put their argument before me. They would be willing to come to terms with me, but if they surrendered the arms and ammunition their credibility and reputation across the border would be ruined. I insisted on the surrender and they finally agreed. At a jirga in Wana the Bromi Khel accompanied by clan elders surrendered the arms and ammunition and promised loyalty to Pakistan.

The surrender was an unusual event in the tribal areas. The *Khyber Mail* of July 24, 1979, noted that it was "the first such occasion." A tribesman rarely surrenders anything, least of all weapons, which are permitted in the tribal areas. Other tribes in the agency had watched how the Bromi Khel were dealt with; had we been unsuccessful others would have been encouraged to slip across the border to make similar attempts. In the delicate situation that prevailed in the region such attempts could have caused problems for the administration. In any event, this was the first and last attempt to smuggle weapons on any scale into the agency.

Case II: The surrender of the Mahsud Robin Hood. Maees Khan, like his father, Gujar, had established his reputation in the region as an outlaw operating from the territory of his clan, the Shabi Khel. His base was a tangled, desolate, and inaccessible area of mountains that lay between North Waziristan Agency, Bannu District, and South Waziristan Agency. Following in his father's footsteps, Maees kidnapped people from Bannu and held them for ransom. His bold personality, his successes, and his assistance to and concern for the poor created a Robin Hood reputation for him in the agency. There appeared no way for the administration to deal with him. Various attempts to capture him were foiled by his daring and superior intelligence networks. Shortly before my appointment as PA, he had stopped work on the proposed main road passing near his area, Shaktu, by shooting at the executive engineer of the Public Works Department and at the APA. An unsuccessful attempt had been made to cultivate his tarboor and rival, Sifat Khan, although he was known to be anti-Pakistan.

In the spring of 1979 I established contact with Maees through his relatives. Initially, he was suspicious and refused to respond to my overtures, although I emphasized my respect for his father and for him. I suggested that times had changed and were changing. If he surrendered to me I would treat him with respect and honor. Perhaps a future administration would not be so sympathetic. After considerable negotiations through junior officials, Maees agreed to surrender to me on certain condtions. His past record would be ignored and he would be treated as a man of honor, a Pukhtun. I reassured him on both scores and he agreed to come to Tank.

At this point some complications arose. Certain Mahsud maliks at Tank were not entirely pleased at the prospects of their Robin Hood giving himself up., He was useful to them when they wished to express their displeasure with the adminstration. He could be relied upon to snipe at government installations or kidnap officials. I renewed my attempts to persuade Maees, promising him a new life, a life of honor. I even promised to make him a malik of the agency, the first I would be appointing in my tenure.

Maees finally agreed to surrender and come down to Tank escorted in honor by a large contingent of agency elders. The *Khyber Mail* headlined the event, "Notorious Mahsud hostile surrenders," and concluded the article with the statement that Maees "was the Agency's most famous hostile and his surrender after years of hostility has brought new hope of peace and tranquility to a large and most backward area of the Agency" (*Khyber Mail*, April 23, 1979).[7]

In Tank, Maees stood out even among the striking figures who congregate in the PA's office. He had about him a certain air of innocence and wonder. This was his first visit to Tank; he had never crossed Jandola for fear of arrest. In his way of life he was carrying on a tradition established by his father. The tradition had begun as jihad against the British. To his supporters, Gujar was *Khalifa* (a religious title for leader, from "caliph"). Talking to him convinced me of his sincerity. Maees was simply coming to terms with Pakistan, however late in the day. A visit to Peshawar was arranged. Accompanied by a host of Shabi Khel maliks, Maees called on the home secretary, NWFP. He later recounted the considerable impression Peshawar made on him.

We established a warm relationship, and Maees often visited me. Initially he felt uneasy without his gun and knife, but after I reminded him he was my malik now, he grew accustomed to moving in Tank without them. Not long after, his cousin Sifat Khan kidnapped three men from Bannu. A jirga of elders failed to procure their release. Maees demonstrated his mettle by attacking Sifat's settlement. Machine-gun fire was exchanged for a few days until the kidnapped men were released. Malik Maees was proving a strong and loyal friend in an isolated and inaccessible area.

Case III: The killing of the Ladha College lecturer. While having dinner in their college at Ladha, on October 12, 1979, two lecturers complained to the cook about the amount of vegetable oil in the eggs. The cook took offense and disappeared into the kitchen only to reappear with a shotgun. He fired point-blank at the two, wounding them severely, and then escaped into the night. The case of Muhammad Rahim, alias Garam ("hot") the cook, would reverberate in the entire province.

I heard about the incident the following morning at Tank. The story troubled me; something was missing from it. From prima facie evidence Garam appeared guilty of murder, but I was certain that he had a strong motive to act as he did. My instincts told me that at the bottom of the matter lay the Pukhto code. Routine administrative action was taken to press for Garam's surrender. The Char Khel, Garam's lineage, were arrested in Tank and their khassadars and food-grains suspended. Jirgas were also formed. Too much pressure could be counterproductive, as Garam would escape into Afghanistan, the traditional way out for culprits in such cases.

News of the shooting caused wide-spread outrage in the province. The mass media discussed it in detail to support the argument that the tribal areas, especially Waziristan, were not safe for nonlocal staff. The death of one of the lecturers was widely announced in the press. Pressure increased on me to arrest and punish Garam. Matters were made worse because of the public school recently approved for the agency. Garam's action reopened the debate: If college lecturers were not safe how could I guarantee the safety of the staff and boys of a public school? Why waste money in Waziristan? In any case the Ladha College, with its ratio of one student to one teacher, itself was under scrutiny and now there was a plausible additional argument for closing it down. I had no answers until we contacted Garam. A council of elders of the Shaman Khel, to which the Char Khel belong, was sent to the agency. They located Garam, but he refused to talk to them.

Anti-Pakistan elements among the Shaman Khel bolstered Garam's resolution not to surrender. They warned him he would be handed over to the martial law authorities and, under Martial Law Regulations, promptly hanged. Indeed, a campaign to hang him was waged in the press by the relatives of the dead man and members of the Teachers' Association. I sympathized with them but could not let a lynch-mob mentality prevail in the agency. In the midst of these arguments Garam sent me a message that he was prepared to surrender if I would give various guarantees. I answered that he would receive a fair trial and that justice would be meted out under the Frontier Crimes Regulations. I would guarantee no more. Garam was worried about the political influence of the relatives of the deceased in Charsadda. I assured him that justice recognized no hierarchy or influence. I also sent word to his family, that if he remained an outlaw wanted for murder, hiding from place to place, their future would be uncertain and dark; on the other hand, I would make sure that he was treated justly to the best of my abilities. He must trust me.

Shaman Khel elders felt that the PA could, in comparison with district authorities, ensure fair terms for Garam and insisted to the Char Khel that he surrender. The more pressure I put on the Shaman Khel the more pressure they applied to Garam's family. The elders' presence alone was said to be costing them between 10,000 to 12,000 rupees a day; jirgas break up if hospitality is below standard. They threatened to burn Garam's home if he did not surrender. Garam's parents capitulated on his behalf. The women of Garam's family brought three sheep and knives to the jirga asking for nanawatee. The jirga could slaughter the women and the sheep with Garam's knives. The impasse was over. The council of Shaman Khel elders decided to impose a fine of 40,000 rupees on their own clan to pay as compensation to the complainants; of this 30,000 rupees would be paid to the family of the deceased in Charsadda and 10,000 rupees to the other lecturer from Bannu. Garam would surrender to the PA at Ladha.

The details of the case now came to light. As I had suspected, Garam had been provoked into committing his wrong and unlawful act. There was a history of animosity between the two lecturers and Garam. The lecturers emphasized that they were "superior" officials of the government of Pakistan. Crude jokes were made about Garam. "A servant is treated like a wife," they suggested to him. In the agency, one's honor is involved in such remarks. Apparently pushed beyond endurance Garam had decided that that particular Friday would decide matters one way or other. He had worn clean clothes and applied *attar* ("scent"), the traditional manner in which Muslim warriors go out to jihad. In the morning the lecturers threatened Garam with termination of service and ordered him not to enter the college. He had pleaded with them not to provoke him and then, as a final gesture of appeasement, brought some eggs from home which he cooked for them. When firing the shots Garam had said "I shall yet make you true Muslims."

Mahsud elders unanimously supported Garam: He had "done Pukhto." They themselves, given such provocation, would have done the same. Even the principal of the college agreed that Garam had been provoked and stated that one of the two lecturers was in the habit of using a sharp tongue to the lower staff. The principal testified to finding Garam "very obedient and expert in his field of service" (statement dated October 17, 1979). He had earlier called a staff meeting to ease tension between the lecturers and the lower staff, including Garam. At one stage, according to the principal, when queried about the bill Garam had asked, "Am I a thief or are these professors animals?" Arrogance in the agency is rarely allowed to pass unchallenged; arrogance accompanied by verbal insults provokes drastic action.

In the second week of November an interesting development took place. I had sent a Dre Mahsud jirga, one of the most important and representative of its kind, to Peshawar. They were to ask for nanawatee from the family of the deceased and as a gesture of goodwill pay compensation money of about 50,000 rupees to them (in addition to the 30,000 rupees collected by the Shaman Khel the Dre Mahsud jirga contributed 20,000 rupees). When they arrived in Charsadda the Dre Mahsuds were received by the assistant commissioner, but the local villagers had little idea of how to treat them. The Dre Mahsud offered *fateha*, prayer for the deceased, but their money was refused. It was seen as a substitute for Garam, not a gesture of goodwill. The villagers feared incorrectly that Garam would go scot-free if the money was accepted. Nanawatee was apparently obsolete in Charsadda, and the locals were perplexed by the concept. To me this example provided an interesting contrast in the behavior of the nang and qalang groups. The concept of nanawatee had played a key role in Garam's surrender and in Charsadda it was unknown. A fundamental concept of Pukhto in the tribal areas had dropped from use in the qalang areas.

On November 19 at Ladha Fort, accompanied by the Shaman Khel elders, Garam surrendered.[8] While I addressed the Shaman Khel, assuring them of my personal guarantee of justice under law and in the light of custom, Garam wept. In the reply on behalf of the tribe an elder described the variety of "tears in the eyes of a man"; they flow from anger, fear, and gratitude. Garam's tears, now that the tension was over, were of the last kind.

Case IV: Mahsud networks and strategy. Social networks and their place in modern politics have interested social scientists studying traditional societies (Boissevain 1974, Mayer 1966). Official and kin networks and the ability to utilize them effectively give the Mahsud a clear edge in dealing with their cousins, the Wazirs. It also makes them a difficult tribe for the administration to deal with and allows them to subvert the laws of the land. Without reference to the ideal code of honor or behavior, the tribesman may, in a crisis, use tactics that violate established law and administrative precedence.

In late October 1979, General Zia-ul-Haq, in a national broadcast, announced a more vigorous implementation of martial law. The emphasis was on cleaning up urban areas by removing illegal encroachments and combating social crimes. The lash was to be administered in public to those found guilty of violating Martial Law Regulations. Reports of public lashings in Rawalpindi and Lahore were being discussed widely in Tank when a young major arrived as local martial law administrator. He was not a Pukhtun. When as a matter of courtesy he called on me at Tank, I advised him not to forget that although in the settled area, he was dealing with Mahsuds who belonged to the agency. Not heeding the advice, and wishing to do his duty in letter and spirit, the major, accompanied by the assistant commissioner of Tank, launched a vigorous campaign to clean up the Tank bazaar. In the process, shops too near the main road were closed and makeshift shops along the road knocked down. Some of the shops that were closed were owned by such Mahsud elders as Gulab Khan and Sher Badshah. A background of hostility exists in Tank between Mahsuds and non-Mahsuds, who represent the majority population. The latter now attempted to put the Mahsuds in their place. This they felt, would be an excellent opportunity to use the larger administrative framework to cut the Mahsuds down to size.

The Mahsuds reacted on two levels: On one level, direct and unrelenting pressure was applied to the major. Telegrams were sent off and telephone calls made to the president of Pakistan, governor of the NWFP, and other important men in Pakistan warning them of imminent tribal revolt if the undue harrassment did not cease forthwith. Various delegations of elders immediately left for Dera Ismail Khan, Kohat, and Peshawar to canvass civil and military officials. Elders like Sher Badshah, who enjoy the personal and visible friendship of active generals holding key positions in Pakistan, mobilized their contacts. General Alam Jan telephoned his colleagues in the Frontier from Quetta to inquire what hell had broken loose in Tank. Telegrams and telephone calls were soon coming in to Tank to the assistant commissioner inquiring about the situation and advising reversion to the pre-October situation. On another level, and as part of their strategy, the Mahsuds refused to cooperate with the Tank administration. They locked their shops and threatened to shoot if they were tampered with.

The major came to see me, and his perplexity was apparent. He had no idea that the Mahsuds would or could launch such a massive counterattack. He was fearful now of losing more than just face. I hurriedly arranged for informal meetings with Mahsud elders, including Sher Badshah, in which the major appeared to them to be sympathetic and reasonable. The matter was now out of his hands, however, and his superior, the brigadier at Dera Ismail Khan, who was also not a Pukhtun, arrived in Tank. The anti-Mahsud lobby had reached the brigadier through their networks in Dera Ismail Khan, and he was determined not to be impressed or outflanked by the Mahsuds. He was clearly out of humor with them. Officials, too, from the settled districts saw this as a good opportunity to chastise the Mahsuds. Although not involved with the Tank administration, I was present and, as a Mahsud representative, felt that I was in a tight position. But I need not have feared. The Mahsuds ran circles around the administration.

The Mahsud case was first pleaded by their oldest malik, reputed to be almost a hundred, who rose to speak eloquently: "Jinnah, the creator of Pakistan, invited us to leave our homes and settle in Pakistan. We left our homes. We sacrificed by settling here. We gave our lives fighting for Pakistan in Kashmir." He reached the climax of his speech by a series of questions: "Is this how we are to be treated? Is this how we will be humiliated and insulted? Are we not safe in Pakistan?" and a threat: "If our shops are touched we will all migrate back to the Agency for good." Others echoed the same theme. The content of the arguments ranged from maudlin to threatening, angry to placatory.

The martial law authorities had not bargained for such an emotional and excitable jirga. The brigadier suggested that the site of the shops be inspected. In the bazaar, where thousands of people were gathered, Sher Badshah strode up to the brigadier boldly and proceeded to argue in Pukhto. To add insult to injury he asked the brigadier if he spoke Pukhto. The brigadier, plainly irritated, curtly replied, "speak in the national language, Urdu," upon which Sher Badshah switched to impeccable English acquired from his service in the British Indian army. This visibly increased the brigadier's irritation. Once again Jinnah, the creation of Pakistan, and the sacrifices in Kashmir were invoked. Sher Badshah then asked a rhetorical question: "Can we be anti-Pakistan—when I have two sons in the Pakistan army, one a major and the other a captain?"

Messages continued to arrive from senior officials in Peshawar and Islamabad expressing concern over the growing "Mahsud problem." It was past lunch time, and no solution was in sight. The brigadier decided to return to the town hall with the jirga. He was determined to end the crisis. In a private meeting he asked my advice. The matter, I suggested, could be handed over to a jirga constituted by him, and the shops be opened until the verdict was announced. In the circumstances this was the best way out. In effect it meant putting the problem on ice. He agreed to the solution and announced his decision to the jirga. He was plainly exhausted by the Mahsud encounter. Sensing victory, the Mahsuds thrust home an unrelated final demand. Some of their shops had been sealed by the assistant commissioner for dealing illegally in food rations. The Mahsuds demanded that these shops be opened. The brigadier conceded to the demand to the chagrin of the assistant commissioner. Within minutes, the jirga said the customary *doa* ("prayers") and dispersed. The crisis was as abruptly over as it had begun.

The brigadier confessed that this was his first Mahsud jirga and that he was mentally and physically exhausted by the end of it. The major was removed from Tank the next day and no replacement posted in his place. The shops, both cement and makeshift, opened to business as usual the next morning. The Mahsuds were jubilant, and news of their victory was flashed from Karachi to Quetta. They had demonstrated their organizational and tactical skill, as well as their skillful manipulation of networks in Pakistan.

Case V: The surrender of Sappar Khan, outlaw of Baluchistan. The origins of this case trace back to a period before the creation of Pakistan. The case is complicated because it involves the administration of two provinces, indeed two countries, and tribes living across the Durand line in Afghanistan. Larger events, notably the invasion of Afghanistan in December 1979, played an important part in the choices made by the actors.

Sappar Khan, son of Patorai, a Mando Khel Pukhtun, lived in his village, Deragai on the banks of the river Zhob, a few miles from Fort Sandeman in Baluchistan.[9] When Sappar became involved in a land dispute with a neighboring clan, the case was referred to the PA of his agency and decided. Sappar felt the administration had been unfair to him and took to the hills, adopting a life of crime, raiding, and kidnapping. At the head of a growing band of followers, Sappar soon established a name for himself in the region, and eventually combined forces with the notorious Kharoti outlaw Nemat.

Shortly before 1947, Nemat's father, a member of the Kharoti tribe living in Afghanistan, was killed in an encounter with the Scouts' unit of Fort Sandeman, the Zhob militia. Nemat swore to take revenge, *badal*. In 1956 he ambushed a Zhob militia party and killed two officers. Nemat henceforth became a "most wanted man" in the Zhob and South Waziristan agencies; the Afghans promptly appointed him "colonel" in the Pukhtunistan militia.

Sappar's difficulties with the administration were compounded by his continued rejection of the Zhob administration's requests to dissociate himself from Nemat. At an abortive meeting of reconciliation, Sappar's son was shot by rivals and taken into custody by the government. In retaliation Sappar kidnapped three Scouts soldiers, whom he exchanged for his son.

In the 1960s and 1970s, eighteen major offenses were recorded against Sappar Khan, including the blowing up of railway bridges and the kidnapping of government civil and military personnel. His following and reputation grew. Various jirgas and raiding parties failed to stop him. He eluded the administration by a successful strategy of moving between distinct administrative structures and tribal zones.[10] When pressure increased in Zhob Agency he would arrive in South Waziristan, from there cross into Afghanistan, and then when the time was ripe, return to Baluchistan to strike again. He appeared in Waziristan as a Pukhtun "guest" seeking shelter among the Wazirs and was honored as such. Wazir territory formed Sappar's base of operations. Timely warnings through Wazir networks always ensured his escape.

In November 1979, Sappar Khan struck again. He kidnapped Lance-Naik Baramat Khan of the Zhob militia in a perfectly executed textbook operation. The Baluchistan Scouts were furious at Sappar and the impunity with which he operated. The colonel of the Scouts was determined to recover his man. He informed me that Sappar had escaped with his victim to my agency and was near the Durand line. General Alam Jan, as the senior officer of the Baluchistan Scouts, was equally anxious to recover his soldier. The general and colonel, themselves Pukhtuns, now felt that their honor was at stake and talked of commando raids across borders to capture Sappar wherever he was and whatever the cost. To me, military action in solving tribal problems implies the failure of the political administration. Thus, I advised patience, and devoted my energies to recovering the soldier.

Through Wazirs, some of whom were close to the Mullah, I exerted pressure on Sappar Khan. After lengthy negotiations the soldier was handed over to me. With a suitable escort I sent him back to report to the colonel at Zhob, who was delighted. [11] When Alam Jan called to thank me on behalf of the Baluchistan Scouts he framed a challenge, half in earnest: "If you bag Sappar Khan I will appreciate your value as a PA in the greatest traditions of the Agency."

First, I gathered information on Sappar Khan, his party, and his movements. He appeared to be an obstinate man to deal with but also a shrewd leader, as illustrated by his choice of base west of Zallay Sar, in Afghanistan. Not only was it out of my reach, as it lay across the border, but the area was shared by three major tribes. Each tribe could thus justifiably claim he was outside their territory.

Next, I began to send messages to him through the antigovernment Wazirs who harbored and supported him and whom he could trust. Simultaneously I contacted "Colonel" Nemat through Abdul Maalik, in an attempt to gain his trust. Our communication was dense with words like "honor," "trust," and "Pukhto." Nemat then approached Sappar on my behalf; his honor was now tied to mine.

The Russian involvement in Afghanistan in late December forced many outlaws and Pukhtunistanis to contemplate long-term future prospects; many surrendered. The cry for jihad against the invading force was in the air. To be seen as indifferent to the Islamic cause could mean identification with the invaders. Stories of death and rape in Afghanistan were rampant; tribal honor was at stake on various levels. During the interchanges with Sappar, involving demands from him and assurances from me, I emphasized the current events. Sappar was aware, and it was pointed out to him, that he could not sit indefinitely in turbulent Afghanistan with five adult daughters in his camp: Honor and tor were involved. Sappar's Wazir advocates insisted on an itbar nama, because, they argued, in the Mullah's case trust had been betrayed by the PA. I insisted that Sappar trust the PA. Gradually he began to feel he could depend on me to extract the best terms for him if he surrendered, which he finally agreed to do but only with a guarantee from the PA, Zhob Agency, that the cases against him would be withdrawn. Insisting that if I were to be his advocate he must come to me unconditionally, I assured him that I would treat him as an honorable man, a guest, and would obtain the best terms from the PA, Zhob Agency, for him. After lengthy and intricate negotiations he agreed.

I informed the colonel at Zhob that Sappar would surrender on itbar, or trust, as an honorable Pukhtun, and that he would not be jailed or slighted in any way either by me or the Zhob authorities. He would be welcomed as a malik, and the jirga accompanying him would be afforded formal courtesy and hospitality. Sappar was prepared to face a formal trial by jirga for his offenses, as is the custom in Zhob Agency. I requested compassion in view of the fact that such a notorious person was prepared to walk in and throw himself at our mercy. The officials at Zhob cleared matters from their seniors at Quetta, the provincial capital of Baluchistan, and agreed to these terms. The IGFC was delighted at the prospect of Sappar Khan's being caught—or as he put it "bagged"—without a shot or loss of life.

A large jirga including the most respected elders of the agency, both Mahsuds (Gulab Khan, Abdul Maalik) and Wazirs (Jalat Khan, Bangul), escorted Sappar Khan to Tank. In January 1980, Sappar Khan formally surrendered. Nemat, too, surrendered and swore loyalty to Pakistan. Accompanying the jirga was another Pukhtunistani,

Nemat Kari Khel, who, like his Kharoti namesake, was an officer in the Afghan militia holding the rank of colonel. Neither Nemat had crossed into Pakistan territory for at least two decades, fearing arrest. On behalf of the government I accepted their surrender, forgave them their past crimes, and promised cordial relations in future. The jirga guaranteed the future good behavior of the three men.

When Zhob was informed that a jirga would accompany Sappar as his "security," another crisis arose that almost aborted the surrender. The officers of the Zhob militia, on learning that Nemat Kharoti would accompany Sappar, were indignant at the thought of his arriving at Zhob and leaving scot-free. He had the blood of the Scouts on his hands. The "honor" of the colonel and the Zhob militia was at stake. The jirga accompanying Sappar was welcome as long as it did not include Nemat. Although I knew the reponse of the jirga, I sounded out its elders. The jirga answered flatly: no Nemat, no Sappar. They, too, had given their word. They would go, as they had come, in a group to Zhob or return to the agency taking Sappar with them. With some difficulty I persuaded Zhob to turn a blind eye to Nemat for the sake of the larger cause.

It was a remarkable return for Sappar Khan. Four buses and as many cars drove from Tank to Gul Kach, crossed into Baluchistan, and then, escorted by the Zhob militia, arrived at Zhob a full day later. Some of the most senior elders of the agency–Gulab Khan, Abdul Maalik, and Jalat Khan–and some of its most notorious anti-Pakistanis–the two Nemats–formed part of this triumphal return.

The colonel hosted tea for the guests, and Sappar's rivals arranged a dinner in their village, a gesture indicating desire for peace. It also signified the Pukhto tradition of hospitality and itbar. I was in constant touch by telephone with Zhob. After the first day of euphoria and goodwill, the jirga sat down to work out an agreement between the administration, Sappar, and his rivals. This took about a week, and proceedings almost ended abruptly on more than one occasion. As the Wazirs had proved their worth in persuading Sappar Khan to surrender, the Mahsuds now exhibited their skill in council. The wisdom and experience of Gulab Khan and Abdul Maalik were displayed in full measure during this week. Had it not been for them the jirga may have failed. Both men had reasons to avoid the trip in the first place; Gulab Khan was severely ill with malarial fever, and Maalik's mother lay on her deathbed. Their personal rivalry was suspended in Zhob, Maalik keeping Gulab warm at night by tending his fire to keep out the bitter cold. Maalik's gesture was in keeping with Pukhtun ideal-type behavior. In turn, Alam Jan, whose family is aligned with Gulab Khan, was on the phone from Quetta to the colonel at Zhob, emphasizing that the Waziristan maliks, especially Abdul Maalik, should be treated as honored guests.

The jirga concluded by announcing its decision regarding the land dispute. Both parties were, by and large, satisfied. The jirga bound the rival parties to sureties worth 200,000 rupees each. Most important, it undertook to stand surety for Sappar Khan's future good behavior. Sappar's base in Waziristan was thus effectively removed. The manner of the surrender as much as the surrender itself of Sappar Khan and the two Nemats, made a considerable impression on the tribes living in the two agencies and on the governments of NWFP and Baluchistan; concepts of honor and trust had been employed successfully between administration and tribes.[12]

Case VI: Wazir conflict in Birmal. An instance of the general goodwill being exhibited by Wazirs coincided with my last weeks in the agency in June 1980. The Zilli Khel clashed with the Toji Khel in Birmal over a land boundary, and gunfire was exchanged. The intratribal conflict was typical of clans sharing boundaries (Ahmed 1980a, chapter 5). Traditionally, the administration attempts solutions only if its own roads or buildings are involved, because outside such "protected areas" there are few practical ways of implementing decisions. Quick to take advantage, foreign agents encouraged both sides to stiffen their positions. The activity of these agents coincided with a reported Soviet summer offensive on Urgun, the Afghan headquarters near Birmal.

It was suggested that the Scouts be deployed near Zallay Sar to prevent Wana Wazirs from joining their kin in Birmal. I turned the proposal down because the use of Scouts implied a failure of the political process and would also add another dimension to the conflict. If a Scouts solider were killed in the operation, the affair would be cast in a totally different light.

Initially I allowed Wazir elders from the clans and the tribes to attempt a reconciliation. A temporary truce faltered. When the elders failed, my junior staff stepped in. Meanwhile, more firing was exchanged and men were injured. The foreign agents, also, stepped up their activities. The Zilli Khel, recalling their discipline during the days of the Mullah, organized a chalweshti for the Birmal conflict. In a jirga they declared a fine of 10,000 rupees for those Zilli Khel failing to appear for battle against the Toji Khel. A meeting of almost 3,000

Zilli Khel warriors was held to chart out a course of action. Life came to a standstill in Birmal as the Zilli Khel and Toji Khel faced each other in trenches across an area of almost twenty square miles.

Seeking a solution, I secretly communicated with Niaz Muhammad, who responded by a tour of the area. His strenuous efforts halted the gunfire, but peace was still far. Various forms of agreements broke down at the last minute. The situation threatened to spill out of Birmal and into the Wana plain. Once in the Wana area it could become complicated, and the administration would be directly involved. At this juncture I decided to trade on the goodwill the Wazirs harbored for me; I would apply the "romantic model" of administration. A jirga of Wazir elders was called at Wana. I was bedridden at the time with an attack of malaria, and my wan appearance in the jirga hall at Wana perhaps added to the urgency of the moment.[13] My address lasted only a few minutes. The Wazirs, I told them, had behaved magnificently during my tenure. They had removed all doubts regarding their loyalty to the government. The fact had been observed and noted at the highest levels. The Birmal affair, however, was slipping out of control. Although it was an internal matter, I could not patiently watch brother killing brother. Moreover, I said, foreign agents had been active in heightening tension. With matters across the border already unsettled such a situation could become detrimental to the people of the agency. As their PA I would not use either the carrot or the stick. I would let them decide the matter. They were men of honor and I expected them to behave with honor; my own honor was now at stake.

Three days were given to them in which to proceed to Birmal, hold meetings, and bring me news of an agreement. A Zilli Khel elder attempted to present his point of view. I silenced him by saying that both Zilli Khel and Toji Khel were equal in my eyes and I would not take sides. Let the elders of the tribe, I said, decide. If they failed I did not have to specify what steps the administration could take. The events of 1976 were still fresh in their minds.

Within hours after the jirga I received reports that my address had been favorably received. Elders were already moving to Birmal, determined to bring peace. An extension of the three-day period was asked, which I granted. By the end of June an agreement between the Zilli Khel and Toji Khel was declared. Peace rarely comes so cheaply or easily in intratribal conflict in the tribal areas.

8

The political agent
as anthropologist

In emphasizing the role of the anthropologist as social actor over that as social observer, there is a danger of transforming anthropology as science to anthropology as autobiography. Nonetheless, autobiography must be part of a discussion of his role as social actor.

For purpose of analysis the roles of actor and observer must be kept separate, which creates a dilemma for the anthropologist. Where does one role conclude and the other begin? Is it possible for the anthropologist to switch off at will the emotional and intellectual signals, hostile or friendly, flowing around and between people? If not, are not both roles affected and to an extent compromised? The anthropologist is expected not only to transcend his fieldwork situation but, in a manner, one aspect of his own self. In this study I have shifted the problem of the actor versus observer around. Rather than accept the division of the two roles as a dichotomy, anthropologist as actor versus observer, I am suggesting a conjunction of roles, the anthropologist as actor *and* observer.

The anthropologist finds himself in the field to prove some thesis, as I, too, set out to do in Waziristan. I was taking a calculated risk that could have proved professionally disastrous. I had argued that tribal behavior, however deviant in the contemporary situation, could approximate or revert to the ideal if the opportunity was afforded, the behavior acknowledged, and the idiom couched in the vocabulary of the tribal code. My task as anthropologist was complicated, for I was an integrated part of the fieldwork.

I came to the South Waziristan Agency in late 1978, fresh from my doctoral studies in anthropology at the School of Oriental and African Studies, London (having completed preliminary requirements in 1974–5). The year before, 1976–7, I had been posted as political agent, Orakzai Agency. Thus, I had the opportunity in Waziristan of combining field and theoretical knowledge. These stood me in good stead, for the times were not propitious in the region. Not only was the agency, one of the most turbulent in the NWFP, smoldering with resentment from the 1976 action in Wana, but Soviet involvement in Afghanistan was increasing overtly and dramatically.

Let us pose the question of whether, on the basis of data presented in the study, my tenure as PA in the agency could be considered successful. To keep the various pressure groups, some opposed to each other, on the PA's side over a long period is an almost impossible task. (A senior colleague expressed the PA's position succinctly: "After a year in Waziristan, every day becomes like a year.") I am certain that many people were dissatisfied with me, and I did have notable failures, for example, I failed to have a new adda sanctioned. Still, in maintaining general peace, ending conflict, and extending the sphere of the government (the traditional definition of success) the answer to the question may be on balance, affirmative.[1] The answer is supported by some of the cases quoted in the last chapter (and the official letters of commendation reproduced as footnotes in the same chapter).[2] And yet I was in no way better than my predecessors in the agency nor especially qualified to administer it. Let me, therefore, discuss the factors that, I think, assisted me during my period in the field.

First, developments in Afghanistan prompted strong Islamic feelings that diverted attention to larger issues outside the agency and helped to close ranks in the tribal areas. The fight of the Afghans was seen in terms of jihad against the kafir and enemies of Islam. As a Sunni Muslim, I was expected to sympathize with current notions of Islamic themes, especially jihad, and, in turn, I could expect understanding from tribesmen (mainly Sunni Muslims on both sides of the border). Many potential tribal troublemakers in the agency such as Pukhtunistanis thus became open to negotiations with the government. I am certain, for example, that the Mullah's decision to remain neutral in agency affairs was prompted by the Afghan struggle.

Second, a network of official and personal contacts in the land provided invaluable assistance in my relationships with tribesmen, apparent in some of the cases in this book. Fortunately, these contacts cut across tribal and political boundaries. Moreover, I was able to establish relationships with those elders unknown to me previously by determined efforts on my part (Abdul Maalik) or on the basis of other links (such as with the Wali of Swat as in the case of Mullah Powindah's grandson, Shahzada).[3] These relationships often created moral dilemmas, as in the case of Ba Khan. While at Tank, I learned that Ba Khan had been arrested in Wana by local field officers, and had been accused of creating trouble for the junior officials at Wana. The officers concerned were apprehensive about my obvious sympathy for him. As responsible officials, they had their reasons for the arrest. The officials were assured that I would not interfere with their action. Let an impartial jirga, I suggested, decide the case according to custom. Ba Khan's son and father visited me in Tank, not to plead for his release but to express confidence in the administration. In addition to the support of tribesmen I benefited immensely from the friendship and support of my colleagues, both senior and junior, who on more than one occasion saved me from error.

Third, to introduce a more subjective note in the discussion, perhaps my desire to succeed lay in an inner psychological compulsion. No Pakistani administrator sensitive to illiteracy, poverty, and corruption, the contemporary Third World syndrome of despair, can remain unmoved in the rural areas of Pakistan. He is among his own people and compelled by a moral imperative to bring some tranquility and harmony into and around his work to the best of his abilities. These, it is argued in the study, are sometimes more possible to achieve through honor, trust and affection than through guns and soldiers. A related compulsion lay rooted in my schooling, a product of the British educational system. Through the process of osmosis, certain values of that system may have touched me. Perhaps the ideal liberal ethos, with its key concepts of justice, fair play, and honorable behavior, accounted in some way for my response to the Wazirs. On my arrival in the agency, the Wazirs clearly required special attention because of their situation as the underdogs. To my mind this ideological position was reinforced by various Islamic themes of justice and generosity toward the downtrodden.

Finally, I attempted consciously to translate theoretical knowledge of systems into administrative policy. The literature assisted me in clarifying and conceptualizing ideas about tribal groups, their structure, and their organization. In particular, an understanding of segmentary tribal theories and their related concepts such as agnatic rivalry proved helpful. Nikkat, which is directly related to tarboorwali, is a characteristic articulation of the segmentary principle. I was scrupulous in translating this aspect of theory into practice: If the leader of one Mahsud bloc was seen at the PA's home, which implied familiarity with the PA, the leader of the rival bloc was invited shortly afterwards. Maalik commented on this aspect of my tenure as the most important: "Yours has been one of the quietest and most peaceful tenures as you have been fair and neutral. I consider you like a brother and so do my rivals like Alam Jan; this is exceptional." Neutrality, not familiarity, was the key to the system.[4]

My neutrality was emphasized by my distance from Waziristan. In the early jirgas I declared that I was not a Pukhtun (as Pukhtun identity is reckoned through the patrilineage, my mother's Pukhtun descent does not qualify me).[5] I had never served in Waziristan before. I was, therefore, neutral between the tribes and their rivalries. However, my distance did not imply lack of sympathy. I would be fair and sympathetic to their demands. It was no more than my official duty as an officer. It was also my religious duty as a brother Muslim (a duty underlined by the lineage of my father, who claimed descent from the Holy Prophet).

The opposite position is adoped by many political officers in contemporary Pakistan.[6] Intimacy with the tribes is suggested. Although it is certainly the easier method of establishing early rapport, the rapport may prove to be short-lived. Overidentification with one or another faction triggers intricate patterns of rivalry and often creates complications. Alliances with one or the other group often result in antagonizing rival blocs and upsetting tarboorwali. The neutrality of administration in local politics is thereby compromised. Officials are soon accused of being potical and doing poticali, that is, practicing deception in the manner of "politicals." Apart from academic theories of segmentary systems, I applied other, more popular and romantic notions about Pukhtun tribesmen with favorable results.

The romantic theories are one consequence of Pukhtun resistance and courage in the colonial encounter. As we know, Pukhtuns were mystified and romanticized by the British (Chapter 3). Paradoxically, the theories were propounded with the most fervor by colonial administrators whose duty it was to rule the Pukhtuns (Bruce 1900, Caroe 1965, Elliott 1968, Howell 1979, Woodruff 1965). The theories maintain that Pukhtun behavior is determined by Pukhtunwali, irrespective of material considerations or rational explanation. When dealing with Pukhtuns there is always the chance of a "rush of blood to the head," Caroe observed (O. Caroe, personal communication, and 1965). Those colonial officers who sought alternative and simpler answers than their civilization could provide found them reflected in the Pukhtun way of life. Their romantic notions of and affection for the Pukhtun tribesman were, without doubt, sincere. Shortly before his death, Howell confessed to Caroe that "often in his dreams he found himself in Waziristan, and his heart flying in those precipitous gorges" (O. Caroe, personal communication).

The empirical validity of these theories exposes some of the weaknesses of more academic explanations of human behavior. For instance, "transactionalists" argue that man interacts with, and within, society to maximize profit (Bailey 1960, 1970, 1972; Barth 1966, 1972, 1981). For these anthropologists, social relationships between people are defined by "a ledger kept of value gained and lost" (Barth 1966, p.4). When entries in the profit column of the ledger outweigh those in the loss column the individual is maximizing his relationships and optimizing his chances. As we have seen in this study, an application of such a theory to explain Pukhtun behavior may be inadequate. At least some aspects of Pukhtun behavior may be explained by the romantic theories.

The romantic model of the political officer is in part a logical extension of the romantic theories. The model reflects an idealized and romantic code. Its key symbols are "honorable behavior," "courage," and "trust." The officer behaves in a certain way because he is expected to do so by local society.[7] He identifies with the group—tribal or peasant—in his charge. For him, the group's code is suffused with a special aura; they are *his* people. Such identification with the people is sometimes seen as excessive by colleagues (Masters 1965, Woodruff 1965).[8] The model is not a theoretical abstract; in Waziristan, officers have died upholding it.

The romantic political-officer model derived partly from identification with the tribe and its values. In Waziristan the model faced an interesting, if inevitable, problem. Officers perceived the Wazirs and the Mahsuds as providing two overlapping but distinct models and expressed their preference for one or the other. Pettigrew, for instance, felt that "the Mahsud simply has more character than the Wazir" (1965, p.2). The tradition has been carried on in Pakistan. Omar Afridi does not conceal his affection for the Mahsuds (1980). One PA, who wrote of both tribes, did so in two separate books (Johnson 1934a, 1934b) and thus treats the two tribes as distinct units.

Political officers writing of "their" tribes is a tradition as old as anthropology itself, and I believe that we may profit from such ethnographic notes.[9] Making allowances for cultural irreducibility, especially in the context of colonialism, I believe that such writings can provide a rich and authoritative source of ethnographic material for the social sciences, as recent literature in anthropology also suggests (Hart 1975, Lindholm 1980, Pastner 1979).

In reading the work of the colonial administrator, we know what his position is. As the representative of a more powerful and putatively more civilized mother country, he is administering—and in this case writing about—isolated and primitive groups. The position of the contemporary political officer commenting on his own society may prove more complex. In contrast to his predecessor in office, the colonial officer, he may wish to overidentify with his group. In doing so he falls into the trap of what I have called the "narcissistic ethnic study," that is, of studying his own society and discovering in an expression of overt subjective identification how much there is to admire in it (Afridi 1980, foreword). Omar Afridi's *Mahsud Monograph* is an excellent example of a "narcissistic ethnic study." Omar is a nang Pukhtun political officer commenting on nang society. So far, examples of narcissistic ethnic studies are rare in the social sciences because most studies, especially those of tribal groups, have been conducted by "outsiders," usually Western scholars.

The narcissistic ethnic study raises certain interesting theoretical and methodological questions for professional anthropology. Does the author of this type of study unconsciously gloss over what are, or imagined to be, defects in society? Or because of kin identification and extension of the local understanding of concepts such as "honor" does the writer consciously throw a curtain over facts that may be thought to compromise the group? Can such studies be objective? Balanced by this set of questions is the obvious advantage of insight into and access to the society being studied. Nothing is secret or hidden. With the emergence of native Third World sociologists and anthropologists studying their own societies, the narcissistic ethnic study will have to confront and tackle the psychosociological questions it raises.

Let me conclude this chapter on the political agent as anthropologist by quoting a letter written by my friend Adam Kuper, Professor of Anthropology at Leiden University, shortly after I took charge of the agency: "The new job has very Kiplingesque reverberations; the Great Game still. It sounds irresistible. Honestly I envy you your chances. I just get landed with more committees!" He concluded the letter, "Of course you must write the modern account of it all—the Caroe of our days—and of course we expect you single-handed to bring peace and prosperity to the region, discomfiting the bad guys"

(A. Kuper, personal communication).[10] The present study is an attempt to write a "modern account of it all." I am not so sure about the proposal at the end of the letter.

The difference between the good and the bad guys is not clear in Waziristan. Jekyll and Hyde exist in every man. Shifting alliances, changed circumstances, and differing temperaments of new actors determine the dominance of one over the other. The individual must draw some form of opportunity cost curves for himself that advise him to follow one rather than another course of action. As the tribesmen say, each person pursues his *gata* ("profit"). The multiplicity of models that confront tribesmen and administrators compounds the difficulty in identifying behavior simplistically. The bad guys often turn out to be the good guys and vice-versa. The question is, do they change or does one's perception of them? Until the 1970s, when the Mullah was cast as a villain by the administration, he was generally acknowledged as a good guy. The transformation is as much a function of a personal relationship with the PA as with traditional rivals.

My failures and successes in the cases point out the principles of tribal behavior and organization. My own analysis of the causes of failure and success help us, it is hoped, to understand better both the anthropologist and his subject. The autobiographical nature of the discussion in this chapter underlines the range and intensity of problems facing Muslim actors involved with religion and politics in Muslim society.

9

Islam and segmentary societies: the problem of definition

Defining Islamic tribal society

In Chapter 1, I incautiously promised that the study would consider the question of who speaks for Muslim society. At the end of the study I appear to have no definite answer. The same question, perhaps differently worded, teases the minds of men and is at the heart of the social and political issues in Waziristan. The definition and location of spokesmen and chiefs reflects a crisis within society. The very title *badshah,* "king," has been applied to each major actor: the malik (the word itself means king), the PA, and the Mullah. Does the malik speak for society? Although he alone among the three comes from within society, the teeman does not reflect much confidence in him. The PA speaks more *to* society than *for* society. Only the Mullah appears to have won a following that cuts across boundaries of lineage, hierarchy, and age. For a while he spoke for society, but in his heart he, too, wished to speak to them and not for them, and it was not long before the PA had wrested the title of spokesman—badshah—back from him. The method by which the PA won back his title underlines precisely the structural weakness of the PA's position in society.

The internal tension between the main groups these men represent has not been resolved. The disparate nature of the three groups—the first characterized by tribal code, lineage identity, cousin rivalry; the second by Indo-British secular, liberal service traditions; the third, by Islamic lore as locally understood—suggests that the problem may be irresolvable. The reason may be that the major actors are all Muslim, each one claiming to know and speak for society. The basis of their claims is rooted in the characteristic traditions of their groups, and thus ensures that each leader will perceive society and its fundamental issues from a different perspective.

The most basic Islamic terms—mullah, kafir, jihad—present us and their users in Waziristan with problems. For example, our definition of jihad–"a holy struggle in the way of Allah,"–surely does not correspond in all cases to that understood in Waziristan. For Maees, the Mahsud Robin Hood, jihad is his life of crime (Chapter 7); for the Wazirs, their battle against the Mahsuds. The use, or misuse, of the concept of jihad by the Mullah is the most appropriate illustration of the point. It tells us more about the Muslim society within which jihad is articulated than Islamic theology or law. Aware of the ambiguity in his usage of the term, the Mullah turned to a cultural interpretation. His political acumen lay in recognizing the shadow areas of the meaning, from which he manipulated successfully. More universal interpretations of jihad, which the orthodox would approve–indeed, applaud–however, are exemplified by the Mahsuds fighting the kafir in Kashmir (Chapter 3) or the Wazirs fighting them in Afghanistan (Chapter 7). The difficulty lies, both for us as well as the actors, in attempting to reconcile the two disparate interpretations. What, for instance, was the Mahsud response to the Mullah's jihad?

Undaunted by the Mullah's branding them as kafir, the Mahsuds responded with consummate skill. Their response to the campaign of the Mullah was the mystification of Pukhtunness. The Wazirs were condemned as deviating from the Pukhtun ideal; by following the Mullah they had become "without honor" and "without shame." In mystifying Pukhtunness the Mahsuds underscored the essentially subordinate role of mullahs in the Pukhtun universe; the Wazir "maulvi sahib" was reduced to a plain "mullah." The mystification also provided the Mahsuds with a counterattack that neatly and effectively canceled the Mullah's condemnation of them as kafir. Rejecting the status as a religious leader, the Mahsuds saw the Mullah as a diabolical figure, the devil himself, *shaitan*. There is hope for the kafir (he can convert to Islam), none for the shaitan (his defiance of God is unpardonable) in Muslim mythology. Point and counterpoint, thrust and counterthrust in society between protagonists are articulated through an Islamic idiom. The use of the idiom is as generalized as it is imperfectly understood.

The opposed catergories in society, Mullah versus shaitan, Muslim versus kafir, and the passion they arouse would indicate the importance of religion in Waziristan. The question arises, how Islamic are these tribes? Sociologically and culturally they may be defined as Islamic, as indeed they so view themselves, exemplified by the high incidence of Islamic symbolism in Muslim society. What is significant is not that the symbols seem to appear everywhere but that they do so in the least expected situations. Whether despoiling electric poles (Chapter 6), shooting college lecturers (Chapter 7), or stealing cattle, the tribesman invokes some aspect of religion.[1] The strength and ubiquity of Islamic symbols in Muslim society cannot be challenged. What can be challenged is their use in society and the assumption of theological support it implies. Neither the Wazir jihad against the Mahsuds nor Garam's shooting of the lecturers is justified by Islam nor is it in the Islamic cause. The understanding of religion is not the issue, however; the affective and conative power of its symbols in society is. Correcting the misuse or misunderstanding of Islam by Muslim tribesmen is a task for the orthodox ulema. The concern of the anthropologist is to examine how society perceives religion, not how religion views itself.

In spite of the strength of Islamic symbols in society, many anthropologists continue to study Muslim groups without reference to the Islamic framework (Ahmed 1976).[2] The tradition in anthropology of studying tribal society in isolation perhaps derives from the study of non-Islamic African tribes (Fortes and Evans-Pritchard 1970, Gluckman 1971, Middleton and Tait 1970).

Recently, the question of relating Pukhtun identity to a larger Islamic identity has engaged anthropologists (Anderson 1980, Beattie 1980, Canfield 1980, Tavakolian 1980). Although this is a move in the right direction, the exercise in itself may serve little purpose. The debate generated could be sterile. We may more usefully confront the problem, as the tribesman himself views it, by examining the relationship in terms of Islam *and* Pukhtunness and not Islam *versus* Pukhtunness. To the tribesman, Islam provides specified political and socioreligious formations within which his Pukhtunness operates. The two are in harmony and *he* sees them as a logical construct. Islam is so much a part of the Pukhtun structure as to suggest that the dichotomy is false.

The case studies in this book have illustrated that Islam and Pukhtunness coalesce and overlap. Indeed, the success of the Mullah is partly explained by his recognition of this integration. The mosque, as we know, remained the base of the Mullah's operations and remains a key symbol of Wazir identity. Once Islam was equated to kinship, his success in leading and consolidating the Wazirs was ensured. No dichotomy separates Islam and Pukhtun.

Although the cultural function of religion in society is recognized in anthropology, the study of religion remains largely confined to holistic analysis of systems, beliefs, and rituals (Banton 1978; Gerth and Mills 1961; Keddie 1978; I.M. Lewis 1978; Weber 1962, 1965, 1968; Werbner 1977).[3] Anthropological studies of Muslim society also reflect this methodological position. In the main, anthropologists use religion as an explanation either of how large-scale social and economic organizations (the *igurramen* in Morocco and the Murids in Senegal, respectively) cross administrative borders or of the dialectics of historical process (holy lineages, like the Sanusi, taking to arms).[4] The observation is not to be misconstrued as criticism. These studies without doubt fill important gaps in the literature. Rather it points out specified methodological techniques. In the Waziristan study I suggest a complement to this perspective. Others have also indicated this direction (Antoun 1979, Antoun and Harik 1972, Swartz 1968).[5] We should consider examining ongoing social drama through the eyes of the main actors at a dynamic and critical level of political life. First, we should make extensive use of contemporary extended case-study material; second, we should examine events through the eyes of the actors; and third, we should select case studies on the basis of the interaction in society of the key actors (particularly the mullah who remains one of the least studied). We may then arrive at a coherent and accurate picture of the structure and organization of contemporary Muslim society. For such studies, perhaps tribal rather than peasant or town society still provides the best material. Islamic tribal society remains relatively free of the consequences of modernization.

Anthropology has made important and original contributions in the study of Islamic tribal societies, a small percentage of the population in comparison with peasant groups. Even these studies show a methodological bias, however, by conceptualizing the universe in wholes and blocs. This bias is evident whether the discussion is of religious organizations, such as Sanusi or Tijaniya, or of tribes, such as the Berbers or Bedouin. Although I am in partial agreement with the conceptualization of these organizations and tribes as wholes, I suggest that the methodology could usefully be complemented by the suggestions I have made. I should now perhaps explain how I have defined *tribe* in my study.

The definition of *tribe* remains problematic in the literature and symptomatic of a deeper crisis in the discipline. A chapter title in a work by Godelier poses the question, "The concept of the 'tribe': a crisis involving merely a concept or the empirical foundations of anthropology itself?" (1977). The question has yet to be satisfactorily resolved in the literature (Dupree and Albert 1974, Helm 1971,

Tapper in preparation). Are tribes to be placed in a discrete category by themselves or are they to be viewed as a stage in social evolution – band, tribe, nation? Some scholars assume the former position, others the latter. For instance, the subtitle, "From Tribe to Nation in North Africa," of the book *Arabs and Berbers* (Gellner and Micaud 1973) suggests that the authors view tribal society as a *phase* in social progress. I am not certain whether this was their intention, but I have been arguing against this position in the present study. The Waziristan tribes see themselves as self-sufficient, autonomous groups who have successfully perpetuated their systems for centuries. This has allowed the Pukhtun tribal system to transcend, as it has incorporated, the stereotypical divisions of society, nomad versus sedentary, urban versus rural. Pukhtuns remain consciously Pukhtun, whether nomad or sedentary, urban or rural.

For our purposes let me attempt to define tribe by comparing the main characteristics of the Waziristan tribes with those of other tribes. How are the Waziristan tribes different from other tribes—for instance, those in India or in Brazil? Most important, the religion, language, culture, and history of the tribes of Waziristan are recognizably part of larger systems spreading beyond the region in which they live. Islam, Pukhto, Pukhtunwali, and the history of the region in various degrees provide frames within which society functions. In contrast to tribes in India or Brazil, the Waziristan tribes are aggressive and dominating in the presence of, and in relationship to, larger state systems. Their guns and inaccessible areas are important to their claim of cultural independence and political freedom. The tribesmen refer to themselves as *qabail*, or tribal, and the tribal areas as *ghair ilaqa*, translated as "area outside government control" and distinct from *ilaqa sarkar*, or "government area." The Mahsuds in Tank see themselves as qabail and distinct from the rest of the local Tank population. Equally important, the Tank citizens see the Mahsuds as different. The difference of perceptions presents continuing problems to the administration, as we saw in Case IV, Chapter 7.

To the native tribes of Waziristan we have added a third, more recent, tribe. By conceptualizing the administration as the third major tribe of Waziristan we acknowledge the influence of the external cultural and political systems it represents. Of most importance for political analysis are the role and personality of the chief of the third tribe, the PA. The conceptualization presupposes participation in the Waziristan arena and implies a leaning toward one tribe or the other as part of policy. The British did not have to divide what they already found divided. Their problem was how to rule effectively in spite of the division. The imperial dictum *divide et impera* is not the answer here; a society that is severely divided becomes unmanageable.

A serious question arises out of the imprecise and sterile nature of the debate around the word *tribe*. Is any heuristic purpose served by defining *tribe*? Changing economics and political boundaries, migrating populations, and demographic shifts in the last decades of the twentieth century suggest a negative answer. No sooner are we sure of a definition than a legitimate exception presents itself as a consequence of one of these factors.

I will call on Professor Leach once again to provide the last word on the subject of *tribe*:

> It now seems clear that, in this whole region, the concept "tribe" is of quite negative utility from the viewpoint of social analysis. The significance of particular features of particular tribal organizations cannot be discovered by functional investigations of the more usual kind. It is rather that we come to understand the qualities of "Tribe A" only when we measure these qualities against their antithesis in "Tribe B." [Leach 1977, p. xv]

Islamic segmentary societies

One of the major contributions of anthropology to Islamic tribal studies is the notion of segmentation in tribal structure. An argument could be made to interpret the Waziristan study as traditional segmentary politics in the classic mold of the segmentary theory. The argument would not be entirely wrong. The first important elaboration of segmentary theory in the discipline appears with the Nuer study by Evans-Pritchard. The individual is defined through the patrilineage and is part of a genealogical charter with "nesting" attributes; smaller lineage groups, starting from the household elder, fit neatly into larger ones and form balanced "segments." All members on the genealogical charter trace their links to a common apical ancestor. The relationship discourages growth of chiefs in society—members are "cousins" and therefore equal—which remains acephalous and egalitarian. Although the main rivals within the group are usually father's brother's sons, male cousins, they tend to unite in the face of external threat.

The theory became and remains popular, particularly in examining Islamic tribal groups. Studies of the Berbers of the Atlas by Ernest

Gellner, the Somali nomads by I. M. Lewis and the Swat Pukhtuns by Fredrik Barth are highly regarded examples. Perhaps Gellner's work best exemplifies the segmentary position. The application of the theory to Islamic tribal groups was made by Evans-Pritchard himself in his study of the Cyrenaican Bedouin. In a sense the segmentary theory had returned home to the genealogical charters of Islamic tribal groups, from which it had originated a century earlier in the writings of Victorian scholar-travelers, notably W. Robertson Smith.

Recently there has been considerable and mounting criticism of segmentary theory, particularly in America. The criticism is led by Clifford Geertz and some younger American anthropologists, such as Dale Eickelman and Lawrence Rosen. (Is the line-up itself suggestive of the segmentary principle, reflecting agnatic rivalry between British and American "cousins," each segment being led by a lineage elder?) The following, in capsule form, are some of the major criticisms against segmentary theory: segments are neither balanced nor is there equality between segments; on the contrary, there is disparity in political resources, which is exacerbated with the emergence of lineages claiming seniority; and in times of political crises groups do not combine according to segmentary patterns. In spite of the criticism, satisfactory alternative explanations have not been put forward.

The present study has illustrated the usefulness of the segmentary theory. The degree of segmentation and segmentary consciousness is high in Waziristan society and locally is so perceived (nikkat and tarboorwali being two of its manifestations). Society is acephalous and egalitarian, each member claiming to be a malik. Political action is articulated on the basis of the relationships defined in and by the genealogical charter. The agnatic rivalry between Wazirs and Mahsuds may be interpreted as a fundamental and homologous articulation of segmentary opposition. Mahsud inheritance of poorer lands, which presupposes junior lineages on the tribal charter, reinforced their solidarity and sharpened their strategy. Indeed, it may be stated that the genesis of the Waziristan problem is lodged in the genealogical charter; to understand the charter is to unlock the mysteries surrounding the problem. We may conclude that the segmentary theory retains its usefulness in examining Islamic tribal groups.

Having accepted the usefulness of the segmentary theory, I must also point out the dangers of applying it too literally. My criticisms are structural and cultural; first, the structural criticism.

When conceptualizing the tribe as a political unit in segmentary argument it would be well to keep in mind the present administrative boundaries, which do not always correspond to tribal boundaries. The discrepancy is one continuing legacy of the colonial period. Districts and agencies, indeed, the international Durand line, were created in the last century by the British, often with a fine disregard for tribal boundaries. Major tribes like the Mohmands or, as in the present case, the Wazirs, were divided in two by the international border. Other tribes were untidily distributed between district and agency boundaries (the Afridis, for example, are in Kohat District and Khyber Agency). The Ahmedzai Wazirs were separated from their Utmanzai Wazir cousins, who were confined to North Waziristan Agency, and placed with their traditional rivals, the Mahsuds, in South Waziristan Agency. Like other tribes in the region, for three generations the Ahmedzai Wazirs have confronted the fact of the borders created by the British. On either side of the Durand line, differing political, educational, and economic factors have widened the gap between Wazir and Wazir. New political realities have enforced the creation of new social boundaries, which take precedence over traditional alignments. Although we may conceptualize the entire Wazir tribe as a unit, we must keep in mind the administrative realities. The Islamic district paradigm contains wide-ranging theoretical ramifications for segmentary theory and is therefore important.

The Wazir thinks of himself as part of a larger tribal configuration, crossing administrative borders, but his empirical restriction to the agency is most evident in times of need. In spite of appeals for assistance, no kin arrived to participate in the desperate struggle against the Mahsuds. The boundaries of the Wazir universe, *in fact*, coincide with the administrative boundaries of the agency. (The boundaries work both ways, however: Wazirs wishing to escape the agency administration may cross the international border to their kin.)

The argument is graphically depicted in Figures 9 and 10 and Map 4. Figure 9 shows in encapsulated form the Wazir-Mahsud genealogy (derived from Figure 1). In the ideal, segmentary theory suggests that the Ahmedzais would be assisted by their Wazir kin when in conflict with the Mahsuds. The Mahsud clans, in turn would unite against the Ahmedzais (the unity of the Dre Mahsuds remained largely unshaken by internal politics and was a formidable factor in defeating the Wazirs).

Map 4 reminds us that although Wazirs live in Afghanistan and North Waziristan Agency also, the Mahsuds are restricted to South Waziristan Agency. Not only are the Utmanzai Wazirs separated by

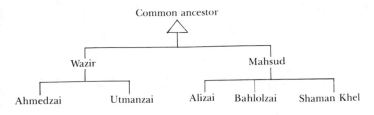

Figure 9. Wazir-Mahsud lineage

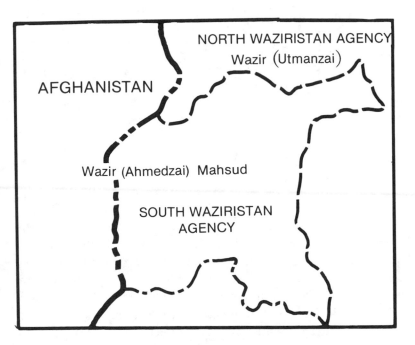

Map 4. The agency

administrative boundaries from their Ahmedzai cousins, but Ahmedzais themselves are divided by the international boundary.

If we superimpose Map 4 onto Figure 9, the importance of administrative boundaries in affecting tribal life will be made clear (Figure 10).

My second criticism of the segmentary theory is cultural. Aspects of social behavior and organization provide important variables in under-

Figure 10. Wazir-Mahsud lineage and the agency

standing Waziristan society. The response of the Wazirs reflects "the dynamics of cultural autonomy" (Parkin 1978). Partly psychological and partly religious, it crystallized into a political movement. The Mullah was simultaneously cause and effect of the phenomenon. Traditional segmentary alignments were reordered by the Mullah or, more correctly, by his politics. The classic articulation and expression of segmentary lineage politics was thus affected in Waziristan. The segmentary theory has not explained successfully the emergence of charismatic religious leaders who negate segmentary philosophy during their ascendancy. By omitting cultural factors from analysis, segmentary theory is clearly reduced. Both criticisms are partly satisfied by the Islamic district paradigm, which illuminates factors and processes of change.

The Islamic district paradigm

In Chapter 1, I pointed out the sociological rather than the theological content of the word *Islamic* in the district paradigm.

Nonetheless, the paradigm suggests a certain exclusivity in Muslim society. Its applicability to other societies may be somewhat limited. The reason perhaps lies in two characteristic features of Islam that other societies, monotheistic (Christian) or polytheistic (Hindu), may or may not share. Let me simplify for purposes of the argument. First, Islam does not sanction an official priesthood. The Prophet's well-known saying "there is no monkery in Islam" testifies to this. Yet we have seen the Mullah appropriate for himself the role of high priest and the Wazirs acknowledge that role. It is this ambiguity that proves difficult to resolve in an Islamic district paradigm, and yet it provides its dynamics. By comparison, the priesthood in Christianity or Hinduism is defined by sets of rules based on theological literature and custom; it is clearly separate from the domain of Caesar. Whatever conflict exists between Church and State—and for Christianity it forms one of the main themes of medieval European history—their respective roles remain defined in orthodox religion. Today, the priest remains largely confined to a religious role.

Second, Islam possesses a highly developed sense of community, *ummah*, which transcends national and tribal boundaries. The concept of ummah dominates Muslim political thinking in cycles every few decades, as in the Pan-Islamic movements. The Hindu community, in contrast, is defined within the geographical entity called *Bharat mata* ("Mother India"); those leaving its shores risk losing caste. Contemporary administrative boundaries confining Muslim groups within them negate the principle of ummah. These boundaries also create rival loyalties based on the district, province, or state. In the Islamic district paradigm, the administrator wishes to maintain boundaries while the religious groups wish to expand them. (In a different context, reflecting the same principle, we saw the Mullah's attempts to involve tribes outside the agency and the resistance of the administration.) The problems of the paradigm are related in a direct manner to the original template of Muslim society.

To understand our contemporary paradigm better we must, therefore, refer to the earliest—and for Muslims the authentic—model of society. The paradigm provided by early Islam is fundamentally different in structure and organization from our contemporary model. In the early model, the caliph combined in one role the functions of tribal elder, government spokesman, and religious leader. The caliph spoke for temporal as well as religious issues in society. The functions of the malik, the PA, and the mullah were fused into one at the appropriate level of society. It is the division of functions and creation of separate roles that cause problems in our contemporary paradigm of society. The division, as we know, is one legacy of the European colonial period: the malik in part and the PA in whole are a product of that period.

In certain ways Muslims are the same everywhere, and yet their societies are different everywhere. The general application of the Islamic district paradigm to Muslim society, therefore, presents us with problems. With this in mind let me continue to simplify and suggest areas where the paradigm may be most usefully applied.

First, it may be employed in those Muslim majority countries that have a colonial background similar to that of Pakistan. Of primary importance to the paradigm is the British colonial experience and the administrative and educational structures and values derived from it. Bangla Desh, Malaysia, and Nigeria are countries that fall into this category. The total population of such countries may account for about half of the entire Muslim population of the world.

Second, the paradigm may partly be applied to those Muslim nations ruled by other colonial powers, the French in Morocco or the Dutch in Indonesia. This could prove a useful exercise, if only to reject the paradigm, and thereby illuminate interesting discrepancies in religious roles within the Muslim world. Does the mullah exist in, for instance, Morocco? If not, who performs his functions in rural society? The *agurram* of the holy lineage? What sociohistorical factors account for the mullah's absence in Morocco? The answers would help us understand why he exists in Iran and South Asia. Conversely, they may help explain the relatively less important political position of institutionalized Moroccan-type holy lineages in Pakistan. Other related questions would also be clarified: can the role of the malik be compared with that of the tribal chiefs—the *caids*? How does the role of the contemporary Moroccan official caids compare with that of the PA? How much of the colonial period of these countries is reflected in their present administrative structures?

India provides a third category for the paradigm: large Muslim groups living as a minority in a nation that has constitutionally declared itself secular. Although the Indian Muslims live within the administrative structure devised by the British, the major clause of the paradigm is missing: Neither the contending groups nor their main leaders are Muslim. The issues in Muslim society are different; indeed, Muslim society itself is different in some ways from those in the former categories.

In concluding, let me throw caution to the wind and cross into Africa from Asia to apply the paradigm. My example is based on the case of the mullah of Kano in Nigeria.[6] Briefly, Haji Muhammad Marwa arrived in Kano from the United Republic of Cameroon, and in the 1960s and 1970s organized a religious movement, a jihad, demanding change in society.[7] Several warnings were delivered to Marwa from the governor, ordering him to cease his activities or face expulsion from Kano. With his expulsion, matters would revert to normal, the administration calculated. It was the application of the conspirator-agitator theory of administration discussed in Chapter 5 and so popular in Pakistan. The characteristic response of the officials, derived from a common British administrative mold, is an aspect of the paradigm.

In late 1980, Marwa led his followers in a series of revolts against the administration, culminating in an attack on the governor of Kano. The main mosque at Kano was almost captured. The Nigerian army and air force were eventually called in to quell the revolt. Reports in early 1981 suggested that more than 1,000 people were killed in the carnage, including the mullah, who died from a gunshot wound. The administration accused Marwa of employing *juju*, or black magic, to influence his followers. His followers believed in his magical powers and with bows and arrows were prepared to face the army, which was using bazookas and bullets. Reports of missing girls and boys also pointed to the mullah and suggested nefarious deeds. A high-powered tribunal has been appointed by the president of Nigeria to report on what are called the Kano disturbances.[8]

Certain similarities with the Waziristan case are clear: the emergence of an *outside* charismatic mullah with powers of oratory and organizational skills who understands both social structure and psychology; accusations by detractors of employing black magic to influence followers; the real and symbolic importance of the mosque to the mullahs, who ultimately derive their authority from religion; and the revolt against established *native*, not colonial or imperial, authority (the governor of Kano can be equated with the PA of South Waziristan Agency). The ambiguity of declaring jihad against Muslim rulers of the land is apparent in both cases. The social structure and organization of the tribes provide further similarities; in both areas, patrilineal, segmentary tribal groups live in low production zones. International interest and outside money, mainly from the Arab world (directly, it was believed, in Nigeria and indirectly, through remittances of laborers, in Pakistan) also add to the complexity of the cases. Disorder and conflict are created in society, the only solution to which appears to be bloodshed. Still, tanks and bazookas do not necessarily win in any permanent manner arguments based on deep ethnic or religious divisions. (It would seem that they did in the earlier Nigerian example of Biafra but not in the Pakistan Bangla Desh one.)

Do the events that took place in remote parts of Nigeria and Pakistan predict future political patterns in Muslim society? Are the Kano and Wana mullahs to be seen as modern revolutionary leaders or as traditional leaders reflecting traditional Muslim structure and organization? Are we witnessing a shift in style and loci of leadership away from urban, Westernized bureaucratic elites? May we relate these movements to the current waves of religious revivalism surging in many Muslim countries? Finally, can universal principles of behavior, suggesting predictive models, be adduced from these case studies? Although we may tentatively answer in the affirmative, it is too early to provide long-term and clear answers. To make matters worse, there is almost no literature or information on such leaders and movements in the contemporary Muslim world. The Kano and Wana examples foretell what may be in store for Islamic governments and societies in the coming decades. Their examples suggest the strength and universality of what I refer to as the Islamic district paradigm in this study and the need for a fuller investigation.

The Waziristan study has attempted to raise several methodological and theoretical questions some of which invite, in my view, hypotheses of underlying cultural, demographic, and possibly psychological mechanisms. Although speculative and exploratory in nature, the study, it is hoped, has indicated areas for future research. The formulation of questions as well as the provision of answers must surely remain one of the major heuristic functions of social studies.

Appendixes

Tor (honor of women) cases

The following three representative tor cases from the two major tribes occurred recently in South Waziristan Agency. An interesting connection between male labor migration abroad and local morality is apparent, as in the first case. The close relationship of spouses, which makes death so agonizing when it occurs, is apparent from a glance at the diagrams. Tribal mechanism to deal with such cases is also illustrated. The severity of punishment clearly demonstrates determination to uphold the ideal-type model by and in society. The tor model is universal among the Pukhtun (Ahmed 1980a).

Tor case 1

A had been in Dubai for an uninterrupted period of two years when he returned to find his wife, B, pregnant. He suspected C, his maternal cousin, who was a truck driver working usually in Karachi. A shot B and arrived at C's house with the intention of killing him. C was away and therefore escaped. C's father mobilized a tribal jirga to save his son's life. The jirga decided that C, though not proved guilty, was not blameless either. He would pay a compensation of 40,000 rupees to A. C left hastily for Dubai to avoid trouble and earn money to pay the installments to A (see first figure on next page).

Tor case 2

The second case is more complicated than the first one. E, wife of F, was in the habit of fetching water from a nearby stream at sunset for her household. F became suspicious and followed her one evening. He saw E dallying with A. F surprised the pair and with a knife managed to slash open E's throat. A fled to his settlement and barricaded himself inside with his sister B and nephew G. F broke into the house and shot A and his nephew G.

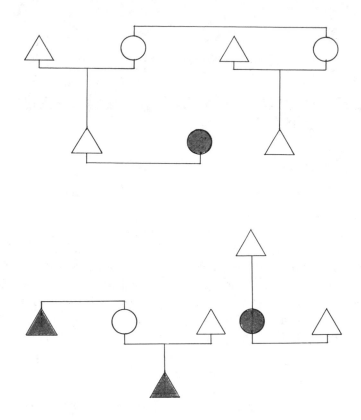

A jirga was assembled to decide the case. The jirga decided that the killing of *A* was in accordance with Pukhto. *G*, however, was innocent and his killing was unjustified. *F* was to pay 50,000 rupees as fine to *G*'s father, *C*. In spite of the jirga's decision, the dead woman's father, *D*, and her brothers followed *F* into the forest and tried to shoot him. *F* was hit in the hips and hands but managed to grapple with *D* and his sons and disarm them. The assailants escaped. *F* fainted from lack of blood. He was rushed first to a hospital in Wana and then to Peshawar.

The jirga was offended by *D*'s behavior and gathered the tribe outside his house to punish him. A fine of 50,000 rupees was demanded. *D* claimed he was too poor to pay such a sum. The jirga threatened to burn down his house if he did not pay. *D*'s lineage kin stood surety for him and asked for time. Time was allowed. *D*'s kin helped him make the payments.

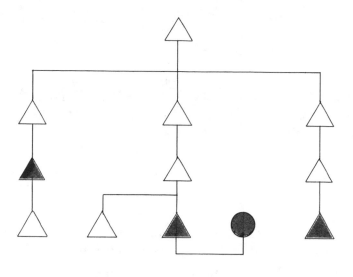

Tor case 3

C, about thirty, was married to D, who was half his age. D and E, a lad her own age, developed a relationship. C followed D early one morning after prayer. He killed first E and then D. E's male kin were tense for a few days, but later, emotions subsided. B, the elder brother of C, is a malik. B had had A's father killed shortly before this incident. A therefore conspired with E's relatives and had C killed on their behalf. No badal followed because, according to their plan, the kin of A and E both denied direct involvement.

Agreement between British and Wana Wazirs

No. XIX

Announcement regarding allowances and tribal responsibility made to and accepted by the Wana Wazirs on 10th November 1921.

Preamble.—Owing to their sincere desire for peace and the betterment and free development of the tribes on the lines of their cherished institutions, the Government of India have decided to announce the following generous lines of policy by which they propose to be guided in the future in regard to the occupation and administration of Wana Wazir country.

(1) Though it is the intention of Government to remain for so long as it pleases in occupation of the Wana Wazir country, it has no intention of introducing into that country the regular administration of a settled district, but it will administer it on tribal lines in accordance with tribal customs and usage.

(2) Allowances and other privileges will be granted as Government may deem proper having due regard to services rendered and especially to the degree in which the co-operation of maliks and tribesmen is forthcoming for the restoration and maintenance of law and order.

(3) The conditions for the payment of allowances will be—

(a) To the maliks for their services in actively helping the Khassadars scheme.

(b) To the maliks for the maintenance of order in their sections. Those sections which have cleared their account and such individuals as have rendered conspicuous service will be permitted to count their allowances from the date of this announcement. Amnesty will be granted to all Wana Wazirs including Militia deserters, who return to their homes, Government reserving the right to recover Government rifles by whatever means they choose.

(c) Proprietary rights of Wana Wazirs in all produce will be respected, but the Government reserves to itself the right to levy after the next five years as the due of the Supreme Government a light toll in kind whether on flocks or otherwise.

(5) No land revenue whatever will be demanded for the next twenty years, the matter to be further considered on the expiry of that period.

(6) There will be no interference in women cases which shall be settled by Wana Wazir jirga when Wana Wazirs only are concerned and when Wazirs and other tribes are concerned, by joint jirga of Wana Wazirs and that tribe.

(7) No court fees whatever will be levied for the next five years, thereafter for the succeeding years an eight anna court fee will be levied. The matter to be farther considered on expiry of that period.

(8) No forced enlistment will be imposed.

(9) All cases will be dealt with by jirga except offences committed against the Government or Government servants or in the Government settlements.

November 8th, 1921

J. G. MATHESON, *Major-General Commanding, Waziristan Force.*

APPENDIX C

Statement given by Mahsuds to British

No. XIV

Translation of the Statement given by the Maliks of the Dre Mahsuds, dated 25th September 1924.

1. We, the Maliks of the three Mahsud clans, were summoned to attend on 23rd September 1924 in case of some fires made over Government officials between Sararogha and Razmak and we were asked to submit a written agreement for taking responsibility.

We unanimously beg to say that we have already submitted a similar agreement at Ladha in July 1922, which we hope will be in the office of Political Agent. The same agreement is quite correct and we are still bound to that.

2. We also agree that if any *badmash* [bad character] will fire on a Government official on road or on a fort from a distance of one mile, the Khassadars and the villagers of the neighbourhood will not be held responsible for the mischief. The Political Officer will trace out culprits and if they were found guilty the officer will send for their Maliks who would bring forth the badmashes from the settlement. If they failed in bringing them the chief maliks of their sections will then produce them for trial. If no trace of the badmashes could be found the fine imposed will be paid up by the three Mahsuds.

3. If Kabul hostiles will commit such mischief as mentioned above in paragraph 2, we will not be held responsible for their misdeed as they are hostiles to the Government as well as enemies to us, and if any body will feed them he will be liable to punishment.

4. If on convoy days badmashes will attack the convoy on road and the Khassadars declined to oppose the enemy then in this case the Court of Enquiry will be held for the loss sustained, and the members will be taken from the three Mahsuds as detailed below:—

Bahlolzai Maliks.. one.

Alizai Maliks... one.

Shaman Khel Maliks.. one.

Political Tahsildar.. one.

Khassadar Sardars .... two.

The members will only give their opinion and it will rest aside with the Government to give the final orders.

5. If on convoy days the Khassadars on picquet duty will be attacked by badmashes, the villagers near the spot will turn the chighas out to help the Khassadars.

6. The following Maliks will be held responsible for this agreement :—

Malik Mehr Dil Mal Khel.

Malik Marwat Khan Shaman Khel.

Malik Khan Shaman Khel.

Malik Aziz Khan Shingi.

Malik Hayat Khan Michi Khel.

Malik Khan Mir Shabi Khel.

Malik Suhail Khan Galleshai.

Malik Mehr Dad and Baz Abdullais.

Malik Pir Rahman, s/o Harap Shabi Khel.

The minor Maliks will assist the above mentioned Maliks.

(Here follow the signatures.)

The domicile certificate

DOMICILE CERTIFICATE.

Certified that Mr_____

Son of Mr_____ Caste_____

Sub Caste_____resident of_____

Tehsil_____ Suth Waziristan Agency is a "Bonafide"

member of_____ and is entitled to all benefits/tribal

allowances paid to the tribe whose membership he claims

      That he shares all losses of his tribe and shoulder the tribal territorial responsibilities.

POLITICAL TEHSILDAR

ATTESTED.
ASSISTANT POLITICAL AGENT.
L A D H A

C O U N T E R S I G N E D .

Dr. Akbar S. Ahmed
Political Agent
South Waziristan Agency.

No._____

Date With Seal.

List of political agents, South Waziristan Agency

1.	Mr. A. J. Grant	1895–1898
2.	Mr. A. W. Mercer	1898
3.	Mr. H. D. Watson	1899–1900
4.	Mr. S. S. Waterfield	1900–1901
5.	Mr. P. W. Johnston	1901–1903
6.	Captain Bowring	1903–1904
7.	Mr. Evelyn Howell (ICS)	1905
8.	Mr. Crump	1905–1908
9.	Captain Patterson	1908–1909
10.	Captain James	1909–1910
11.	Major Dodd	1910–1914
12.	Mr. T. B. Copeland (ICS)	1914–1916
13.	Mr. J. A. O. Fitzpatrick, CIE, CBE (ICS)	1916–1919
14.	Major Crosthwaite	1919–1920
15.	Mr. Fitzpatrick	1920–1921
16.	Maj. A. E. B. Parsons, OBE (IA)	1921–1923
17.	Maj. J. W. Thomson Glover	1923–1924
18.	Capt. W. R. Hay (IA)	1924–1925
19.	K. B. Maulvi Ahmad Din	1925
20.	Capt. W. R. Hay (IA)	1925–1928
21.	Maj. C. E. U. Bremner, MC	1928–1930
22.	Maj. H. H. Johnson	1930–1934
23.	Maj. H. A. Barnes	1934–1937
24.	Capt. Abdur Rahim	1937–1938
25.	Maj. H. A. Barnes	1938
26.	Maj. Abdur Rahim	1938–1940
27.	Maj. A. J. Dring (IA)	1940–1942
28.	Mr. C. B. Duke (ICS)	1942–1943
29.	Mr. P. T. Duncan (ICS)	1943
30.	Mr. G. C. S. Curtis, OBE (ICS)	1943–1946
31.	Maj. J. O. S. Donald (IPS)	1946

32. Capt. R. V. E. Hodson (IPS)	1946
33. Capt. W. G. Raw (IPS)	1946–1947
34. Mr. P. T. Duncan (ICS)	1947–1948
35. K. B. Muhammad Nawaz Khan (PCS)	1948–1951
36. K. S. Attaullah Jan Khan (CSP)	1951–1953
37. K. S. Ghulam Sarwar Khan (PCS)	1953–1956
38. Sayed Darbar Ali Shah (CSP)	1956–1959
39. Lt. Cdr. Izzat Awan (PCS)	1959–1962
40. Mr. Fakhruzzaman Khan (PCS)	1962–1964
41. Sahibzada Muhammad Ayub (PCS)	1964–1967
42. Sardar Hizbullah Khan (PCS)	1967–1968
43. Mr. Fakhruzzaman Khan (PCS)	1968
44. Capt. Omar Khan Afridi (CSP)	1968–1971
45. Mr. Aziz-ul-Hassan Khan (PCS)	1971–1973
46. Mr. A. R. Abbassi (PCS)	1973–1974
47. Mr. Inayatullah Khan (PCS)	1974–1975
48. Mr. Abdul Karim Khan, Daur (PCS)	1975
49. Mr. Abdullah (CSP)	1975–1977
50. Alhaj Taj Muhammad Khan (PCS)	1977–1978
51. Dr. Akbar S. Ahmed (CSP)	1978–1980
52. Mr. Rustam Mohmand (CSP)	1980–

Note: CSP = Civil Service of Pakistan; IA = Indian Army; ICS = Indian Civil Service; IPS = Indian Political Service; PCS = Provincial Civil Service (NWFP). A unified administrative structure replaced the CSP and PCS after the abolition of the service cadres in 1973.
Source: PA's office, Wana and Tank.

List of commandants, South Waziristan Scouts

1.	Maj. R. Harman	1900–1902
2.	Lt. Col. R. Harman	1902–1905
3.	Maj. Jacob	1905–1906
4.	Capt. R. S. Paul	1906–1907
5.	Maj. R. S. Paul	1907–1909
6.	Maj. G. Dodd (political agent)	1910–1913
7.	Maj. J. C. Simpson	1914–1915
8.	Captain Davis	1915–1920
9.	Maj. C. D. Bennett	1920–1922
10.	Maj. G. H. Russell	1923–1924
11.	Maj. S. P. Williams	1924–1929
12.	Capt. H. H. Johnson	1929–1930
13.	Major Cosby	1930–1934
14.	Maj. Skrine	1934–1936
15.	Maj. D. H. R. Williams	1936–1941
16.	Maj. Woods	1941–1942
17.	Lieutenant Colonel Woods	1942–1944
18.	Lieutenant Colonel Venning	1944–1947
19.	Lt. Col. A. C. S. Moore	1947
20.	Lt. Col. K. M. Chambers	1947–1948
21.	Lt. Col. D. K. Old-Rini	1948
22.	Lt. Col. Khush Waqtul Mulk	1948–1950
23.	Lt. Col. J. H. Harvey Kelly	1950
24.	Lt. Col. Abdul Jabar	1950–1953
25.	Lt. Col. Abdul Hafiz Afridi	1953–1954
26.	Lt. Col. Amanullah Khan	1954–1955
27.	Lt. Col. Mohammad Nawaz Khan	1955–1957
28.	Lt. Col. Karamatullah Khan	1957–1962
29.	Lt. Col. Mohammad Ishaq	1962
30.	Lt. Col. Mohammad Mobin Khan	1962–1964
31.	Lt. Col. S. A. R. Durrani	1964–1966

32.	Lt. Col. Abdul Matin	1966–1969
33.	Lt. Col. Ahmad Khan	1969–1972
34.	Lt. Col. Ali Gohar	1972–1973
35.	Lt. Col. Raja Khan	1973–1975
36.	Lt. Col. F. G. Khattak	1975–1979
37.	Lt. Col. Muhammad Mumtaz Ali	1979–1980
38.	Lt. Col. Javed Yunas	1980–

Source: Commandant's office, Wana

Notes

1. Models and methods

1 *Mullah* is a generic name for a religious functionary – a Muslim or "Mohammedan learned in theology and sacred law" (*Oxford English Dictionary* 1975, p. 792). A discussion of the mullah and his role in society will be found in Chapter 5. Throughout the text I shall refer to the Waziristan Mullah with a capital *M* to distinguish him from other mullahs.

2 *Waziristan*, refers generally to the area of North (Shomal) and South (Janobi) Waziristan agencies. The name derives from the Wazir tribe. *Wazir* in Arabic and Urdu means "minister." Elders of the tribe claim that they once served as advisers to the rulers of Afghanistan.

3 Analysis will be based on what anthropologists term "the extended case method" (Gluckman 1961, 1969) and "situational analysis" (Velsen 1964, 1969), that is, an advocation of theory and method that rest on extensive use of diachronic case-study material. In place of the technical anthropological term *father's brother's sons* for male cousins, I shall employ the lesser jargon, agnatic rivalry, when defining rivalry between males descended in the patrilineage from a common ancestor.

4 The name popularly acquired by the international border demarcated in 1893–4 between Afghanistan and British India, now Pakistan, after the British official in charge of the demarcating mission.

5 The district was the basic and key unit of administration in British India (Woodruff 1965). It included subdivisions and thanas (a further subdivision) and was part of a division, several of which formed a province. The agency in the tribal areas corresponded to the district in the administrative universe. Although I call this intermediary level a district to help conceptualize the unit of analysis, district (or agency) boundaries do not always correspond to ethnic ones, a fact that continues to create political problems for the modern state. In certain cases new ethnicity – district ethnicity – was formed, such as Hazarawal in Hazara District (Ahmed, 1982a). Pakistan, like India, retains the administrative structure it inherited after independence in 1947. Most districts and agencies remain profoundly rural in character and somewhat isolated from national developments. The vast literature on the subject is, for the most part,

memoirs written by British district officers. For a fresh contribution, see Hunt and Harrison (1980); the latter was once a member of the Indian Civil Service.

6 I shall refer to the paradigm as district rather than agency because the former is older in history and more widely known; indeed, it is the forerunner of the agency. Also see Ahmed 1982b.

7 Senior district officials in British India, who usually belonged to the elite Indian Civil Service cadre, were often seen as distant and superior by society. The Indian Civil Service, according to its critics, was neither Indian, nor civil, nor a service. After 1947 the Civil Service of Pakistan, which replaced the Indian Civil Service, drew similar criticism.

8 The statement is supported by examples from the highest political level in Pakistan. The head of state has usually been a serving or retired government official (civil or military): Ghulam Mohammad, Iskander Mirza, Ayub Khan, Yahya Khan, and Zia-ul-Haq to name those who have ruled Pakistan since the mid-1950s. Mr. Bhutto (1971–7) is the one exception.

9 For a fuller discussion, see Ahmed and Hart, 1982.

10 The Soviet invasion of Afghanistan in December 1979 has increased interest in debates about the nature of Islamic tribal society; for example, see Anderson 1980, Beattie 1980, Canfield 1980, Tavakolian 1980. The interest also resulted in the "Revolutions and Rebellions in Afghanistan" session at the Annual Meeting of the American Anthropological Association held in Washington, D.C., December 1980.

2. Waziristan: land, lineage, and culture

1 The sedentarization process of these nomadic groups in the context of larger political developments is discussed in Ahmed 1981c.

2 In "The Burkis of Pakistan: Reemergence of Ethnicity and Primordial Loyalties" (in preparation-a), I discuss Burki ethnicity and its reemergence as a result of the success of kin Burkis living first in India (East Punjab) and after 1947 in Pakistan (West Punjab). The emphasis on their rather obscure language reconfirms boundaries around the Burkis and acts as a diacritical feature to distinguish them from the Mahsud. They provide a rare example of a "hill" group consciously identifying with their "plain" cousins to the point of emphasizing the tribal name of the latter (Burki, rather than Urmar). In Pakistan it is usually the other way round, with hill groups providing ideal-type templates for their cousins in the plains.

3 Population figures, indeed most statistics, in the tribal areas even today are based on rough estimates provided by elders. A confidential note of a British political agent recorded the dilemmas in census work in Waziristan: "The Mahsud approaches all topics from an acquisitive point of view and not least the matter of enumeration. When Mahsuds are questioned as to their numbers they give the answer which best serves their interests.

Certain tribes whose hearts – to use an expression beloved of the Japanese – are not good, habitually underestimate their numbers, probably believing that the enquiry is made in order to assist Government to fine them adequately and thinking that in any case one does not give one's order of battle to one's enemy. Other tribes appear to be habitually truthful; and others believe that they and their maliks have much to gain in the consideration of the Political Agent by making themselves out to be more numerous than they actually are. Thus it can be seen that a numbering of the Mahsuds presents unusual difficulties" (Curtis 1946, p. 15).

4 The point made in note 3 regarding population "estimates" must be kept in mind when discussing figures in the tribal areas. If the reproduction rate strains demographic possibilities it is partly explained by the Mahsuds' need to exaggerate their numbers to official enumerators.

5 Due to shifting boundaries between the agency and Dera Ismail Khan (DIK) District the figures appear as "estimates," like those for population. Some official records give the agency figures as 2,556 square miles, whereas others give 3,936 square miles.

6 The tribes refer to themselves as *mizh*, "we," the first person plural. Howell (1979) appropriately entitled his account of the Mahsud, *Mizh*. In Waziristan, *Mahsud* is pronounced as "Mahsit."

7 For a discussion of Pukhtun tribes, clans, and sections, see Ahmed 1980a, chaps. 4 and 5.

8 The nikkat division in the agency is based on late-nineteenth-century population figures, which are constantly challenged. Bruce 1929 provides a detailed picture. The point is admirably made by Curtis: "But no matter how carefully he may assess the importance of tribal and party claims, no matter how shrewd the advice of his Assistant Political Officer, no Political Agent can ever hope to make a distribution of benefits which Mahsud tribal opinion will accept as fair" (1946, p. 5).

9 In 1979, after considerable effort, I obtained permission from the government for a public school in Wana. The school was to be the first of its kind in the tribal areas and of a high standard. Once it was approved the laws of nikkat were set in motion. Mahsuds argued that it should be in Mahsud territory on the basis of nikkat. The Zilli Khel Wazirs argued that it should be in Wana but on their lands on the same basis. The matter created a political controversy. The name, too, was debated. Birmal, the Wazirs insisted; Preghar, after the highest peak in the agency in Mahsud territory, the Mahsuds suggested. In the end I called for a Waziristan jirga and informed them that I was requesting the government to rescind approval and offer it to some other agency. This ended the debate. The school would be in Wana. I suggested a name neutral to both tribes, the Waziristan Public School, which was generally approved.

10 Jalat Khan's male ascendants were described by a political officer in 1903

thus: "In this section are the two houses of Bannocha and Gulan, who, with the Gulsher above mentioned, were formerly the leaders of Wana. Gulan owed his position more to his father Karim Khan, who built the large Wazir kot [settlement] near the tahsil [or thana] . . . Some years ago Gulan was killed when returning from the tahsil by his half-brother Fatteh Khan. The latter then fled to the Abdur Rahman Khels and became a hamsaya [client] of Khalo. He was subsequently killed after returning to Wana by Ata Muhammad and Shergai, the sons of Shahzaman, Gulan's cousin on the father's side and brother on the mother's. To this day Khalo cherishes an absurd idea that he should get sharm [compensation; lit., 'shame'] for Fatteh Khan. Gulan left a son, Guldin, who is now a boy of about 15. He will never come to any good" (Johnston 1903, p. 11). Many contemporary political officers would be inclined to agree with the conclusion of the note when commenting on the role in recent Waziristan history of the son of Guldin, Jalat Khan.

11 *Chalweshti* derives from the number forty, the traditional ideal unit for tribal warfare. In the next chapters we will meet the word again in the case study concerning the Mullah. Earlier, the word *chalweshta* was used for semiofficial "tribal police" (Aitchison 1933, p. 604); see Elphinstone (1972) for the earliest discussion in English. Today, words like *chalweshti* and *nanawatee*, so important to nang Pukhtuns, are obsolete in the settled districts, where qalang Pukhtuns live.

12 Not all names are suggestive of extraethnic influence. Many Mahsuds possess traditionally nang names, such as Yaghistan ("rebellion") Khan, an Abdullai of Makin, or Khon Khel ("Blood clan"). Others possess more individualistic names like Sangi mar Jan ("beloved precious stone").

13 A political officer will hear time and again echoes of the statement made by Jaggar, an Abdur Rehman Khel Mahsud, to Howell: "Let it be 'field' and blow us all up with cannon, or make all eighteen thousand of us Nawabs" (Howell 1979, p. 96). "Eighteen thousand" refers to the almost mythical figure of the original Mahsud population, and in this statement the basic principle of *tarboorwali*, a code of equality and rivalry with cousins, is illuminated.

14 "Such as would excite the envy of an Athenian demagogue," remarked Howell (1979, p. 96). Mulaqat lists are prepared by the junior staff with scrupulous attention to nikkat, and the mulaqat is a formal affair announced in public places. Mulaqats are important in winning over tribesmen.

15 Nanawatee, as word and concept, is obsolete in Charsadda; the amnesia reflects on the transition of Pukhtun society from nang to qalang (see case III in Chapter 7).

16 The intensity of tarboorwali at the household level is fierce and may express itself in the most bizarre manner. A Mahsud commented on his cousin's holding a high government post in Peshawar and the airs he had

acquired in the civil service: "He doesn't visit us now and my hand cannot reach him where he is. But I await the day he dies and is brought home for burial. I will disgrace his funeral rites by firing on the corpse." At least in one instance tarboorwali has taken a more fortunate and less deadly turn. The male descendants of the maliks Gulab Khan and Abdul Maalik have entered one of Pakistan's elite public schools, Aitchison, or Chief's, College in Lahore, and continue the rivalry on its playing fields.

17 I met Mir Badshah in Multan, in 1969, shortly before he died, at the house of his eldest son Alam Jan, then a major in the army and later, while I was PA, SWA, general, Frontier Corps, Baluchistan. Although of great age, Mir Badshah was still lively and exhibited a keen interest in life and events around him.

18 "In Waziristan what the Apostle Paul describes as 'Patient continuance in well doing' pays very low returns. The tendency is to ignore those who are quiet and to reward, perhaps not the actual wrong doer, but those who assist in allaying trouble. It therefore pays to belong to a tribe which understands that 'Sweet are the uses of hostility'. Opportunities for pleasing the Political Agent by bringing a trouble maker to terms will continually be arising. A glance through the list of *Lungi* [allowance] -holders will show how much more profitable it is to belong to a tribe whose maliks subscribe to this belief than it is to one whose maliks are simpler folk. The Michni Khel for instance who have a long record of friendliness with Government cannot boast one single *Lungi*-holder" (Curtis 1946, p. 3; also see Johnston 1903).

19 "The Mahsuds were most exhausting people to deal with, and I well remember my weariness and despair after a morning spent with them, whether in jirga or mulaqat" (O. Caroe, personal communication; also see Afridi 1980, p. 1). The Wazir is equally culpable as a mulaqati: "I think the Ahmedzai Wazir must be the most persistent mulaqati and the most boring one there is" (Johnson 1934a, p. 2).

20 In early 1979 a son was born to me in Tank. Waziristan elders congratulated me, repeating the theme that as he was a son he would be lucky (*bashtawar*) for me. The birth of a girl is traditionally ignored in Waziristan. For a discussion of the role of women in Pukhtun society, see Ahmed and Ahmed 1981.

21 Approximately ten rupees equal U.S. $1. Inflation from figures quoted in Ahmed 1980a is a result of remittances from the Arab States.

22 The Wazirs and Mahsuds mentioned in the text are *dwa-kora*. Abdul Maalik suggested the rapid inflation in land prices by contrasting those before 1947 with those in 1980. About 1947 he bought unirrigated land near Tank at 1 to 2 rupees per canal (one-eighth of an acre); today it is worth more than 1,000 rupees per canal. The cost of land in Tank is high, 50,000 to 60,000 rupees per canal, almost as expensive as in the cities, such as Peshawar.

23 The incorporation and popular usage of foreign loan words in Pukhto reflect both the importance of the words per se as well as their function as a link between administration and tribe in the tribal areas. Derivates of root words carry many shades of meaning in society. *Political* may also imply chicanery and trickery, as mentioned in the text. Such ambiguous words are distinct from borrowed foreign words like *radio* or *telephone*. Certain English words from the colonial encounter in Waziristan are now permanently used, *machine* for "machine-gun," *bombari* for "bombing," and contrast with modern foreign words such as *boring* for "boring tube-well equipment." While being briefed by my field officers shortly after taking charge of the agency, I was confused by the references of a Wazir official to *Gujarzai*, or "place of Gujar." We were talking of the famed father of Maees, the Shabi Khel outlaw (see Chapter 7, case II). Later on I discovered *Gujarzai* was not the "place (*zai*) of Gujar" but the "son (*zoi*) of Gujar." In Waziristan, *zoi* (Yusufzai – son) is pronounced as *zai*.

24 Although I refer to the tribes of Waziristan as Pukhtuns, the word is locally pronounced as *Pushtun*. I use *Pukhtun* to preserve the large cultural unity in the context of the NWFP and for purposes of the argument, which relates Waziristan to other tribes of the province.

25 When I traveled from Waziristan to Hazara as consultant sociologist for the World Bank Hazara Forest Project in 1979–80, the contrast in the two areas constantly impressed me. There is a high degree of differentiation in structure and organization of the two societies within the Pukhtun universe of the Frontier Province. In the tribal areas, guns, silent fortresslike settlements, Scouts' posts and ever-ready soldiers, were prominent; no women were visible. There was silence and widespread desolation in the agency countryside. In Mansehra, the northern district of Hazara, on the other hand, people appeared relaxed. Off-duty soldiers from army units, in various stages of dress, lounged around the Mansehra rest house where they were camped; songs from radios floated in the air, men and children loitered, students sat in groups talking, and women were busy helping their men in the green fields; no guns were visible. The contrast may be further underlined by the administrative history of the two areas. In Waziristan the history of assassinations of senior military and civil officers still necessitates escorts and guards for officials. In Hazara the earliest images of administrators derive from *kaka* ("uncle") Abbott, who used to stroll into the villages with sweets in his pockets for children (Caroe 1965) and after whom Abbottabad, the district headquarters, was named.

26 Normally, a nonstop journey by road from Wana to Peshawar takes about twelve hours. It is a hot, dusty, and tiring experience. The road is poor throughout and in some patches, as between Tank and Pezu, it is almost nonexistent. The Shahur Tangi, the main gorge at the entrance to the agency, may often be blocked for a full day as a result of heavy summer

rains. At times the crossing of streams, such as that at Chaghmalai before the Shahur Tangi, may take hours. The Chaghmalai crossing involves a treacherous stretch of water between 100 and 400 yards wide and between 1 and 3 feet deep, depending on the season.

The daily English newspaper the *Pakistan Times* usually takes three days to arrive at Wana and, like a character from a Somerset Maugham short story, I could only keep abreast of world and national affairs well after they took place.

27 Foreign visitors have also commented on the hostile looks of the Waziristan tribes (Stephens 1953).

28 This was illustrated to me by the visit of Professor Wali from the Quaid-i-Azam University, Islamabad, the first Mahsud to earn a Ph.D. degree (1980). The professor, I assumed, would be respected in society and pointed out to the younger generation as a man to emulate, but in various meetings where Mahsud elders were present I noted the haughty indifference with which they treated him. The gun, the diacritical feature of Pukhtunness, had been abandoned and given up for the pen. He was reduced to being a teacher of children.

In June 1980 when elders heard I was being considered for the post of vice-chancellor, Iqbal Open University, Islamabad, they were incredulous. Groups and individuals pleaded with me: "You want to become a teacher [*ustaz*, from Arabic] when you are king of Waziristan. How many bodyguards will you have? Not one." Even the educated tribesman is not impressed by learning or degrees. My friend General Alam Jan, when on the phone from his headquarters at Quetta, would invariably preface his conversation with a good-humored but irate burst against the concept of a political agent being referred to as "Doctor Sahib" by the telephone exchange: "The only damned doctor should be the agency surgeon. I'm sure the great old PAs like Major A. J. Dring [PA 1940–2] must be revolving in their graves at the thought of the agency being run by a doctor. In Waziristan you must be 'PA Sahib' not 'Doctor Sahib'."

29 Among the Mahsuds who have done well in Karachi is Sakhi Jan. He was elected chairman of one of the union councils (an electoral ward) there in spite of severe local opposition.

30 Mahsud self-apperception, as united and dangerous, is confirmed by Sir Olaf Caroe, who likens "the Mahsud to a wolf . . . the wolf-pack is more purposeful, more united and more dangerous." In comparison, the Wazir is like "a panther . . . sleeker, and has more grace." Caroe concludes, "Both are splendid creatures" (O. Caroe, personal communication). Although Caroe has romanticized the Pukhtuns he found that Mahsuds "were not enchanting people to deal with" (ibid.). Even to those who write with warmth of Pakistan and its peoples, the Mahsuds "at times are simply savages" (Stephens 1953; p. 129).

31 It has been suggested that Ibn Battuta, the fourteenth-century traveler, may have passed through the Suleman mountains and this area on his way to India (Battuta 1929, p. 360). If so he is one of the few visitors to India to have used this route.

3. History as an expression of agnatic rivalry

1 For an overview of Waziristan tribes in the Great Game see Ahmed 1979, 1980a, and 1980b.

2 It was Kipling who popularized the mirrorlike reflection between the British and the Pukhtun. His famous poem, while despairing that East and West could ever meet, concludes with an exception: "But there is neither East nor West, Border, nor Breed, nor Birth, / When two strong men stand face to face, though they come from the ends of the earth!" (Rudyard Kipling, "The Ballad of East and West," 1889).

3 Lawrence inscribed a note to the South Waziristan Scouts in his book *Revolt in the Desert* (1927), now preserved in a glass case in the Wana mess. The note reads: "This disgraceful looking book was written by me: but its squalid type, degraded blocks, and quite untruthful introduction are responsibilities of the publisher. However it is the only edition still in print, and therefore the only one I can offer the South Waziristan Scouts in memory of a very good day and night they gave F/Lt Smethans and myself [signed] T. E. Shaw, Miranshah, 3/XI/28"

4 See Lockhart 1897 for a contemporary account of Mullah Powindah. Termed the "pestilential priest" by Kitchener, then commander-in-chief of the British Indian army, and a "first class scoundrel" by Curzon, the viceroy of India, he remained an active thorn in the side of the British until his death. His grandson surrendered to me and swore loyalty to Pakistan, an incident that drew a comment from, among others, Sir Olaf Caroe ("He has, moreover, won the support of Shahzada Tajuddin, grandson of the legendary Mulla Powindah, stalwart and crafty opponent of all that was attempted by the British Raj in that inhospitable land. The Shahzada, it seems, has actually pledged loyalty to Pakistan" [Caroe 1980, p. 89]) and the national press (for example, the *Pakistan Times*, under the heading "Tribal leader surrenders," July 1, 1979).

5 In the 1940s the influential spokesmen of Waziristan supported the idea of a separate homeland, Pakistan, for the Muslims of India. When Jawaharlal Nehru arrived in Razmak to canvass for a united India, he received a stormy welcome. Mehr Dil, father of Mir Badshah, actually assaulted him with a stick.

6 Reflecting the romantic mystique of Waziristan are the contents of this letter written by Sir Olaf Caroe regarding Sir Evelyn Howell, shortly before the latter's death. "When I met him in Cambridge about four years ago . . . he said so many years had gone by. But he would feel happier in

the mountain ranges of Waziristan. It was, he said, precisely because that was the most dangerous period of his life that it had become the period that he loved most. Often in his dreams he found himself in Waziristan, and his heart flying in those precipitous gorges." (O. Caroe, personal communication). The affection for the Pukhtun was genuine to people like Howell, and the feeling is made explicit in official reports such as his *Mizh* (1979), not written for public eyes but as a confidential document. Along with the serious writing of officials like Howell are a number of popular novels set in Waziristan (e.g., Breem 1979). The worst of the genre border on the absurd and describe people and places not even remotely accurate. For instance, in *Sadhu on the Mountain Peak*, by D. Macneil, the intrepid hero Ogilvie in the heart of Waziristan meets maliks with Hindu names like Ram Surangar, is housed in palaces with marble floors and statues, and at night is sent a chosen girl by his host to keep him company (1971, pp. 78, 165) – all highly improbable in Waziristan.

7 The frontispiece of the semiofficial history of the South Waziristan Scouts, written by its Pakistani officers in Urdu, is a portrait of Colonel Harman (Khan, n.d.).

8 Maj. A. J. Dring, PA from 1940 to 1942, makes the same point in a personal story of when he accompanied a punitive column into Mahsud territory: "The hostiles were out in very large numbers; they got above the military pickets and disaster followed. Every single thing went wrong. One regiment came literally running from the hills into camp. We got bogged down seven miles from Razmak, all wires were cut and I spent no less than four and a half weeks in a hole in the ground utterly cut off. On that short march the column suffered at least eighty killed, including the British colonel of one of the regiments" (Allen 1977, pp. 204–5).

9 See Howell 1979, and for a first-hand account, see Pettigrew 1965, in his chapter, "The Shahur."

10 The day after discussing the deaths of British political agents for the documentary *Khyber* while sitting on the same tennis court at Tank which had proved so fatal to my predecessor Dodd in 1914, Dr. Andre Singer, the producer, and I were involved in a serious motor accident just outside the Shahur Tangi. The driver, traveling dangerously fast, braked and swerved to avoid some donkeys that suddenly appeared from behind a knoll. We overturned thrice at great speed. Had the accident been fatal the doubtful honor of being the first Pakistani political agent to die on duty would have been overshadowed for me by its distinctly nonromantic manner: death neither by bullets from an ambush nor an assassin's knife but as a consequence of the sudden appearance of donkeys. Whatever its other virtues the donkey seldom inspires romantic allusions in Frontier literature.

11 Howell provides a dramatic eyewitness account of the assassination of Colonel Harman in the Wana mess in 1905 by a Shabi Khel Mahsud

(Caroe 1965, app. D). Officials beyond the borders of the agency were not safe either. In 1923, Major Finnis, political agent, Zhob Agency, was killed by Zilli Khel Wazirs operating in Baluchistan.

12   At one stage Lord Curzon, pushed beyond endurance, recorded: "No patchwork scheme – and all our present recent schemes, blockade, allowances etc., are mere patchwork – will settle the Waziristan problem. Not until the military steam-roller has passed over the country from end to end, will there be peace. But I do not want to be the person to start that machine" (Howell 1979, pp. 35–6).

13   See Appendix B for a typical and early example of such a treaty between the British and the Wana Wazirs (Aitchison 1933, pp. 615–16). The tribes' freedom to live by their own customs and traditions is guaranteed in such treaties. In return tribes signed a "statement of intention," which stipulates the nature of fines, etc. See Appendix C for an example of a statement signed by such Mahsud elders as Mehr Dil, father of Mir Badshah, and Pir Rahman, father of Abdul Maalik (ibid., pp. 610–11).

14   The British signed treaties, subsequently ratified by the government of Pakistan (Instruments of Accession), clearly specifying terms and conditions, rights and duties of the rulers, etc., with the wali of Swat, and the nawabs of Amb and Dir. All important matters – defense, foreign policy, ecclesiastical affairs, etc. – would be the direct concern of the central government.

15   Jaggar's extended family still lives in Kabul. His nephew and cousins, living as dwa-kora in Waziristan, described the migration in religious terms of jihad against the British. Kin feeling for Waziristan remains in the Kabul Mahsuds. In 1980, messages were received through tribal kin networks from a minister in Kabul, a Mahsud, advising the agency administration not to allow the Afghan refugees to form camps on the border in order to avoid possible future retaliatory action.

16   "They live in poor country. Nevertheless such is the influence of their leading family (that of K. B. Mehr Dil Khan) that they do not accept one anna of Afghan money. This point must never be overlooked" (Curtis 1946, p. 183).

17   Mahsud presence is announced by occasional sniping at the Razmak camp, a feature that has initiated a voluminous correspondence between the political agents of North and South Waziristan agencies. The correspondence assumes strident urgency when such important persons as the president or governor are visiting Razmak; both PAs then tend to disown the Mahsud groups living around Razmak.

18   Afghanistan supports the claim that Pukhtuns in Pakistan wish to secede and form an independent country called Pukhtunistan.

19   The use of the term displays the fine sense of irony the Waziristan tribes possess; both the concept and function of *badshah* are external to history and society in Waziristan.

20 The *Guardian* felt that I described such characteristics of tribal society "rather ruefully" (Nancy Banks-Smith, *Guardian*, July 30, 1980) in Granada's 1980 TV documentary *Afghan Exodus*. It was more accurate when it quoted me as saying it was "a very free society" (ibid.).

21 Just how elite members and their families of the Indian Civil Services considered themselves is brought out in the collection of anecdotes and reminiscences, *Plain Tales from the Raj* (Allen 1977). For a more serious account of the Indian Political Service, see Coen 1971.

22 The head office of the PA is a veritable secretariat, with numerous assistants and offices full of dusty and decaying files. The PA is assisted by what is called the English Office. The office superintendent, a senior and experienced assistant, supervises the head office, which is divided into various branches. The accountant, the reader, the khassadar accountant, the education clerk, the record keeper, the rationing assistant, the food inspector, and the supervisor also assist the PA in their specified charges.

23 In our first mulaqat, Jalat Khan informed me that he had just returned from Peshawar to investigate my affairs. He knew the extent of my property as well as my official history and that of my adult agnatic kin. He carried a warm letter of introduction from a mutual friend, Arbab Sikander Khan, the NAP leader, which helped ensure our cordial relationship during my tenure.

24 These are traditionally recognized ways of attracting official attention. "Government officials being fired on are the Mahsud and Wazir equivalent for presenting a petition" (Howell 1925, p. 10).

25 Howell, who served both as PA, South Waziristan Agency, and resident in charge of North and South Waziristan agencies, recorded the pressures: "A trans-border agency is a charge which imposes upon the holder a heavy strain, physical, mental, and, we may perhaps add, moral. It is not every officer, even amongst members of a picked corps, who is fit or by temperament apt to carry the burden, and even amongst the few who are there are fewer still who can stand the strain for long at a time. Consequently changes of incumbency are of necessity frequent, and Government are for ever being compelled to change their tools just as these are becoming shaped to their task" (Howell 1979, p. 98). Sir Olaf Caroe's comments on my taking charge as PA were, "I wish you well in your hard and exhausting post in South Waziristan – a very testing job" (O. Caroe, personal communication).

26 It was a case typical of the Frontier, resulting from a sense of betrayed honor. In 1946 the PA, Major Donald, was kidnapped by the Shabi Khel on the central Waziristan road. During captivity he had promised his captors there would be no retaliation. He had perhaps also developed some sympathy for his kidnappers, a common phenomenon, as we know from instances of hostages forced into captivity in the contemporary world. When the Shabi Khel were bombed (among them Abdul Maalik's

family) and persecuted after his release, Donald, no doubt feeling he had let the empire *and* his tribes down, shot himself in the study of the PA's bungalow at Tank. When I inquired about the incident, Sir Olaf Caroe, who was then governor, assumed part of the blame: "You . . . ask why Donald committed suicide. I should have thought the story itself provided the answer; he could not take any more; he felt he had let down not only himself but also me (to be egotistic) and his father, and perhaps the Mahsuds too. I think, he loved them in a queer sort of way. Wavell [viceroy of India] blamed me for making him go back and said I really killed him. My answer to Wavell was "Sir, I am pretty sure you as a Wykehamist [from Winchester College] like me, in that position, would have done the same. Donald's father had been Resident [of Waziristan] in his time" (O. Caroe, personal communication). Many of the older clerical staff, including the PA's stenographer who was a junior assistant to Donald, remember him as a sensitive and God-fearing individual and recall the incident at the PA's house in Tank vividly.

There is a story attached to Donald. Major Faheem Attaullah, son of Attaullah Jan, who was once PA, South Waziristan (1951–3), visited me in Tank in 1980. As a child he had heard a story that Donald's ghost haunted the room in which he committed suicide. One night, he recounted, the room was used by a visiting Englishman, who had not been told the story. At breakfast next morning the guest appeared disturbed and his face was pale. He had obviously not slept. On enquiry, Attaullah Jan was told that a ghost had awakened his guest at night. It was sitting on the edge of his bed and made awful noises as it wept. For the record, let me say the ghost made no appearance during my stay at Tank.

27 For a generalized history of the South Waziristan Scouts written by its officers, see Khan (n.d.). See Appendix F for names of Scouts' commandants.

28 The Tank Zam public school has some hundred children attending classes. Of these only three are girls. The first and only Mahsud girl, the daughter of Abdul Maalik, was entered after I spent hours convincing her father of the benefits of female education. Perhaps his example will be followed by other Mahsuds in the future.

29 Usage of "caste" in the domicile certificate (Appendix D) has been standard terminology in official documents since the British India days. It also reflects a failure on the part of Pakistani authorities to comprehend its significance in a Muslim tribal society.

30 The timber permit allows one truckload of timber to be exported from the agency and in theory is to be issued to a bona fide agency tribesman by the PA for the specific purpose of constructing a house. To prevent deforestation the commissioner, DIK, has imposed a limit of about sixty-five permits a month each for North and South Waziristan agencies. In practice, the maliks, more than a thousand in number, and other

pressure groups ensure that the permits are divided and subdivided monthly among themselves according to nikkat at advertised mulaqats. Registers in the offices of the PA and commissioner, DIK, provide a check against dishonesty in the distribution. By the last week of the month the monthly quota is usually exhausted, and the PA may have to run a deficit budget. The permits are in reality sold off to middlemen and can earn anywhere between 2,000 to 5,000 rupees, depending on the market. Thus various means are employed to acquire a permit. Senior officials or politicians in the land are approached with stories, which are usually concocted, for a letter of recommendation to the PA.

31 This is where Dodd was gunned down in 1914.

32 P. T. Duncan, who had served as PA earlier, in 1943, was killed during a jirga at the Sararogha Scouts' fort by a young Mahsud whose father had lost his life fighting the British. The Mahsud has been advised that if he wished to take *badal*, the primary law of the Pukhtun code, he had best get on with it and kill Mr. Duncan, for soon there would be no Englishmen left and London was a long way from Waziristan. The PA's badragga shot the assassin on the spot.

4. Strategy and conflict in Waziristan

1 Baddar, mentioned earlier, then belonged to the Wazirs; it was shortly to be captured by the Mahsuds.

2 The Maulana Mufti, based in Dera Ismail Khan, was to become an eminent leader in Pakistan politics. His simple habits, austere living standards, and reputation for incorruptibility made him a respected and popular figure. He headed the Jamiat-i-Ulama-i-Islam (party of religious scholars of Islam), the JUI, as president and generally opposed the politics of the central government, led by General Ayub Khan in the 1960s and Mr. Bhutto in the 1970s. Against the latter's PPP, he allied with the Pukhtun nationalists, the NAP, and was chief minister, NWFP, from 1972 to 1973. Until his death in 1980 he proved a strong and loyal patron to Mullah Noor Muhammad.

3 The figure was given to me by the APA, Wana, in 1976. Manual labor was provided free by Wazirs and perhaps this accounts for the low total cost of building the mosque.

Catherine Asher, who has just completed a project called "Legacy and Legitimacy: Sher Shah Sur's Patronage of Imperial Mausolea," made the following remarks after seeing photographs of the Wana mosque: "The mosque recalls those of the late 18th and 19th centuries – when forms of embellished Mughal style became associated with the architecture patronized by the power elite, regardless of religious affiliation. However, its use in the 20th century here in the South Waziristan Agency, easily can be associated with a revival of Islamic based authority, much in the same way that the earliest phases of the Mughal style were distinctly associated with Islamic religion, society and concepts" (C. Asher, personal communication).

4 For the convenience of the reader, all references to communications from the PA or APA will be cited in the text as here. They are listed in the References under "Political Agent's Office (1966–80)."

5 Prominent, among others, in Mr. Bhutto's mold were M. Khar, H. Sherpao, and M. Bhutto, leading, respectively, the provinces of Punjab, NWFP, and Sind. Mr. Bhutto's enigmatic and charismatic personality continues to fascinate biographers (Burki 1980a, Schofield 1979, Taseer 1980).

6 Pirzada served with me as tehsildar during 1976–77, when I was political agent, Orakzai Agency. He remained a staunch supporter of the Mullah and kept me abreast of developments in the South Waziristan Agency. His pro-Wazir views were balanced for me by the arguments of Moeen Khan Mahsud, my assistant director, Rural Development Department, Orakzai Agency. Because of my friendship with Pirzada, his father and his brother Shahzada, both key men of the Mullah, were to prove loyal friends to me when I was PA, South Waziristan Agency. On taking charge I had Moeen Khan transferred to South Waziristan Agency as my assistant director, Rural Development Department, where he proved a valuable informal link between me and key Mahsud elders; see Chapter 8.

7 It is significant that in a lengthy top-level meeting held by the governor, NWFP, with the political agents in July 1972 to review law and order, which I attended as deputy secretary, Home and Tribal Affairs Department, there was no mention of Noor Muhammad. Either Peshawar was, like most bureaucratic centers, engrossed myopically in more immediate problems, or the presence of Arbab Sikander as governor and Maulana Mufti as chief minister, both putatively supporting the Mullah, discouraged the subject.

8 *Kharai* is from *Khar*, the Peshawar city, and its use, which is derogatory, implies non-Pukhtun ethnicity. Supporters of the Mullah claim that in identifying the officials with certain political parties he was perhaps not far off the mark as their subsequent careers illustrate. The PA was posted on promotion shortly afterward to the key job of secretary to the PPP chief minister of the NWFP. The APA was accused by the Mullah of PPP sympathies because his sister was a secretary and confidant of Begum Bhutto, the wife of Mr. Bhutto. The colonel left service to join the NAP and in 1977 successfully contested the National Assembly seat on the NAP ticket from Mardan District.

9 The Mullah's antipathy to Haji Pasti is perhaps explained by memory of his father's employment as mullah with Pasti's father.

10 The "Special Report regarding Mahsud-Wazir dispute" from PA, SWA, to commissioner, DIK, July 7, 1975, provides a graphic and detailed account

of the clashes over this period in which many men were killed and wounded.

11 Lal Bacha, the driver, and Taj-ul-Mulk, the Mahsud bodyguard of the political agent, were among those who escorted the Mullah back to Wana. Taj-ul-Mulk described the scene: "Wazirs were mad with joy. They were crying and congratulating each other. When we arrived at Michan Baba [a few miles from Wana] some fifteen thousand Wazirs had gathered and they stopped our convoy to welcome the Mullah and kiss his hands. There was frenzy in the air. People knew me and recognized me. Someone could have said – here is a Mahsud – kill him. I was prepared. I aimed my gun at the head of the Mullah. I am the best marksman of the PA's bodyguard. I would not go alone. I told Lal Bacha, if anything happened he should run for it. But matters passed without an incident. It was a black day for us."

12 The event was described to me by the then commandant of the Scouts, the major commanding a Scouts wing in the operation, and numerous other eyewitnesses.

13 When I visited Wana in June 1976, shortly after the incident, I was struck by the strained atmosphere in and around the camp. The market was literally a plowed field with bulldozers and tractors standing on it. Nothing remained of the shops or their goods. Sandbags and armed soldiers were visible in the mosque. Sullen and dazed groups of tribesmen huddled around the camp. A captain of the Khyber Rifles from the Khyber Agency, who had been at school with me and had arrived with Scouts' reinforcements, built up a dark picture: "We will be over-run and slaughtered. The Wazirs will swamp us." The attack on the Wana camp in 1894 was perhaps in his mind.

14 Condoms, commonly known in Pakistan as French leather (from "letter"), or FL, became a snide symbol of the moral depravity of the Mullah to his detractors. "Boxes of FLs were found in his rooms" remains a common statement of condemnation and judgment of morality, and "If he was a religious man why did he need them?" a common question. Such sentiments are often to be heard in official circles when the Mullah is discussed.

15 The Ismaili leader Hasan-i Sabbah, born in the city of Qumm in the middle of the eleventh century, became famous as the legendary Old Man of the Mountain. The sect he founded was said to be based on assassinations and practice of the black arts. The word *assassin* derives from Hashishiyya, the followers of Hasan-i Sabbah. Hashish is the Arabic name for Indian hemp, *cannabis sativa*, which was used extensively by the Hashishiyya.

16 On my first tour to Sholam, bordering Birmal, one week after I arrived in the agency, senior officers of the South Waziristan Scouts arranged for tea on top of a knoll commanding the plain. The armored cars of the Scouts

had been deployed and the Scouts were out in force. The formality of the tour was contrasted with my later trips in the summer of 1979 without armored cars or even heavy trucks (see Chapter 7). A Scouts' officer, associated with the action in 1976, had accompanied me. I asked some Wazirs to point out the direction of Birmal, where, I believed, Musa Nikka, their ancestor, was buried. I said I would like to pay homage to the ancestor of the Wazirs, who was also a renowned Muslim leader. They pointed toward the northwest. The officer interjected and asked the Wazirs, "Do you believe in Musa Nikka or do you believe in your Mullah? Who is greater?" Immediately the atmosphere became strained. The Wazirs fidgeted and one of them said, "Both in their own ways are great, but Musa Nikka is the founder of the Wazir tribe." At which the officer asked, "Are you people Muslim first or Wazir first?" No one answered the question. The Wazirs are a religious people and intensely resented the stigma this implies. Such jibes against the Wazirs were common after the action of 1976. As a result of the little exchange, many Wazirs came up to me in the next few days and complained bitterly of such attitudes. They suggested that if I were to be so openly identified with men involved in the 1976 events, I would not be a very successful PA as far as the Wazirs were concerned.

5. *Order, ideology, and morality in Waziristan*

1 Azam Warsak is a small Zilli Khel market settlement that sprang up after the 1976 action and is not on standard Waziristan maps (Surveyor-General 1922–3, sheet 38-H).

2 For comments on and explanation of society by Muslim saints and men of ideas, see Ahmed (forthcoming).

3 I am referring to Noor Muhammad as Mullah, for the designation is generally better known than maulvi; the latter is preferred by the Wazirs. Disparagement is not meant nor is any meaning attached to my usage. The title "maulvi" in Pukhto is a loan word from Persian (and Urdu) and implies formal literate tradition. Noor Muhammad may well have developed the wish to be addressed as maulvi during his Multan education, a wish his followers gladly complied with.

4 Pasti and Jalat had both requested me to allow them to speak in public on behalf of the Mullah to the governor. Both wished to make explicit a political point: that of loyalty to the Wazirs. Pasti, given his history of opposition to the Mullah wished to "clarify his position," as he expressed it to me, and to address the Wazirs through the governor. Jalat wished to express continued loyalty to the Mullah and Wazir cause. The point was underlined in the presence of the large Mahsud gathering. Both men spoke as they wished. Their speeches were duly communicated to, and appreciated by, the Mullah in jail and the Wazirs in the agency.

5 *Ulema*, plural for *alim*, or Muslim learned in legal and religious studies; *alim* derives from *ilm*, knowledge of the Holy Quran, sayings of the Prophet, and religious tradition.

6 An earlier Arabic meaning of *mawla* is "client" or "affiliated group."

7 *Sartor* is literally "black head", and the name implies one whose head is uncovered as a result of poverty, grief, or some personal obsession; here it would signify an obsession with the cause of Islam. *Baba* is a term of respect for an elder.

8 Dara Shikoh, scholar and eldest son of Shah Jehan, the Mughal emperor, reflected Indo-Persian Sufic intellectual tradition when he observed, "Paradise is there, where there is no molla [mullah]" (Schimmel 1981, p. 362). Khushal Khan Khattak, the warrior-poet of the Pukhtuns wrote: "An hour spent in their [religious functionaries] company / And I'm filled with disgust" (Mackenzie 1965, p. 79). Muhammad Iqbal, the Muslim poet and philosopher of South Asia, expressed a similar thought in a more philosophic vein: "Banish from the house of God the mumbling priest whose prayers / Like a veil creation from Creator separate" (Iqbal 1970, p. 135; also see Malik 1971).

9 Minhaj-ud-din, a young Mahsud scholar expressed views on mullahs in his master's thesis thus, "It looks interesting to many of the long bearded man, claded in white religious outfit, claiming to be the standard bearers of the religion and looting those poor people who made their money mostly by life staking dacoities or very hard labour" (Mahsud 1970, p. 90).

10 I was shown the wide-angle door viewer by officials in 1976 and again in 1978 as proof of the Mullah's "devilry" and black magic. My suggestion that it was commonly used in many houses in the West to detect callers was greeted with some skepticism. To many, the device remains literally "the magic eye," *de jado starga*.

11 Nalkot is discussed in relation to certain methodological assumptions of anthropological fieldwork in Ahmed, "The Reconsideration of Swat Pathans: A Reply to Fredrik Barth" (in preparation-b). Also see Ahmed 1982c.

12 A demiofficial (DO) letter from commissioner, DIK, to PA, SWA, March 29, 1980, no. 106, comments on the political dealing with one such emergent fakir: "I agree the district administration has no control over Faqir Ali Mohammad, but the successful anti-state tour of South Waziristan Agency speaks of the utter ineffectiveness and incompetency of the so-called Dre Mahsud Khanans [leading Mahsud maliks]. Despite such heavy odds, Akbar, I always expected my trusted Doc to excel and flatten the Bhittani Faqir. It demonstrates Akbar wields more influence in the Agency and the adjoining Bhittani area than the consumers of the big chunk of our exchequer. They have outlived their utility and now the affairs be left to our worthy Doc to have solo flight. It pleases me to record 'well done, Akbar.'"

13 Two standard and opposed contemporary accounts, one critical (Badauni 1895–1925) and the other laudatory (Fazl 1927), have provided material for subsequent arguments regarding Akbar's theological position.

14 For an illuminating discussion of Ibn Khaldun, see Mahdi 1971.

15 In its usage of *Mohammedans* instead of *Muslims*, as in this quote and that in Chapter 1, the *Oxford English Dictionary* continues to offend Muslims. *Mohammedans* implies "followers of Mohammed." Muslims believe they are among those who have "submitted' (*Muslim* and *Islam* derive from *submission*) to Allah and are his followers only. *Mohammedan* has been dropped from circulation even by the traditional and conservative Orientalist scholars who once used it as a substitute for *Muslim* (for example the title, *Mohammedanism*, of Gibb 1949); editors of the *Oxford English Dictionary*, please note for future editions.

16 The war between Iran and Iraq begun in late 1980 provides an example of Muslims employing the concept of jihad against each other. A front-page headline in the *New York Times* in November 1980 read: "Leader tells Iraqis to wage 'holy war' against Iranian foe." The war, the Iraqi leader explained, was "to defend the ideals of the Holy Prophet" (Nov. 10, 1980). The Iranian ayatullahs, too, appeal to their nation to die fighting for Islam. The idiom of jihad barely conceals the deep rifts dividing Iran and Iraq on the basis of endless and complex encounters in history. Ethnic (Iranian–Persian vs. Iraqi–Arab), and sectarian (Irani–Shia vs. Iraqi–Sunni) factors further embitter the combatants.

17 *Jihad* has been translated in the contemporary world in dramatically nontraditional ways. For instance in April 1981 an Indonesian Muslim group, calling itself Komando Jihad or Holy War Command, hijacked a DC-9 passenger airplane belonging to the Garuda Indonesian Airways. Indonesian commandos successfully foiled the attempt at Bangkok airport, killing all five hijackers. Although the idiom of jihad was employed during the hijacking the case remains clouded in obscurity. Jihad is also used for other daily, even secular, activity. There is at least one daily newspaper called *Jihad* in Pakistan.

6. *Economic development and reinforcement of ideology in Waziristan*

1 The World Bank is conducting an economic study of migratory labor from Pakistan and Bangla Desh to the Middle East and the impact of remittances sent home through the Pakistan Institute for Development Economics and the Bangla Desh Institute for Development Studies. To the best of my knowledge no anthropologists are attached to the study, and an important, perhaps key, dimension is therefore unrepresented. For a speculatory paper by a World Bank official, see Burki 1980b.

2 The executive engineer, Buildings and Roads Department, like other

heads of government departments, relies on the political administration to put pressure on recalcitrant tribesmen. As an example, the executive engineer would complain to the APA that Malik A had "eaten up advances" and refused to work on the scheme for which he has been nominated. If the APA's inquiries corroborated the executive engineer's complaint, he would arrest and jail the malik. An awkward situation could arise if the PA had cordial relations with the malik. If he expressed sympathy for the malik, as usually happens, the executive engineer would feel let down.

3 Alam Jan recounted to me that in 1922, when his father, Mir Badshah, opened the first primary school among the Mahsuds in his area at Karamma, he was violently opposed by the mullahs. They organized a protest, and a *lashkar* ("war party") gathered, with a drummer beating his drum, to burn the school down. It was seen as a symbol of British imperialism. Mir Badshah met the lashkar and refused to close the school. Firing was exchanged in which several horses were killed, including the mullah's from under him. Two people also died, including the drumbeater. Opposition to Mir Badshah's school ended after the incident, and it is today one of the leading high schools of the agency. Alam Jan fears, however, that the mullah's party still want revenge and indeed, its members have promised to harm him when and where possible.

4 The traditional policy of fining or arresting those tribal groups in whose territory the incident took place proved unsuccessful. Shahzada had shrewdly selected poles from almost every major clan. A clear collision course with the Mahsud tribe had been set for me. Shahzada, permanently living deep in Shabi Khel territory, was safe from direct government action. Mahsuds exhibit a general and distant respect for Shahzada and in such cases sit on the fence watching with interest how administration will tackle this rather difficult person. Both too much and too little pressure on Shahzada can be counterproductive; he reacts to one as a personal challenge and to the other as general recognition of his strong position. Tackling the issue involved secret meetings, the exchange of promises, increase of allowances, tact, and the covert threat of action. I finally established personal contact with Shahzada. In this the links between Mullah Powindah and my wife's great-grandfather, the first wali of Swat, were of some assistance. It was suggested that we were "kinsmen" and ought to be supporting, not opposing, each other. The delicacy of the regional situation as events in Afghanistan unfolded also assisted. "I now realize your true intentions," Shahzada later wrote to me, "at this delicate stage of Pakistan's history and with conditions such as they are across the border we cannot allow the struggle for Islam to be interfered with. I have called off the jirga in which I was to make certain announcements" (Shahzada, personal communication).

7. *The anthropologist as political agent*

1 The refugees created considerable problems for the political administration through sheer numbers alone. In South Waziristan Agency there
were estimated to be almost 50,000 refugees. In North Waziristan Agency,
which had a population of about 250,000, there were some 130,000
officially registered refugees (Ahmed 1980b).

2 A paper I wrote on the Birmal area was circulated with a Frontier Corps
report arguing a "forward policy" (1979).

3 "I have been directed by the Governor to convey his appreciation for the
effort that has been put in by the political authorities and the South
Waziristan Scouts in pushing forward to the Durand line. The establishment of the new posts at Zallay Sar near Azam Warsak and Domandi
(Zarmelan) is indeed a land-mark in the history of tribal administration.
You may also kindly congratulate all those under you for their help to make
this a reality" (DO letter from chief secretary, NWFP, to PA, SWA, July 28,
1979, No. PS/CS-NWFP/79–263). On July 19, 1980, at a farewell dinner
given for me by the Scouts, the commandant, also, referred to these two
posts: "It was during his tenure that we were able to occupy without firing
a bullet the strategically important border posts of Zallay Sar and Zarmelan
situated on two very important military approaches from Afghanistan
into Pakistan."

4 "The surrender of such a large number of hostiles is the result of your
personal interest in the affairs of the agency you are in command and your
foresightedness to safeguard the borders of Pakistan. Your excellent work
is highly appreciated and commended. Please also convey the appreciation of your subordinates for this assistance" (DO letter from commissioner, DIK, to PA, SWA, Feb. 28, 1980, No. 1688/67–Poll.) Also see
Khyber Mail, Feb. 18, 1980; *Muslim*, Feb. 24, 1980.

5 In response to the invitation of one of the most turbulent sections of the
Mahsuds, the Abdullai, I visited them in their villages by the Darra Algad
a few miles from Makin in "unprotected area." I was the first PA to do so.
Over the last few years Scouts personnel had been shot at and kidnapped
near Makin. The trip, involving a long walk through ravines and over hills,
was made tense by the fact that my host's tarboor was annoyed about the
visit and had threatened to disrupt it. Rapid gun shots fired in the air
from a distance indicating traditional welcome underlined the risks we
were exposed to; a stray bullet could have cost a life. The headline for June
16, 1979, of *Jihad* read, "First time in history PA Waziristan visits
Kaniguram and Makin." Also see *Khyber Mail*, June 24, 1979.

6 When the Agency council was formed in 1980, I nominated the first
Suleman Khel tribesman ever to be made member. (See also Ahmed
1981c). I was the first political agent to visit the Urmar in Kaniguram, a
trip that resulted in approval of a bridge, obtained with considerable

difficulty, to connect the area with the main road (Caroe 1980; *Khyber Mail*, Jan. 13, 1980).

7 The daily newspaper *Jihad* wrote an editorial on the significance of Maees's surrender under the heading, "Dr. Akbar S. Ahmed's achievement" (April 20, 1979). Also see *Jihad*, April 21, 1979; *Mashriq*, April 23, 1979.

8 "The Governor, NWFP, has been pleased to see the fortnightly report and was particularly happy to note the way you handled the situation and got the surrender of Garam Khan through the tribe. He directed me to convey his appreciation to you. The Governor further observed that the conduct of the tribe in this case has been praiseworthy" (DO letter from the secretary of the governor, NWFP, to PA, SWA, Dec. 12 1979, No. 5640/L–11 (79)/GS).

9 Sappar is a corruption of the name Safar ("to travel"). As he is known in the area as Sappar, I use this name.

10 Ashraf Ghani, an Afghan anthropologist, informed me of a Sappar Khan who led a band of followers during the 1970s in raids against government posts and property in Afghanistan in the areas adjoining Waziristan. It is not clear, however, whether it was the Sappar Khan who features in this study or not. If it was, then it appears that Afghan authorities were as helpless in dealing with him as were their Pakistani counterparts.

11 "Please permit me to convey my deep sense of gratitude to you and your subordinates for unstinted co-operation which you extended to Zhob Militia by recovering L/Nk Baramat Khan of this Corps who was kidnapped by Ferari ["outlaw"] Safar Khan. I will not hesitate to say that where all possible force failed to achieve desired results your political manoeuvre was unique for unconditional and prompt recovery of the individual from Ferari. I must appreciate that this is such a precedence which has never been set by any civil administration, particularly in agency area in the past. I, therefore, extend my heart felt gratitude to you and your staff for this excellent co-operation on behalf of Zhob Militia" (DO letter from colonel, Zhob Militia, to PA, SWA, Jan. 10, 1980, No. 207–6/100/A).

12 The governor of Baluchistan, in a rare gesture of appreciation crossing provincial boundaries, wrote to his counterpart in the NWFP requesting him "to convey his appreciation" to PA, South Waziristan Agency, "The Governor of Baluchistan has conveyed that but for your resolute efforts and skillful handling the surrender of Safar Khan Mando Khel of Zhob would not have been possible. He has requested the Governor NWFP to convey his appreciation to you for this commendable achievement. I am accordingly directed to convey to you the appreciation of the Governor of Baluchistan." (DO letter from secretary, Services and General Administration Department, NWFP, to PA, SWA, April 17, 1980, No. SOI [S&GAD] 1–74/71.)

13 Although the government once thought it was eradicated, malaria is common in and around Tank, which is a low-lying waterlogged area. Apparently the Tank mosquito has developed immunity to traditional methods to kill it. The high rate of malaria among the Mahsuds in Tank is affecting their health (for instance, Gulab Khan in case V, Chapter 7). Many maliks who visited me complained of malaria and displayed its symptoms – recurring temperature, irritability, and fatigue. An interesting study awaits the anthropologist with an interest in tropical disease who is prepared to test the hypothesis that the rapid political success of the Mahsuds (in acquiring land in Tank and leaving the agency – and as a consequence exposure to poor climate and mosquitoes) will affect the characteristics that made success possible (robust health, stamina, household structure, etc.) over two or three generations and, in turn, the relationship with their cousins the Wazirs. The Wazirs remain relatively safe from malaria as they live almost entirely in the agency. A correlation between malarial conditions and successful political activity in Waziristan could thus be established. The implications are enormous for Waziristan society and politics.

8. The political agent as anthropologist

1 It was to the traditional definition of success the commandant referred in his speech at the Wana mess: "It can be safely said that his tenure in the Agency was the quietest period in the Agency's recent history. It was a period of peace and tranquility" (July 19, 1980).

2 A greater purpose is served by including than by excluding such letters, although in doing so I may stand open to the charge of immodesty. Not only do they support the cases I refer to but they are a record of official correspondence in a remote but important area of the world in a critical time. In addition they provide a rare insight into the working of, and interaction between, tribal administrators in contemporary Pakistan.

3 The reputation of Abdul Maalik as an inveterate opponent of the administration had preceded him when I first met him in my Tank office in December 1978. The mulaqat got off to a cold and formal start. Toward the end I put my cards on the table. The gist of my argument was: "You are one of the recognized elders of the agency, yet stories circulate about your capacity and tendency to create mischief regarding agency matters. You have been called an untrustworthy man; a paid agent of the Wazirs. I want to be your friend. I want to treat you with the respect due to an elder of the agency and the worthy son of a worthy father, both of you have been members of the National Assembly. I cannot do this if I am to issue warrants of arrest for you like my predecessors." Maalik melted visibly to the argument. With a smile he gave me his hand: "I will not be the first to withdraw the hand

of friendship. You will know what the friendship of Abdul Maalik means." I was expecting ideal-type behavior from, indeed suggesting it to, Abdul Maalik. He was prepared to prove its empirical validity through his behavior. True to his word Abdul Maalik proved a loyal friend and considerable asset during my stay in Waziristan as the cases in the book illustrate.

4 Omar Afridi (PA, 1968–71) was one of the few PAs Abdul Maalik had had a sympathetic relationship with in recent times. Omar, too, thought well of Maalik and his father, Pir Rahman (Afridi 1980, p. 11).

5 My mother's parents were Pukhtuns. Her father, Nawab Colonel Sir Hashmatullah Khan, was of the Barakzai tribe of Afghanistan. For many years he was senior member of the cabinet of Gwalior State (Kabadi 1938, sec. III, p. 117). He died as chief minister of the state. The *Indian Who's Who* notes, "sound judgement and progressive views are among his chief characteristics" (ibid.).

6 In the Indian Civil Service it was common for officers to be posted outside home areas. For instance, among the officers who served in provinces distant from their homes were Iskander Mirza in NWFP and N. M. Khan and Aziz Ahmed in East Pakistan. Many such officers later rose to eminence in Pakistan, Iskander Mirza becoming president of the country.

7 The discussion of expected idealized behavior in this study triggered the memory of an essay by George Orwell, "Shooting an Elephant" (1956), which I read as a schoolboy. I was intrigued not by the shooting of the elephant by the British officer in Burma but by his reasons for doing so. He appeared to have responded mechanistically to a collective suggestion made by people he loathed. The sequence was enacted *because he was expected to do so*: "The people expected it of me and I had got to do it" (ibid., p. 6). The colonial and ethnic factors add to the complexity of the situation but do not cloud the relationship between actor and audience. Orwell discovered that "a sahib has got to act like a sahib; he has got to appear resolute, to know his own mind and do definite things" (ibid., p. 7). He must live up to expected ideal behavior. His own actions are thus determined by external expectations: "And it was at this moment, as I stood there with the rifle in my hands, that I first grasped ... here was I ... seemingly the leading actor of the piece; but in reality I was only an absurd puppet pushed to and fro by the will of those yellow faces behind" (ibid., p. 6). Structurally, my argument is similar. The problem of Orwell and the elephant, which had eluded me all these years and lay somewhere in my unconscious, was finally brought to the surface and resolved in the light of the discussion in this chapter.

8 The PA's identification with his tribes is revealed in the following popular story: "There was a tale current in the folklore of Indian clubs and messes for which there was perhaps no historical authority but which did enshrine a truth. It concerned a Political Agent accompanying British troops on a

punitive expedition. After breakfast with the officers, he took his lunch in a haversack and disappeared; they did not see him again till evening when, sipping a pink gin by the light of a lantern carefully screened from snipers, he asked: 'And how did things go on your side today? Casualties on our side were half-a-dozen' " (Woodruff 1965, vol. 2, p. 153).

9 For instance, see Howell 1979. Also of note are forthcoming works by King and by Merk and a book in preparation by Ahmed and Hart.

10 For comments on the role of the anthropologist as political officer, see the review by Sir Olaf Caroe of Howell's monograph *Mizh* in *Asian Affairs*: "Akbar Ahmed has prevailed against the odds, and won the respect which Pathans will give only to one whom they regard as a full man" (Caroe 1980, p. 89). Also see a review by Professor Dupree, who stated: "At last! We can add a Pakistani name to the long list of administrator-scholars who have carved out brilliant names for themselves along the Frontier. The names of past greats roll off the tongue like Sir Laurence Olivier spouting Shakespeare: Elphinstone and Edwardes, Bellew and Biddulph, Burnes and Barton, Raverty and Ross-Keppel, Pettigrew and Sandeman, Masson and Merk, Warburton and Goodwin, Howell and Caroe – among others. None, however, have approached the Frontier with such qualifications as Dr. Akbar S. Ahmed" (L. Dupree, reviewing Ahmed 1980a, *Muslim*, July 11, 1980). Also see reviews by K. Ahmed, *Pakistan Times*, Sept. 26, 1980; S. J. Burki, *Middle East Journal* 35:1 (1981):79–80; J. Freedman, *American Anthropologist* 83:2 (June 1981): 468–70; D. M. Hart, *British Institute of Middle Eastern Studies*, 8:1 (1981) 65–69; C. Lindholm, *Journal of Asian Studies* 41:1 (Nov. 1981): 163–5; F. Rahman, *Afghanistan Council Newsletter*, Asia Society, New York, Sept. 1981; and A. Singer, *Royal Anthropological Institute Newsletter*, no. 42, Feb. 1981. I am grateful for the notice, but I must point out that there are Frontier officers far more worthy of praise than I. Although the reviews make the important point of underlining the continuity in administration after independence, the comparison may obscure a fundamental fact: The native officer is part of society. He is neither a colonizing agent nor an alien social entity; he remains an integrated part of the larger whole.

9. Islam and segmentary societies: the problem of definition

1 A revealing and delightful story is recounted by Minhaj-ud-din Mahsud illustrating the point. It also reflects the attitudes of Mahsud tribesmen to dacoity (non-Mahsud cattle from the settled district are fair game), prayer (rigidly observed), and invocation of saints and God (constant and fervent appeals in endeavor, however dubious or illegal its content): "Mr. Mattak Khan is an ideal man I can quote. In his youth he has been a famous dacoit having a gang of daring and skillful fighters and artful thieves. He has a notorious record in this regard. But he has all along been very religious

minded. He prays regularly, observes fasts, pays *zakat* (compulsory alms) – even from his stolen things. He serves religious leaders with great zeal and honesty.

"One of his stories goes thus: He and his gang came out on an expedition of stealing cattles from a village in Jandola. He was telling me that they prayed their later afternoon (third) prayer at such and such place and started for the destination: prayed their evening prayer at such and such place and again moved ahead. At mid-night after the night prayer they reached the spot.

"Like the rest prayers of this day, they humbly prayed to Allah, besought great *pirs* and vowed to shrines to bless them with success. They held positions and started breaking through into the cattle band. After having successfully stolen the cattles, they made for their homes. Soon a group of armed villagers followed them. It was the morning prayer time; they prayed to Allah to save them and help them carry the cattle safely. They vowed that out of these cattles so many will be sacrificed and given in charity in the name of Allah and they called upon *pirs*; through their tactics they were successful in bringing the cattles to their homes. Honest to their promises, they slaughtered some sheep and goats at shrines, gave some of them to Maulvis in charity – Maulvis have established that they are the most rightful receivers of charity. The Maulvis well in the know about these cattles, accepted these under the pretence that these were *halal* (pure) for them as they did not steal these and were given to them in the name of Allah and holy persons" (Mahsud 1970, p. 92).

2 For one such example, see Barth 1972. Perhaps by reexamining his earlier work (Barth 1981) he has acknowledged the criticism.

3 The following comment by Geertz is apt: "For an anthropologist, the importance of religion lies in its capacity to serve, for an individual or for a group, as a source of general, yet distinctive, conceptions of the world, the self, and the relations between them, on the one hand – its model *of* aspect – and of rooted, no less distinctive 'mental' dispositions – its model *for* aspect – on the other. From these cultural functions flow, in turn, its social and psychological ones" (Geertz 1973, p. 123). For a successful employment of religious and cultural functions in recreating history, see Geertz 1980.

4 See, for example, Asad 1970; Berger 1970; Dupree and Albert 1974; Eaton 1978; Eickelman 1976, 1981; El-Zein 1977; Evans-Pritchard 1973; Geertz 1968; Geertz, Geertz, and Rosen 1979; Gellner 1969a, 1969b, 1981; Gellner and Micaud 1973; Ghani 1978 and in preparation; Gilsenan 1973; Jamil 1965; Mayer 1967; Meeker 1979, 1980; Mitchell 1969; Shariati 1979; Vatin 1980.

5 For South Asia see Bailey 1960, 1970; Mayer 1966; Nicholas 1965.

6 Although a flourishing and standard literature exists on African Islam south of the Sahara (Behrman 1970; Bello 1962; Cunnison and James

1972; Holt 1958; Jamil 1965; I. M. Lewis 1969; W. A. Lewis 1965; Lewis and Kritzech 1970; Martin 1976; Nimtz 1981; O'Brien 1971; Smith 1960; Stewart 1973; Trimingham 1960, 1964, 1965, 1980), analysis remains mechanistic and traditional in method, the notable exceptions being Cohen 1969, 1972, 1981; Lubeck 1981; and Paden 1973. Too few studies analyze the interaction of religion, politics, and ethnicity in explaining macro social and political processes worked around extended case studies. The Nigerian case would require analysis within this framework to explain satisfactorily the emergence of the mullah of Kano. I am indebted to M. Crawford Young for information on West Africa.

7 For one of the few sociological comments on Marwa's movement see Lubeck 1981; for a factual account see Okoli 1981.

8 The four-man judicial tribunal is headed by a justice and called the Kano Disturbances Tribunal of Inquiry. An understanding of the events in Kano within the context of the Islamic district paradigm, in which tribal administration and religious organization interact, will remain incomplete unless those who could comment professionally on such interaction are consulted. Anthropologists, in particular, may have a useful contribution to make in analyzing the Kano disturbances.

References

Original sources

Bruce, C.E. (1929). *The tribes of Waziristan: notes on Mahsuds, Wazirs, Daurs, etc.* His Majesty's Stationery Office for the India Office. Confidential.

Curtis, G. S. C. (1946). *Monograph on Mahsud tribes.* Government of NWFP. Confidential.

Frontier Corps (1979). Forward deployment of Frontier Corps NWFP 3rd paper. Headquarters Frontier Corps Peshawar. Secret.

Frontier Crimes Regulation (1901, validated 1954). Government of Pakistan, Peshawar.

General Staff (1921). *Operations in Waziristan 1919-1920.* Compiled by the General Staff, Army Headquarters, India. Superintendent Government Printing, Calcutta, India. Confidential.

(1932). *Summary of events in North-West Frontier tribal territory. 1st January, 1931 to 31st December, 1931.* Government of India Press, Simla, India. Confidential.

(1936). *Military report on Waziristan 1935.* 5th ed. Government of India Press, Calcutta, India. Confidential.

(1937). *Report of the Frontier Watch and Ward Committee 1936.* Printed by the Manager, Government of India Press.

Howell, E. B. (1925). *Waziristan border administration report for 1924–25.* Government of India. Confidential.

Intelligence Section (1930). *Tribes of Waziristan: Mahsuds.* Vol. 1, Part 1 Intelligence Section "G" Branch at Headquarters, Waziristan. Commercial Steam Press, Dera Ismail Khan. Confidential.

Johnson, H. H. (1934a). *Notes on Wana.* Government of India. Confidential. (1934b). *Mahsud notes.* Government of India. Confidential.

Johnston, F. W. (1903). *Notes on Wana.* Government of India. Confidential.

Lockhart, W. S. A. (1897). *Operations against the Mahsud Waziris: 1894– 95.* Printed at the Government Central Printing Office, Simla, India.

Macaulay, A. (1881). Letter no. 120-P, October 8. In *Waziristan border administration report for 1924–25*, by E. B. Howell. Government of India, 1925. Confidential.

Mahsud, Minhaj-ud-din (1970). Impact of education on social change in South Waziristan Agency. Master's thesis, Punjab University.

Noor Muhammad (1976). Letter dated April 1 to chief minister NWFP (in Urdu).

(n. d.). Personal diaries (in Urdu).

Political Agent's Office (1966–80). Official correspondence, PA's Office, Tank/Wana.

(1977). Political agent's handing-over note, PA's Office, Tank/Wana.

Surveyor-General of India (1922–23). Afghanistan, Baluchistan and NWFP. Restricted Map Sheet 38-H, 5th ed. Survey of India Offices.

Secondary Sources

Afridi, O. K. (1980). *Mahsud monograph*. Foreword by A. S. Ahmed. Tribal Affairs Research Cell, Home and Tribal Affairs Department, Government of NWFP.

Ahmed, A. S. (1973). *Mataloona: Pukhto proverbs*. Pakistan Academy for Rural Development, Peshawar. Reprinted 1975, Oxford University Press, Karachi.

(1976). *Millennium and charisma among Pathans: a critical essay in social anthropology*. Routledge & Kegan Paul, London.

(1977). *Social and economic change in the tribal areas*. Oxford University Press, Karachi.

(1978). The colonial encounter on the NWFP: myth and mystification. *Journal of the Anthropological Society* (Oxford) 9 (3): 167–74.

(1979). Tribe and state in Asia: the Great Game revisited. Paper for SOAS-SSRC Seminar, London. Revised version: Tribes and states in Central and South Asia. *Asian Affairs* 11 (o. s., 67), pt. 2, (June 1980): 152–68.

(1980a). *Pukhtun economy and society: traditional structure and economic development in a tribal society*. Routledge & Kegan Paul, London.

(1980b). How to aid Afghan refugees. *Royal Anthropological Institute News*, no. 39, August.

(1981a). The Arab connection: emergent models of social structure and organization among Pakistani tribesmen. *Asian Affairs* 12 (o. s., 68), pt. 2 (June 1981): 167–70.

(1981b). At the Khaiber pass. *Christian Science Monitor*, June 1.

(1981c). Nomadism as ideological expression: the case of the Gomal nomads. *Nomadic Peoples*, no. 9, August.

(1982a). Hazarawal: formation and structure of district ethnicity in Pakistan. Paper presented at the Annual Meeting of the American Ethnological Society, April 1982, Lexington, Ky.

(1982b). Order and conflict in Muslim society: a case study from Pakistan. *Middle East Journal* 36 (2): 184–204.

(1982c). Review of *Selected essays of Fredrik Barth*, vols. 1 and 2, by Fredrik Barth. *Journal of Peasant Studies*, (London).

(forthcoming). *Muslim society: readings in social structure, thought and development*, Routledge & Kegan Paul, London.

(in preparation-a). The Burkis of Pakistan: reemergence of ethnicity and primordial loyalties.

(in preparation-b). The reconsideration of Swat Pathans: a reply to Fredrik Barth.

Ahmed, A. S., and Z. Ahmed (1981). *Tor* and *Mor*: binary and opposing models of Pukhtun femalehood. In *The endless day: rural women, Asian case-studies*, ed. T. S. Epstein and Rosemary A. Watts. Pergamon Press, Oxford.

Ahmed, A. S., and D. M. Hart, eds., (1982). *From the Atlas to the Indus: the tribes of Islam*. Routledge & Kegan Paul, London.

(in preparation). *Islamic tribes and European administrators: readings in the colonial encounter*.

Aitchison, C. U. (1933). *A collection of treaties relating to India and neighbouring countries*. Government of India, Delhi.

Algar, H. (1969). *Religion and state in Iran 1785–1906*. University of California Press, Berkeley.

Allen, C. (1977). *Plain tales from the raj*. Futura Publication, London.

Al-Muttaqi (1974). Kanz. In *Islam: politics and war*, vol. 1, ed. B. Lewis. Harper & Row (Torchbooks), New York.

Anderson, J. W. (1980). How Afghans define themselves in relation to Islam. Paper presented at the Annual Meeting of the American Anthropological Association, December 1980, Washington, D. C.

Antoun, R. T. (1979). *Low-key politics: local-level leadership and change in the Middle East*. State University of New York Press, Albany.

Antoun, R. T., and I. Harik (1972). *Rural politics and social change in the Middle East*. Indiana University Press, Bloomington.

Asad, T. (1970). *The Kababish Arabs*. Hurst, London.

ed. (1973). *Anthropology and the colonial encounter*, Ithaca Press, London.

Badauni, A. Q. (1895–1925). *Muntakhab ut-Tawarikh*. 3 vols. Trans. by G. S. A. Ranking and W. H. Lowe. Asiatic Society, Calcutta.

Bailey, F. G. (1960). *Tribe, caste and nation*. Manchester University Press.

(1970). *Stratagems and spoils: a social anthropology of politics*, Blackwell Publisher, Oxford.

(1972). Conceptual systems of the study of politics. In *Rural politics and social change in the Middle East*, ed. R. Antoun and I. Harik. Indiana University Press, Bloomington.

Banton, M., ed. (1978). *Anthropological approaches to the study of religion*. ASA Monograph 3, London.

Barth, F. (1959). Segmentary opposition and the theory of games: a study of Pathan Organization. *Journal of the Royal Anthropological Institute* 89, pt. 1.

(1966). Models of social organization. Occasional paper no. 23, Royal Anthropological Institute, London.

(1972). *Political leadership among Swat Pathans*. Athlone, London.

(1981). *Selected essays of Fredrik Barth: features of person and society in Swat; collected essays on Pathans*. Vol. 2. Routledge & Kegan Paul, London.

Battuta, Ibn (1929). *Travels in Asia and Africa*, Trans. by H. A. R. Gibb. G. Routledge & Sons, London.

Beattie, H. (1980). Effects of the Saor revolution in the Nahrin area of northern Afghanistan. Paper presented at the Annual Meeting of the American Anthropological Association, December 1980, Washington, D.C.

Behrman, L. (1970). *Muslim brotherhoods and politics in Senegal*. Harvard University Press, Cambridge, Mass.

Bello, A. (1962). *My life*. Cambridge University Press, Cambridge.

Bendix, R. (1960). *Max Weber: an intellectual portrait*. Heinemann, London.

Berger, M. (1970). *Islam in Egypt today; social and political aspects of popular religion*. Cambridge University Press, Cambridge.

Boissevain, J. (1974). *Friends of friends: networks, manipulators and coalitions*, Blackwell Publisher, Oxford.

Breem, W. (1979). *Leopard and the cliff*. St. Martin's Press, New York.

Bruce, C. E. (1938). *Waziristan 1936–1937*.Gale and Polden, Aldershot.

Bruce, R. I. (1900). *The forward policy and its results; or, thirty-five years work amongst the tribes on our North-Western Frontier of India*. Longman Group, London.

Burki, S. J. (1980a). *Pakistan under Bhutto 1971–1977*. Macmillan Press, London.

(1980b). What migration to the Middle East may mean for Pakistan. *Journal of South Asian and Middle Eastern Studies* 3 (3).

Canfield, R. L. (1980). Religious networks and traditional culture in Afghanistan. Paper presented at the Annual Meeting of the American Anthropological Association, December 1980, Washington D. C.

Caroe, O. (1965). *The Pathans*, Macmillan Press, London.

(1980). Review of *Mizh*, by E. Howell. *Asian Affairs* 11 (o. s., 67), pt. 1 (February): 88–90.

Churchill, W. S. (1972). *Frontiers and wars*. Penguin Books, London.

Coen, T. C. (1971). *The Indian Political Service*. Chatto & Windus,   London.

Cohen, A. (1969). *Custom and politics in urban Africa*. Routledge & Kegan Paul, London.

(1972). Cultural strategies in the organization of trading diaspora. In *The development of trade and markets in West Africa*, ed. C. Meillasoux. Oxford University Press, New York.

(1981). *The politics of elite culture: exploration in the dramaturgy of power in a modern African society*. University of California Press, Berkeley.

Cunnison, I., and W. James, eds. (1972). *Essays in Sudan ethnography*, Hurst, London.

Dale, S. F. (1981). *Islamic society on the South Asian frontier*. Oxford University

Press (Clarendon Press), New York.

Dupree, L., and L. Albert, eds. (1974). *Afghanistan in the 1970s*. Praeger, New York.

Eaton, R. M. (1978). *Sufis of Bijapur, 1300–1700: social roles of Sufis in medieval India*. Princeton University Press, Princeton, N. J.

Eickelman, D. F. (1976). *Moroccan Islam: tradition and society in a pilgrimage center*. University of Texas Press, Austin.

(1981). *The Middle East*. Prentice-Hall, Englewood Cliffs, N.J.

El-Zein, A. H. (1977). Beyond ideology and theology: the search for the anthropology of Islam. *Annual Reviews of Anthropology* 6: 227–54.

Elliott, J. G. (1968). *The Frontier 1839–1947: the story of the North-West Frontier of India*. Cassell, London.

Elphinstone, M.(1972). *An account of the kingdom of Caubul*. Vols. 1 and 2, Oxford University Press, Karachi.

Evans-Pritchard, E. E. (1973). *The Sanusi of Cyrenaica*. Oxford University Press, New York.

Fazl, Abul (1927). *The Ain-i-Akbari*. Trans. by H. Blochmann. Asiatic Society of Bengal, Calcutta.

Fischer, M. J. M. (1980). *Iran: from religious dispute to revolution*. Harvard University Press, Cambridge, Mass.

Fortes, M., and E. E. Evans-Pritchard, eds. (1970). *African political systems*. Oxford University Press, New York.

Geertz, C. (1968). *Islam observed*. Yale University Press, New Haven, Conn.

(1973). *The interpretation of cultures*. Basic Books, New York.

(1979). Suq: the bazaar economy in Sefrou. In *Meaning and order in Moroccan society: three essays in cultural analysis*, by C. Geertz, H. Geertz, and L. Rosen. Cambridge University Press, Cambridge.

(1980). *Negara: the theatre state in nineteenth-century Bali*. Princeton University Press, Princeton, N. J.

Geertz, C., H. Geertz, and L. Rosen (1979). *Meaning and order in Moroccan society: three essays in cultural analysis*. Cambridge University Press, Cambridge.

Gellner, E. (1969a). *Saints of the Atlas*. Weidenfeld & Nicolson, London.

(1969b). A pendulum swing theory of Islam. In *Sociology of religion*, ed. R. Robertson. Penguin Books, London.

(1973). Introduction to *Arabs and Berbers: from tribe to nation in North Africa*, ed. E. Gellner and C. Micaud. Gerald Duckworth, London.

(1981). *Muslim society*. Cambridge University Press, Cambridge.

Gellner, E., and C. Micaud, eds. (1973). *Arabs and Berbers: from tribe to nation in North Africa*. Gerald Duckworth, London.

Gerth, H. H., and C. W. Mills, trans. and eds. (1961). *From Max Weber: essays in sociology*. Routledge & Kegan Paul, London.

Ghani, A. (1978). Islam and state-building in a tribal society: Afghanistan 1880–1901. In *Modern Asian Studies*, vol. 12, no. 2. Cambridge University Press, Cambridge.

(in preparation-a). *Sharia* in the process of state-building: Afghanistan 1880–1901.

(in preparation-b). Disputes in a court of *sharia*.

Gibb, H. A. R. (1949). *Mohammedanism: an historical survey*. Oxford University Press, New York.

Gilsenan, M. (1973). *Saint and Sufi in modern Egypt*. Oxford University Press, New York.

Gluckman, M. (1961). Ethnographic data in British social anthropology. In *Sociological Review* 9: 5–17.

(1969). Introduction to *The craft of social anthropology*, ed. A. L. Epstein. Tavistock, London.

(1971). *Politics, law and ritual in tribal society*. Blackwell Publisher, Oxford.

Godelier, M. (1977). *Perspectives in Marxist anthropology*. Cambridge University Press, Cambridge.

Hart, D. M. (1975). *Emilio Blanco Izaga: colonel in the Rif*. 2 vols. HRAF, New Haven, Conn.

Helm, J., ed. (1971). *Essays on the problem of tribe*. American Ethnological Society, University of Washington Press, Seattle.

Hodgson, M. G. S. (1974). *The venture of Islam*, 3 vols. University of Chicago Press, Chicago.

Holt, P. M. (1958). *The Mahdist state in the Sudan 1881–1898*. Oxford University Press (Clarendon Press,) New York.

Holt, P. M., A. K. S. Lambton, and B. Lewis (1970). *The Cambridge history of Islam*. Vol. 2. Cambridge University Press, Cambridge.

Howell, E. B. (1979). *Mizh: A monograph on government's relations with the Mahsud tribe*. Foreword by A. S. Ahmed. Oxford in Asia Historical Reprint Series, Oxford University Press, Karachi. Originally published in 1931 by Government of India Press, Simla.

Hunt, R., and J. Harrison (1980). *The district officer in India 1930–1947*. Scolar Press, London.

Iqbal, M. (1970). Selected poems. In *Muslim self-statement in India and Pakistan 1857–1968*, ed. A. Ahmad and G. E. Von Grunebaum. OHO Harrassowitz, Wiesbaden.

Jamil, M. A. (1965). *The Tijaniya: a Sufi order in the modern world*. Middle Eastern Monographs, 7, Royal Anthropological Institute, London.

Kabadi, W. P., ed. (1938). *Indian who's who 1937–1938*. Vahibhav Press, Bombay.

Keddie, N. R., ed. (1978). *Scholars, saints, and sufis: Muslim religious institutions since 1500*. Near Eastern Center, University of California, Los Angeles.

Khan, K. (n. d.). *Dastini Parina* (in Urdu). Dar-ul-adab, Peshawar.

Khomeini, Imam (1981). *Islam and revolution*. Trans. by H. Algar. Mizan Press, Berkeley, Calif.

King, L. W. (forthcoming). *Monograph on the Orakzai country and clans*. Introduction by A. S. Ahmed. Oxford in Asia Historical Reprint Series. Oxford University Press, Karachi. Originally published in 1900 by Punjab Government Press, Lahore.

Kipling, R. (1960). *Kim.* Macmillan Press, London.

Lawrence, T. E. (1927). *Revolt in the desert.* G. H. Doran Co., New York.

Leach, E. R. (1977). *Political systems of highland Burma: a study of Kachin social structure.* Athlone, London.

Lewis, I. M., ed. (1969). *Islam in tropical Africa.* Oxford University Press, New York.

(1978). *Ecstatic religion.* Penguin Books, New York.

Lewis, W. A. (1965). *Politics in West Africa.* Oxford University Press, New York.

Lewis, W., and J. Kritzech (1970). *Islam in Africa.* Van Nostrand, New York.

Lindholm, C. (1980). Images of the Pathan: the usefulness of colonial ethnography. *European Journal of Sociology* 21(4).

Lubeck, P. (1981). Islamic political movements in northern Nigeria: the problem of class analysis. Paper presented at the Islamic Political Movements Conference, May 9–11, 1981, University of California, Berkeley.

Mackenzie, D. N. (1965). *Poems from the devan of Khushal Khan Khattak.* Allen & Unwin, London.

Macneil, D. (1971). *Sadhu on the mountain peak.* Corgi Books, London.

Mahdi, M. (1971). *Ibn Khaldun's philosophy of history.* University of Chicago Press, Chicago.

Malik, H., ed. (1971). *Iqbal: poet-philosopher of Pakistan.* Columbia University Press, New York.

Martin, B. G. (1976). *Muslim brotherhoods in nineteeth-century Africa.* Cambridge University Press, Cambridge.

Masters, J. (1965). *Bugles and a tiger.* Four Square, London.

Maududi, Abul-ala (1948). *Al-jihad fil-Islam,* Lahore.

Mayer, A. C. (1966). The significance of quasi groups in the study of complex societies. In *The social anthropology of complex societies,* ed. M. Banton. Tavistock, London.

(1967). Pir and murshid: an aspect of religious leadership in West Pakistan. *Middle Eastern Studies* 3(2).

(1970). *Caste and kinship in central India.* Routledge & Kegan Paul, London.

Meeker, M. E. (1979). *Literature and violence in North Arabia.* Cambridge University Press, Cambridge.

(1980). The twilight of a South Asian heroic age: a rereading of Barth's study of Swat. In *Man* 15(4): 682–701.

Merk, W. R. H. (forthcoming). *Report on the Mohmands.* Introduction by A. S. Ahmed. Oxford in Asia Historical Reprint Series. Oxford University Press, Karachi. Originally published in 1898 by Punjab Government Press, Lahore.

Middleton, J., and D. Tait, eds. (1970). *Tribes without rulers.* Routledge & Kegan Paul, London.

Mitchell, R. P. (1969). *The society of the Muslim brothers.* Oxford University Press, New York.

Nicholas, R. W. (1965). Factions: a comparative analysis. In *Political systems and the distribution of power,* ed. M. Banton. Tavistock, London.

Nimtz, A. (1981). *Islam in East Africa.* University of Minnesota Press, Minneapolis.

O'Brien, D. B. (1971). *The Mourides of Senegal: the political and economic organization of an Islamic brotherhood.* Oxford University Press, New York.

Okoli, E. J. (1981). After the Kano rioting. *West Africa,* no. 3311 January 12.

Orwell, G. (1956). *The Orwell reader.* Harcourt Brace Jovanovich, New York.

Oxford English Dictionary (1975) Concise ed. Oxford University Press (Clarendon Press), New York.

Paden, J. (1973). *Religion and political culture in Kano.* University of California Press, Berkeley.

Pakistan Population Census (1972). Federally Administered Tribal Areas, Census Organization, Interior Division, Islamabad.

Parkin, D. J. (1978). *The cultural definition of political response: lineal destiny among the Luo.* Academic Press, New York.

Pastner, S. L. (1979). The man who would be anthropologist: dilemmas in fieldwork on the Baluchistan frontier of Pakistan. *Journal of South Asian and Middle Eastern Studies* 3(2).

Peters, R. (1979). *Islam and colonialism: the doctrine of jihad in modern history.* Mouton, The Hague.

Pettigrew, H. R. C. (1965). *Frontier Scouts.* Selsey, Sussex.

Pickthall, M., trans. (1969). *The Holy Quran.* Taj Company, Karachi.

Rahman, F. (1979). *Islam.* University of Chicago Press, Chicago.

(1980). *Major themes of the Quran.* Bibliotheca Islamica, Chicago.

Raverty, H. G. (1888). *Notes on Afghanistan and part of Baluchistan: geographical, ethnographical and historical.* Eyre and Spottiswoode, London.

Rodinson, M. (1980). *Muhammad.* Trans. by A. Carter. Pantheon Books, New York.

Schimmel, A. (1981). *Mystical dimensions of Islam.* University of North Carolina Press, Chapel Hill.

Schofield, V. (1979). *Bhutto: trial and execution.* Cass, London.

Shariati, A. (1979). *On the sociology of Islam.* Trans. by H. Algar. Mizan Press, Berkeley, Calif.

Singer, A. (1982). *The Pathans.* Time-Life Books, New York.

Smith, M. G. (1960). *Government in Zazzau.* Oxford University Press, New York.

Spain, J. W. (1962). *The way of the Pathans.* Robert Hale, London.

(1963). *The Pathan borderland.* Mouton, The Hague.

Stephens, I. (1953). *Horned moon.* E. Benn, London.

Stewart, C. C. (1973). *Islam and social order in Mauritania.* Oxford University Press, New York.

Swartz, M., ed.(1968). *Local-level politics*. Aldine, Chicago.

Tapper, R. L., ed. (in preparation). *Tribe and state in Afghanistan and Iran from 1800 to 1980*.

Taseer, S. (1980). *Bhutto: a political biography*. Ithaca, London.

Tavakolian, B. (1980). Sheikhanzai nomads and the Afghan state. Paper presented at the Annual Meeting of the American Anthropological Association, December 1980, Washington, D. C.

Trimingham, J. S. (1960). *Islam in West Africa*. Oxford University Press, New York.

(1964). *Islam in East Africa*. Oxford University Press, New York.

(1965). *Islam in Ethiopia*. Barnes & Noble Books, New York.

(1980). *The influence of Islam upon Africa*. Longman, New York.

Vatin, J. C. (1980). Islam, religion et politique. *Revue de l'occident Musulman et la Méditerranée* 1.

Velsen, J. V. (1964). *The politics of kinship*. Manchester University Press, for the Rhodes-Livingstone Institute.

(1969). The extended-case method and situational analysis. In *The craft of social anthropology*, ed. A. L. Epstein. Tavistock, London.

Wali, M., trans. (1980). *Maqsud-ul-Mominin*, by Bayazid Ansari. Foreword by A. S. Ahmed. University Book Agency, Peshawar.

Watteville, H. de (1925). *Waziristan 1919–1920*. Constable, London.

Weber, M. (1962). *The Protestant ethic and the spirit of capitalism*, Allen & Unwin, London.

(1965). *The sociology of religion*. Methuen & Co., London.

(1968). *The religion of India*. Free Press, New York.

Werbner, R. P., ed. (1977). *Regional cults*. ASA Monograph 16. Academic Press, New York.

Woodruff, P. (1965). *The men who ruled India*. Vol. 1: *The founders*. Vol. 2: *The Guardians*. Jonathan Cape, London.

Newspapers: English dailies

Christian Science Monitor (Boston, Mass.)   *Muslim* (Islamabad)
Guardian (England)   *New York Times* (New York)
Khyber Mail (Peshawar)   *Pakistan Times* (Pakistan)

Newspapers: Urdu dailies

Jihad   Mashriq   Nawai Waqt

Glossary

adda	Market
azan	Muslim call to prayers, said five times daily.
badal	Revenge
badshah	King
badragga	Tribal escort
beghairat	Without shame
Birmal	Most inaccessible tribal area in the Frontier Province; Birmal spreads into Afghanistan
chalweshti	Refers to tribal fighting unit. From the number forty, *chalwesh*
desi hakeem	Native medicine man
din	Religion, Islam, opposed to *dunya*
dolas kassi	(Lit., "twelve men.") The Mullah's cabinet
Dre Mahsud	(lit., "three Mahsud.") Refers to the three Mahsud clans
dunya	World, opposed to *din*
dwa-kora	Owner of two houses, usually one in the agency and the other in the settled areas
fateha	Prayer for deceased
fatwah	Religious instruction
gata	Profit
hujra	Guest room
itbar	Trust
itbar nama	Written guarantee, surety
jaba	(Lit., "tongue.") Word of honor
jihad	Muslim endeavor, in the way of Allah. Popularly understood as religious war
jirga	Council of elders
jumat	Mosque
kacha	(Lit., "unbaked," "makeshift.") Mud, opposed to *pakka*
kafir	Nonbeliever, that is, non-Muslim
Kalima	Muslim declaration of faith (see *shahada*)
kashar	Young, political have-not, opposed to *mashar*
kharai	From *khar*, or city; Peshawar

khassadars	Tribal levies under command of political agent
khel	Lineage
khutba	Sermon
lashkar	Tribal armed force for battle
lungi	Allowances given by the government to individuals (see *muajib*).
madrassah	Religious school
malik	Recognized elder
mashar	Traditional elder
maulvi	Religious functionary or learned religious scholar
melmastia	Hospitality
mian	Religious lineage
mizh	We, first person plural; *mong* in Yusufzai Pukhto
muajib	Allowances given by the government to tribal section or subsection (see *lungi*).
mulaqat	Official meeting
mullah	Religious functionary
munsif	Arbitrator in conflict
naib-tehsildar	Field official, assistant to tehsildar (see *tehsildar*)
nanawatee	(From "go in.") Supplication, suing for peace
nang	(Lit., "honor.") A category of Pukhtun social organization, that is acephalous and egalitarian and opposed to *qalang* society
nikka	Grandfather, ancestor
nikkat	Division based on traditional and established principles between and within tribes
pakka	(Lit., "baked," "solid.") Cement, opposed to *kacha*
parda	(Lit., "veil.") Seclusion, modesty of women
parmat	Permit, timber permit allowing truckload of timber from the agency
pir	Holymen; some acquire a reputation as saint
potical	Political agent or political administration
Pukhto	Language of Pukhtuns but also meaning the essence of Pukhtunness and the Pukhtunwali code
Pukhtun	Member of the Pukhtun tribal group, defined by patrilineage and behavior approximating the Pukhtunwali ideal
Pukhtunistan	Concept of an autonomous Pukhtun state supported by Afghanistan. Pukhtunistanis in Pakistan are suspected of indulging in minor acts of sabotage and are known as anti-Pakistan
Puhktunwali	Composite of *badal, melmastia, nanawatee, tor* and *tarboorwali*; the code of the Pukhtuns
qalang	(Lit., "taxes" and "rents.") A category of Pukhtun social organization, hierarchical with powerful chiefs and opposed to *nang*

qazi	Judge, learned in Islamic theology and law
sayyid	Descendant of Holy Prophet
Scouts	Paramilitary organization consisting mainly of tribesmen. The Scouts, not the regular army, are posted to the tribal areas
shahada	Muslim declaration of faith (see *kalima*)
shahadat	Death in the cause of Islam
shaheed	One who dies for Islam
shaitan	Satan or devil
shariat	Body of Islamic law
tabligh	(Lit., "conversion.") A nonpolitical Muslim organization based in the Punjab
takfir	Declaring someone a non-Muslim
talib	Religious student
tarboor	Cousin, father's brother's son; a rival
tarboorwali	Code of the tarboor, based on cousin equality and rivalry
taweez	Religious talisman
teeman	Tribe, people, nonprivileged groups as opposed to maliks; general populace as distinct from elite malik group
tehsildar	Official, in charge of *tehsil* or *thana* (see naib-tehsildar)
tor	(Lit., "black.") Refers to honor of women. When the woman is dishonored, both male and female are *tor*
tora	(Lit., "sword.") Courage
ummah	Muslim community
wesha	(Lit., "wood.") Refers to timber permit. *Largi* in Yusufzai Pukhto

Index